MAPPING CORPORATE EDUCATION REFORM

Mapping Corporate Education Reform outlines and analyzes the complex relationships between policy actors that define education reform within the current, neoliberal context. Using social network analysis and powerful data visualization tools, the authors identify the problematic roots of these relationships and describe their effects both in the US and abroad. Through a series of case studies, each chapter reveals how powerful actors, from billionaire philanthropists to multinational education corporations, leverage their resources to implement free market mechanisms within public education.

By comprehensively connecting the dots of neoliberal education reforms, the authors reveal not only the details of the reforms themselves, but the relationships that enable actors to amass troubling degrees of political power through network governance. A critical analysis of the actors and interests behind education policies, *Mapping Corporate Education Reform* uncovers the frequently obscured operations of educational governance and offers key insights into education reform at the present moment.

Wayne Au is Associate Professor at the University of Washington Bothell, and is an editor for the teaching magazine and non-profit publishing house *Rethinking Schools*.

Joseph J. Ferrare is Assistant Professor at the University of Kentucky.

The Critical Social Thought Series

Edited by Michael W. Apple
University of Wisconsin—Madison

Contradictions of Control
School Structure and School Knowledge
Linda M. McNeil

Working Class without Work
High School Students in a De-industrializing Society
Lois Weis

Social Analysis of Education
After the New Sociology
Philip Wexler

Capitalist Schools
Explanation and Ethics in Radical Studies of Schooling
Daniel P. Liston

Getting Smart
Feminist Research and Pedagogy with/in the Postmodern
Patti Lather

Teacher Education and the Social Conditions of Schooling
Daniel P. Liston and Kenneth M. Zeichner

Race, Identity, and Representation in Education
Warren Crichlow and Cameron McCarthy, editors

Public Schools that Work
Creating Community
Gregory A. Smith, editor

Power and Method
Political Activism and Educational Research
Andrew Gitlin, editor

Critical Ethnography in Educational Research
A Theoretical and Practical Guide
Phil Francis Carspecken

The Uses of Culture
Education and the Limits of Ethnic Affiliation
Cameron McCarthy

Education, Power, and Personal Biography
Dialogues with Critical Educators
Carlos Alberto Torres, editor

Contradictions of School Reform
Educational Costs of Standardized Testing
Linda M. McNeil

Act Your Age!
A Cultural Construction of Adolescence
Nancy Lesko

Tough Fronts
The Impact of Street Culture on Schooling
L. Janelle Dance

Political Spectacle and the Fate of American Schools
*Mary Lee Smith with Walter Heinecke, Linda Miller-Kahn,
and Patricia F. Jarvis*

Rethinking Scientific Literacy
Wolff-Michael Roth and Angela Calabrese Barton

High Stakes Education
Inequality, Globalization, and Urban School Reform
Pauline Lipman

Learning to Labor in New Times
Nadine Dolby and Greg Dimitriadis, editors

Working Method
Research and Social Justice
Lois Weis and Michelle Fine

Class Reunion
The Remaking of the American White Working Class
Lois Weis

Race, Identity, and Representation in Education, Second Edition
Cameron McCarthy, Warren Crichlow, Greg Dimitriadis, and Nadine Dolby

Radical Possibilities
Public Policy, Urban Education, and a New Social Movement
Jean Anyon

Could It Be Otherwise?
Parents and the Inequities of Public School Choice
Lois André-Bechely

Reading and Writing the World with Mathematics
Eric Gustein

Market Movements
African American Involvement in School Voucher Reform
Thomas C. Pedroni

Rightist Multiculturalism
Core Lessons on Neoconservative School Reform
Kristen L. Buras

Unequal By Design
High-Stakes Testing and the Standardization of Inequality
Wayne Au

Black Literate Lives
Historical and Contemporary Perspectives
Maisha T. Fisher

Hidden Markets
The New Education Privatization
Patricia Burch

Critical Perspectives on bell hooks
Maria del Guadalupe Davidson and George Yancy, editors

Advocacy Leadership
Toward a Post-Reform Agenda in Education
Gary L. Anderson

Race, Whiteness, and Education
Zeus Leonardo

Controversy in the Classroom
The Democratic Power of Discussion
Diana E. Hess

The New Political Economy of Urban Education
Neoliberalism, Race, and the Right to the City
Pauline Lipman

Critical Curriculum Studies
Education, Consciousness, and the Politics of Knowing
Wayne Au

Learning to Liberate
Community-Based Solutions to the Crisis in Urban Education
Vajra Watson

Critical Pedagogy and Social Change
Critical Analysis on the Language of Possibility
Seehwa Cho

Educating Activist Allies
Social Justice Pedagogy with the Suburban and Urban Elite
Katy Swalwell

The Political Classroom
Evidence and Ethics in Democratic Education
Diana E. Hess and Paula McAvoy

Mapping Corporate Education Reform
Power and Policy Networks in the Neoliberal State
Wayne Au and Joseph J. Ferrare

MAPPING CORPORATE EDUCATION REFORM

Power and Policy Networks in the Neoliberal State

Edited by
Wayne Au and
Joseph J. Ferrare

Routledge
Taylor & Francis Group

NEW YORK AND LONDON

First published 2015
by Routledge
711 Third Avenue, New York, NY 10017

and by Routledge
2 Park Square, Milton Park, Abingdon, Oxon, OX14 4RN

Routledge is an imprint of the Taylor & Francis Group, an informa business

Library of Congress Cataloging-in-Publication Data
Mapping corporate education reform: power and policy networks in the neoliberal state/by Wayne Au and Joseph J. Ferrare.
    pages cm.—(Critical social thought)
    Includes bibliographical references and index.
    1. Education and state. 2. Policy networks. 3. Neoliberalism. I. Au, Wayne, 1972–
    editor of compilation. II. Ferrare, Joseph J. editor of compilation.
    LC71.M317 2015
    379—dc23
    2014040610

ISBN: 978-1-138-79198-5 (hbk)
ISBN: 978-1-138-79200-5 (pbk)
ISBN: 978-1-315-76240-1 (ebk)

Typeset in Bembo and Stone Sans
by Florence Production Ltd, Stoodleigh, Devon, UK

CONTENTS

List of Figures   *xi*
List of Tables   *xii*
List of Contributors   *xiii*
Series Editor's Foreword by Michael W. Apple   *xvii*

1   Introduction: Neoliberalism, Social Networks, and the
    New Governance of Education   1
    Wayne Au and Joseph J. Ferrare

2   mEducation as a Site of Network Governance   23
    Diego Santori, Stephen J. Ball, and Carolina Junemann

3   Network Restructuring of Global Edu-business:
    The Case of Pearson's *Efficacy Framework*   43
    Anna Hogan, Sam Sellar and Bob Lingard

4   Mapping the Education Entrepreneurial Network:
    Teach For America, Charter School Reform, and
    Corporate Sponsorship   65
    Beth Sondel, Kerry Kretchmar, and Joseph J. Ferrare

5   International Access Project: A Network Analysis of an
    Emerging International Curriculum Program in China   86
    Shuning Liu

6 Mapping Neoliberal Reform in Chile: Following the
   Development and Legitimation of the Chilean System
   of School Quality Measurement (SIMCE)   106
   *Javier Campos-Martínez, Francisca Corbalán Pössel,
   and Jorge Inzunza*

7 Mapping the Discourse of Neoliberal Education Reform:
   Space, Power, and Access in Chicago's Renaissance 2010
   Debate   126
   Sarah Bell

8 Other People's Policy: Wealthy Elites and Charter School
   Reform in Washington State   147
   Wayne Au and Joseph J. Ferrare

9 Gangsta Raps, Power Gaps, and Network Maps: How
   the Charter School Market Came to New Orleans   165
   Kristen L. Buras

10 Enterprise Education Policy and Embedded Layers
   of Corporate Influence   190
   Patricia Burch and Jahni M. A. Smith

Index   207

FIGURES

2.1   mEducation policy network   24
3.1   Sir Michael Barber's network of relations   47
3.2   Pearson's network cultivated from Barber's relations   50
3.3   Pearson's "Efficacy Framework" network   58
4.1   Graph of TFA's organizational ties   73
4.2   Graph of ties between key organizational and individual
      actors   75
4.3   Directed graph of organizations and key funders   79
5.1   The network of Sunny High IAP international curriculum
      program   99
6.1   Key actors involved in the initial linkages of SIMCE   114
6.2   Key actors involved in SIMCE's renewal   118
7.1   Schools mentioned and unmentioned within the reading
      sample per Chicago's aggregated ZIP codes based on
      median income   135
7.2   Correspondence analysis map of mentioned schools by
      their coded themes   140
8.1   The Yes On 1240 campaign network   155
9.1   Policy ecology of New Schools for New Orleans   174
10.1 The iron triangle of education policy and reform   192
10.2 Enterprise education policy and education markets   197
10.3 Pearson example of interlocking educational services   198

TABLES

4.1	Organizational affiliations of TFA alumnus	76
7.1	CPS schools mentioned in the 389-article sample reporting on Ren2010 and Chicago ZIP codes symbolized by median income	136
7.2	Expectancy of CPS schools' mentioned status per aggregated U.S. Census tract categories based on racial ethnicity majority	136
7.3	School themes as they emerged through the coding process	138
8.1	Yes On 1240 campaign cash and in-kind contributions $50k and greater	151
8.2	Philanthropic support for Yes On 1240 connected organizations	154

CONTRIBUTORS

Wayne Au is an Associate Professor in the School of Educational Studies at the University of Washington Bothell, and he is an editor and contributor for the non-profit, social justice publisher, *Rethinking Schools*. His work focuses on critical educational policy studies, teaching for social justice, curriculum studies, multicultural education, and critical education theory and practice, and his work has appeared in *Teachers College Record*, *Educational Researcher*, and *Curriculum Inquiry*, among others.

Stephen J. Ball is Karl Mannheim Professor of Sociology of Education at the Institute of Education, University of London, and Fellow of the British Academy. His work uses sociology in the analysis of education policy. Recent books include *Global Education Inc.* (Routledge, 2012) and *The Education Debate* (second edition) (Policy Press, 2012).

Sarah Bell has been working as a professional cartographer since 2008 and recently completed her M.S. in Geography from Huxley College of the Environment at Western Washington University. Her research interests include critical cartographies and counter-mapping of a wide range of social and environmental policies.

Kristen L. Buras is an Associate Professor in the Department of Educational Policy Studies at Georgia State University. She is author of *Charter Schools, Race, and Urban Space: Where the Market Meets Grassroots Resistance*, and coauthor of *Pedagogy, Policy, and the Privatized City: Stories of Dispossession and Defiance from New Orleans*, recognized for its outstanding contribution by the Curriculum Studies Division of the American Educational Research Association (AERA). She is cofounder and director of the New Orleans-based Urban South Grassroots Research Collective for Public Education and was granted the Distinguished Scholar-Activist Award by Critical Educators for Social Justice of AERA.

Patricia Burch is an Associate Professor at the University of Southern California. She has authored numerous articles and books on the evolving influence of the private sector on public policy in K-12 education, with particular attention to issues of equity. She is author of *Hidden Markets* (Routledge, 2012) and coauthor, with Annalee Good, of *Equal Scrutiny* (Harvard Education Press, 2014).

Javier Campos-Martínez is a doctoral student in the Social Justice Education concentration at the University of Massachusetts Amherst. He is a current member of the work group "Education Policy and the Right to Education in Latin America and the Caribe" of the Latin-American Council of Social Sciences (CLACSO) and former editor of *Revista Docencia* at the Colegio de Profesores de Chile A.G. A founding member of the Chilean Collective for a New Education, his research interests include the examination of the effects of neoliberalism on schools and teachers' working condition.

Joseph J. Ferrare is Assistant Professor in the Department of Educational Policy Studies and Evaluation at the University of Kentucky. His research interests are broadly situated in sociology of education and policy analysis. He is currently working on projects that examine historical and contemporary inequities in patterns of education attainment, as well as the network governance structures that are seeking to shape these patterns through market-based reforms.

Anna Hogan is completing a PhD as a full-time student in the School of Education at the University of Queensland, Australia. She is researching the role of edu-business in education policy processes both globally and nationally.

Jorge Inzunza is a psychologist at the University of Chile. He participated in the implementation of affirmative action programs in Chile. He completed his Masters in Social and Human Sciences at the University of Paris 10, Nanterre. He served as an advisor to the Chilean Teachers' Union and Editor of the Journal *Docencia* at the same organization. He obtained his PhD in Education at the University of Campinas (São Paulo, Brazil). The main themes of his publications and research are history of education, educational psychology, global educational policies and high-stakes standardized tests. Currently he is working on the dissemination of educational policies and the role of international organizations.

Carolina Junemann is a researcher at the Institute of Education, University of London. Her research interests focus on education policy analysis, the social impacts of policy and more broadly the relationship between educational and social inequalities. She is coauthor (with Stephen Ball) of *Networks, New Governance and Education* (Policy Press, 2012).

Kerry Kretchmar is an Assistant Professor of Education at Carroll University, where she values collaborating with local community organizations and schools to develop effective pre-service teachers. Her research interests include examining the way market-based reforms are impacting teachers, teaching, and teacher education.

Bob Lingard is a Professorial Research Fellow in the School of Education at the University of Queensland in Australia. His most recent book is *Politics, Policies and Pedagogies in Education* (Routledge, 2014). He is also co-editor of the journal, *Discourse: Studies in the Cultural Politics of Education.*

Shuning Liu is a PhD student at the University of Wisconsin-Madison, majoring in Curriculum and Instruction, and Minoring in Educational Policy Studies. Her current research interests involve the role of international education in the formation of social elites. Using a transnational lens, she looks critically at how the educational experiences, identities, and life trajectories of socially elite Chinese students are influenced and shaped by the political economic and social-cultural processes at both local and global levels.

Francisca Corbalán Pössel is an Assistant Professor in the Department of Psychology, University of Chile (Universidad de Chile). She earned a Masters degree in Sociology of Education at the Institute of Education, University of London, and is currently completing a PhD at the same institution. Her interest of study is the neoliberalization of education and urban life in Chile.

Diego Santori is a Lecturer in Sociology of Education and Education Policy Analysis, at the Institute of Education. His interests include the relationships between education policy, economics, and subjectivity and the ways in which their interpenetration produces new cultural forms and practices that shape our possibilities of existence in specific ways. Together with Professor Stephen Ball and Carolina Junemann, he is currently working on a Leverhulme Trust-funded research project on the role of philanthropy in education policy, policy networks and governance.

Sam Sellar is a Postdoctoral Research Fellow in the School of Education at the University of Queensland. His current research interests include large-scale educational assessments, new accountabilities in schooling and the aspirations of young people in high-poverty regions. He is Associate Editor of *Critical Studies in Education* and *Discourse: Studies in the Cultural Politics of Education.*

Jahni M. A. Smith is a PhD student studying Urban Education Policy in the Rossier School at the University of Southern California. She is an international scholar with interests in K-12 education policy, economics of education, and understanding market-based reforms in education with specific attention to equity and quality.

Beth Sondel is an Assistant Professor in Social Studies and Social Justice Education at North Carolina State University. Her research partners critical theory with qualitative research to interrogate the relationship between social justice, democracy, and public schools. In her most recent research, she has looked at the role of Teach For America in the promotion and implementation of market-based reform in New Orleans and elsewhere.

SERIES EDITOR'S FOREWORD

Michael W. Apple

One of the major benefits of the extensive international work that I do is the knowledge I get about the kinds of policies that are affecting education throughout the world. Increasingly, the similarities are striking. Neoliberal reforms now dominate the educational landscape in a wide range of nations. The policies may be talked about and justified in somewhat different ways; but beneath the rhetorical forms of justification, the *practice* is often very much the same. This is not an accident. It is the result of a long-term social/pedagogic project to change people's commonsense about what counts as a good set of goals, a good school, a good curriculum, a good teacher and good teacher education, a good student, and a good system of determining success.

It also involves a shift in authority. Different sets of actors, both up front and behind the scenes, have influence and these actors are often linked with one another in *networks* that are not readily visible unless one looks beneath the surface. The key word here is networks.

As Stephen Ball puts it, "[P]olicy networks ... constitute a new form of governance, albeit not in a single coherent form, and bring into play in the policy process new sources of authority and indeed a 'market of authorities'" (Ball, 2012, p. 9). In the process, policy itself is being privatized (Ball, 2012, p. 8) at the same time as schools themselves are increasingly being commodified and put on a market.

We can see this all around us. Slowly but surely, the selling of public institutions—with education increasingly coming center stage in this—is now a key component of our kind of economy (Lynch, Grummell, and Devine 2012). But "selling education" requires that education is made into a product that can be consumed. And as I noted above, this again requires a larger creative social-political project of changing the basic ways we think about public and private, democracy, and similar things. In particular, the very meaning of the concept of democracy must be radically transformed. Instead of being a "thick" concept that embodies collective participation and mobilization to make our institutions responsive to communities, it must be changed into a "thin" concept. Democracy is to be seen as individual choice on a market. The ideal citizen then is the *consumer*, the possessive individual who acts "rationally" based on self-interest (Apple, 2006).

Anything, and anyone, that stands in the way of such supposedly rational individual choice needs to be challenged. Thus, the collective power of teachers and teacher unions and the historic gains in autonomy and creativity of the teaching profession must be drastically limited. The attacks on tenure, on teacher education, on democratically-arrived-at models of teacher assessment—all of these go hand in hand with the neoliberal agenda. The voices and collective power of marginalized communities, the poor, and people of color must also be limited (see, e.g., Lipman, 2011). And even with the articulate defenses of public schools, teachers, and more thickly democratic practices and policies by figures such as Diane Ravitch (Ravitch, 2014; see also Hagopian, 2014; Apple, 2013; Apple, 2014), at times it feels as if hope is in short supply.

This reality makes *Mapping Corporate Education Reform: Power and Policy Networks in the Neoliberal State* a very significant book. Wayne Au and Joseph Ferrare have brought together a series of critical analyses that map the connections and interlocking influences, people, and organizations that are changing the ways educational policies are made, who makes them, and what these policies actually are, and just as importantly how they are evaluated. The result is a volume that is powerful and illuminating.

Some of the very best work on these connections and interlocking networks of people and organizations is found in Stephen Ball's recent critical analyses (Ball, 2012; 2007)—and such work is represented here. But *Mapping Corporate Education Reform* extends our critical understanding of what these networks are and how they function in significant ways. It accomplishes this both in the wide range of different kinds of analysis and in the areas of policy and practice that it covers. The introductory chapter by Au and Ferrare demonstrates the range of methodologies and approaches to uncovering the networks of influence, at the same time as it wisely and clearly situates all of this within the concerns of so many committed educators and communities that dominant educational policies are having truly damaging effects on an education worthy of its name.

The entire book is also a reminder that neoliberal policies constantly cut across national boundaries, a situation where the connections and mutual influences among the groups that sponsor these policies are often as international as they are intricate. In recognition of this reality, Au and Ferrare provide the reader with a book that is itself international in scope. This too is significant.

There are of course alternatives to the neoliberal policies that now dominate the educational landscape. The influence of the Citizen School and participatory budgeting first developed in Porto Alegre, Brazil that I discuss at much greater length in *Can Education Change Society?* (Apple, 2013; see also Apple, Au, and Gandin, 2009) provides a cogent example of such policies. The efforts of the Center of Research in Theories and Practices that Overcome Inequalities at the University of Barcelona (see Soler, 2011) are also important. Publications such as *Rethinking Schools* also consistently document the continuing practical labor of educators throughout the United States to counter the effects of dominant policies and practices and to build workable alternatives to them.

All of these things are important. But we must also constantly understand the context in which we work and be honest about the ways power now operates to make it harder for a more critically democratic education to be built and defended. *Mapping Corporate Education Reform* is essential reading for more fully understanding this context and for learning what needs to be done to interrupt it.

Michael W. Apple
John Bascom Professor of Curriculum and Instruction
and Educational Policy Studies
University of Wisconsin, Madison

References

Apple, M. W. (2006). *Educating the "right" way: Markets, standards, god, and inequality.* (second ed.) New York: Routledge.

Apple, M. W. (2013). *Can education change society?* New York: Routledge.

Apple, M. W. (2014). *Official knowledge: Democratic education in a conservative age.* (third ed.) New York: Routledge.

Apple, M. W., Au, W., and Gandin, L. A. (Eds.) (2009). *The Routledge international handbook of critical education.* New York: Routledge.

Ball, S. (2007). *Education plc: Understanding private sector participation in public sector education.* New York: Routledge.

Ball, S. (2012). *Global education inc.: New policy networks and the neo-liberal imaginary.* New York: Routledge.

Hagopian, J. (Ed.) (2014). *More than just a score: The new uprising against high-stakes testing.* Chicago: Haymarket Books.

Lipman, P. (2011). *The new political economy of urban education: Neoliberalism, race, and the right to the city.* New York: Routledge.

Lynch, K., Grummell, B. and Devine, D. (2012). *New managerialism in education: Commercialization, carelessness, and gender.* New York: Palgrave Macmillan.

Ravitch, D. (2014). *Reign of error: The hoax of the privatization movement and the danger to America's public schools.* New York: Vintage.

Soler, M. (Ed.) (2011). Education for social inclusion, special issue of *International Studies in Sociology of Education*, 21: 1–90.

1

INTRODUCTION

Neoliberalism, Social Networks, and the New Governance of Education

Wayne Au and Joseph J. Ferrare

This project began when one of us (Wayne) was doing extensive research and public scholarship about the forces advocating for charter school reform in the US state of Washington. The deeper Wayne dug into the politics of charter school reform advocacy at the state level, the more he began to see the same names and organizations popping up in multiple places. The most immediate name was that of Microsoft founder and billionaire, Bill Gates Jr., who was supporting the establishment of charter school laws in Washington State through large personal financial donations. Given the well-known presence of the Bill & Melinda Gates Foundation in supporting charter school reform, Wayne began to wonder about ways that Gates' foundation might also be active in pushing charter school policy in Washington State as well. Then the flood gates opened (pun intended), as Wayne found numerous connections between a central group of non-profits advocating for charter schools and the Gates Foundation. At that point, Wayne called Joe, whose doctoral work focused on using Social Network Analysis (SNA) to map significant relationships in education and was in the midst of another project mapping relationships between Teach For America, charter schools, and corporate sponsors (Kretchmar, Sondel, and Ferrare, 2014, see also Chapter 5, this volume). Together we were able to construct a graph of the connections among wealthy elites, philanthropic foundations, and organizations leading the campaign for charter schools in Washington State (Au and Ferrare, 2014, see also Chapter 9, this volume), a process that illustrated to us how SNA can be combined with critical policy analysis in order to expose power relations operating behind and within current structures of education policy, and one that provided the impetus for *Mapping Corporate Education Reform: Power and Policy Networks in the Neoliberal State*.

Admittedly, the title of this collection is a loaded one. We have terms such as, "corporate education reform," "power and policy networks," and "neoliberal state," and these terms require unpacking within the current political context generally, and relative to the arguments of this specific book. We begin this introduction by addressing the term "neoliberalism" and its implications for the structure of the state and the privatization of public assets. We then extend that discussion into an explanation of what has been more popularly referred to as "corporate education reform" and how it relates to power and policy networks within public education. We continue with an overview of social network analysis as a methodology generally and relative to educational policy analysis specifically, and conclude this introduction with a discussion of each chapter and how we make sense of them as examples of governance structures in the neoliberal state and as examples of different approaches to analyzing these structures.

Neoliberalism

Ball (2012) is cautious with his use of the term "neoliberal," particularly because of how widely it is used and the multiplicity of possible meanings that people ascribe to it—such that it can lose all purposeful meaning. We explicitly recognize this as an issue here, because all words can be sliding signifiers whose exact meaning shifts depending on who is using it, where they are using it, when they are using it, and to what audience they are speaking (Gee, 1996). This can especially be the case with terms like "neoliberal" and "neoliberalism" given the shifts in their temporal, spatial, cultural, and geographic contexts (Davies, 2014): Neoliberalism has existed formally as a state practice since at least the 1972 coup d'etat in Chile, where a leftist social democratic president (Allende), with the explicit aid of the U.S. Central Intelligence Agency and U.S. Secretary of State Kissinger, was overthrown by right wing conservatives and replaced by a corporatist and fascist ruler, Pinochet (Harvey, 2004b).

Pinochet was more than friendly with the interests of corporations domestically and internationally, and with the help of students of free market economist and University of Chicago professor Milton Friedman, he set about deregulating the Chilean economy, opening its markets to foreign interests, defunding social programs, and privatizing industries that were once publicly controlled—doing so with military force and deadly violence. While the Chilean neoliberal experiment benefitted international corporations and Chile's economic elite, it also clearly led to the economic immiseration of the vast majority of the Chilean people. Indeed, and as an aside, this economic immiseration of working people has become so common with the neoliberal project that it is now seen as one of the central functions of neoliberalism generally: to open up new markets for the rich while simultaneously worsening conditions for the poor (Harvey, 2004b).

Suffice to say, with over a 40-year history, one that is highly charged in terms of politics, economics, and human/environmental distress, the concept of neoliberalism has traveled to and through multiple contexts across time and around the globe. Thus, "neoliberalism" carries with it a relatively wide range of meaning, and it means different things to many different people in many different contexts. In this regard, we too are somewhat careful about how and why we use "neoliberalism" here. However, as critical scholars, we also are keenly attuned to the worsening conditions for the people and the planet, and so we know that our scholarly trepidations around the concept of "neoliberalism" are relatively unimportant compared to the devastating effects of neoliberalism in practice worldwide (Harvey, 2014; Roy, 2014).

As editors of this volume, and knowing fully that the contributors may or may not agree with us, we draw extensively on the work of Harvey (2004a, 2004b, 2007) for our understanding of neoliberalism generally, as well as the work of Apple (2001), Fabricant and Fine (2013), and Lipman (2011), for our understanding of how neoliberalism structures education specifically. As a basic definition, Harvey (2007) explains: "Neoliberalism is a theory of political economic practices proposing that human well-being can be best advanced by the maximization of entrepreneurial freedoms within an institutional framework characterized by private property rights, individual liberty, unencumbered markets, and free trade" (p. 22).

Lipman's (2011) definition of neoliberalism is also useful and expands upon Harvey's (2007) explanation. Lipman (2011) defines neoliberalism as,

> an ensemble of economic and social policies, forms of governance, and discourses of ideologies that promote self-interest, unrestricted flows of capital, deep reductions in the cost of labor, and sharp retrenchment of the public sphere. Neoliberals champion privatization of social goods and withdrawal of government from provision for social welfare on the premise that competitive markets are more effective and efficient.
>
> *(p. 6)*

Neoliberalism thus extends into a multitude of institutions and spheres of society such that neoliberalism is also embodied in social and economic policies, ideologies, cultural practices, human relations, relations of production and consumption, and worldviews (Harvey, 2007). In this regard we see neoliberalism as a massive restructuring structure, one that restructures commonsense, restructures relationships between humans and other humans, restructures relationships between humans and products, restructures cultural, capital, political flows, and restructures the state and economy in line with individual self-interest and at a cost to commitments to collective well-being.

Neoliberalism and Wealth Concentration

Harvey (2007) argues that, given the international evidence, neoliberalism has functionally been a scheme to restore the power of economic elites using neoliberal ideology as a justification for more firmly establishing the class position of elites in countries such as Britain and the United States and has created the social, economic, and political environments for the formation of capitalist classes in countries such as India and China. Further, he points out that even in national economies like that of Mexico, which was historically exploited by the capitalist elite in the global north, neoliberalization has only served to concentrate wealth in the hands of domestic elites in those economies. Indeed, because resources are distributed unequally, free market reforms—and the state's facilitation of such reforms—function to redistribute resources, social and economic goods, wealth, and power "upwards" towards those individuals, communities, and corporations already benefitting from high concentrations of wealth. This process also carries with it a simultaneous restriction of access to those same resources and opportunities for those already on the bottom (Fabricant and Fine, 2013).

Neoliberalism, the State, and the Privatization of Public Education

Critical to any discussion of neoliberalism generally, but particularly neoliberalism in education, is the role of the state within the neoliberal framework. Because state regulation and state intervention are seen as obstacles to free market competition, neoliberalism advocates for the existence of a very small state government with limited function. The neoliberal state needs to help maintain the integrity of currency, maintain defense and police forces, and keep some semblance of a judiciary system, all in support of maintaining rights to private property and keeping the markets free and open. Further, the neoliberal state must support the creation of markets in all areas in which they do not yet exist (e.g., education or health care), but once those markets are established, the state must keep its interventions to the bare minimum. The neoliberal state also takes on other functions, such as redistributing wealth upwards to elite classes through changes to tax codes to benefit corporations and the wealthy, and by shrinking government spending on programs aimed at social support (Harvey, 2007).

As the neoliberal state shrinks (itself the result of the neoliberal commitment to deregulation and market forces), responsibilities for governing are increasingly shifted from democratically elected state governments towards private bodies that are unelected and unaccountable to the voting public. As Lipman (2011) notes, this is a radical shift from *government* to *governance*:

> The "triumph of market ideology" is coupled with an erosion of the idea that informed citizens should make decisions based on the general welfare. The shift from *government* by elected state bodies and a degree of democratic accountability to *governance* by experts and managers and decision making by judicial authority and executive order is central to neoliberal policy making . . . Public-private partnerships, appointed managers, and publicly unaccountable bodies comprised of appointed state and corporate leaders

make decisions about urban development, transportation, schools, and other public infrastructure using business rationales. In these arrangements, the state acts as an agent of capital.

(p. 13, original emphasis)

Indeed, this shift from government to governance in the neoliberal state is a critical aspect of *Mapping Corporate Education Reform* because new forms of power, authority, and governance must be created to fill the space that is created by the shrinking, neoliberal state—a point we will address in more detail later in this introduction.

One of the key outcomes of the shrinking neoliberal state is the opening of new markets through the privatization of public goods and services: Within the neoliberal framework public goods and services that were once provided by the state are converted into new markets ripe for exploitation and profiteering by private/corporate interests. Thus, we see major institutions associated with the military, the medical industry, systems of public education, and social services, among others, being opened up as capital for accumulation by private interests. Indeed, this has been a central feature of neoliberalism (to varying degrees) in capitalist economies throughout the world (Harvey, 2007). Neoliberal privatization thus seeks to turn all things public into profitable markets, oftentimes through the outsourcing of formerly public services to private corporations (see, e.g., Burch, 2009), and initiate a process where, "Entire sectors of the social reproduction side of the welfare state, most critically in health care and education, are being rapidly capitalized as entrepreneurs search for new profitable markets" (Fabricant and Fine, 2013, p. 25). Harvey (2004a) calls this neoliberal movement of capital from public projects and institutions into the coffers of private enterprises, "accumulation by dispossession" (p. 74), where the public is being dispossessed of its assets which are functionally being accumulated by wealthy elites.

The shrinking of the neoliberal state, combined with the neoliberal commitment opening new markets through the accumulation by dispossession of public assets, has particularly profound implications for public education in the United States and around the world in at least three ways. First, and in the rawest sense, the neoliberal reconfiguration of public education—as a state institution—is simply about giving entrepreneurs and corporations access to a new and potentially profitable market of public assets to which they did not previously have access. As Fabricant and Fine (2013) explain:

In public education, we have witnessed the ascent of charter schools, virtual learning, market curricula development, and an expansive number of firms engaged in the measurement and assessment of teachers, with a host of entrepreneurs making large and small profits. More specifically, profit making extends from publishers capitalizing on the new standards-based testing curricula, to high-tech companies experimenting and testing their curricula interventions, to real estate operators leasing property at exorbitant fees, to alternative certification programs, and finally for-profit schools. Each of these fragments, pieces of profit making, are part of a new "gold rush" to capitalize the $500 billion of public assets being redistributed from neighborhood K-12 public schooling to the marketplace.

(p. 25)

Second, the creation of the neoliberal public education marketplace reconfigures key aspects of education policy and practice. Specifically, the neoliberal vision of public education is one of a competitive market where students, teachers, schools, and administrators are ranked against each other using high-stakes, standardized test scores as the primary metric for comparison (Au, 2009). In this vision teachers' unions are a barrier to the competitive hiring and firing of "good" or "bad" teachers—as determined by student test scores—and the teaching profession itself is deregulated through quick teacher training programs (i.e., Teach For America), resulting in both the deprofessionalization of teaching and an attack on university-based teacher education programs (Au, 2013; Kretchmar et al., 2014; Zeichner and Pena-Sandoval, 2015). Further, within the neoliberal revisioning, and as something akin to small businesses, public schools need to be deregulated and put into direct competition with each other for students by being turned into charter schools (run by charter management organizations and governed by appointed boards) to be judged, and potentially closed, also based on test scores (Apple, 2006; Fabricant and Fine, 2012).

The third implication of the neoliberal state for public education revolves around the foundational discourse about, and the purposes of, education. For instance, the very language of educational bureaucracies has changed. Borrowing from the corporate sector, high-level district administrators are now referred to as Chief Executive Officers (CEOs), Chief Financial Officers (CFOs), and Chief Operations Officers (COOs), and instead of being concerned with growth in learning, schools are forced to meet growth targets and benchmarks in test scores. Students and parents are subsequently reframed as consumers/customers and teachers, schools, and principals are similarly reframed as service providers (Apple, 2006; Au, 2009; Lipman, 2011). This neoliberal discursive shift does not stand alone, however. It also signals a more profound neoliberal shift in the purposes of education: Under neoliberalism the purpose of education increasingly shifts to the production of "human capital," "adding value," and meeting the needs of the economy, rather than, for instance, serving the social good or meeting collective needs of communities (Lipman, 2011).

Much like the struggle over the U.S. curriculum from 100 years ago—where different forces jockeyed as to whether children would be mainly taught for job training or more humanistic ends (Kliebard, 2004)—we are in the midst of a similar struggle over what children should learn and what schools should prepare them to do with their lives. In the contemporary context of the U.S., public education has been declared in a crisis, particularly compared to other countries, and thus needs to be completely restructured in order for the US to gain supremacy both in the international test score rankings and in the global economy. While the actual research evidence does not support the existence of this exact crisis (Ravitch, 2013), we are experiencing a crisis in the education of working class children generally and working class children of color even more sharply, with neoliberal education policies only exacerbating this crisis (Anyon, 1997; Fabricant and Fine, 2013; Lipman, 2011). Fabricant and Fine (2013) provide a good summary of the process, and are worth quoting at length:

> Various social reproduction functions of the state, such as public schooling, are abandoned, creating the basis for policies that capitalize and redistribute formerly public assets to the private sector, while proliferating, for example, testing cultures as a cheapened substitute for other forms of education. Present educational policies are decreasingly able either to produce meaningful academic growth or avert students' dropping or being pushed out of school. Instead, local schools are underfinanced and pedagogically constrained, providing ever-more degraded learning environments that lead students to early decisions of exit and dead-end jobs. Residents in the poorest communities of color who depend on public education to build the academic capacity and market competitiveness of their children are rendered even more marginal than in the recent past. The continued extraction of capital from the "commons" (regressive tax codes, budget cutting, capitalization of public schooling) only further delegitimates public institutions in the eyes of individuals struggling to carve a better life out of ever-more hostile environments.
>
> *(pp. 23–24)*

Thus, the very purposes of education are redefined as for meeting the labor needs of global economic competition, but this purpose is a mirage because the conditions required for a quality education are undermined by neoliberalism's compulsion for restructuring the state, cutting social spending, and draining resources from the public sector.

Corporate Education Reform, Policy Networks, and the New Governance

The above discussion of neoliberalism, the neoliberal state, and the subsequent restructuring of public education frames both the impetus for *Mapping Corporate Education Reform: Power and Policy Networks in the Neoliberal State* generally, and the work of each of the chapters individually. Indeed, our definition of "corporate education reform" itself extends from this discussion. In broad agreement with other scholars and education activists (see, e.g., Apple, 2006; Fabricant and Fine, 2013; D. W. Hursh, 2006; Lipman, 2011; Saltman, 2012, among others), in sum we define "corporate education reform" as policies and practices that support the:

- defunding of public education through regressive tax policies and budget priorities that cut not only spending on public education, but also state-funded programs that provide social supports to low income communities from which underserved children hail;
- accumulation by dispossession of public monies from public education vis-à-vis the marketization of educational services through private contracts (i.e., testing companies, textbook publishers);
- deregulation of teacher labor practices (anti-union, anti-tenure), teacher and administrator certification (i.e., Teach For America), and school governance (i.e., charter schools);
- reconstruction of access to public education in the form of free market competition (i.e., charter schools and private school voucher programs);
- evaluation-through-comparison of public education students, teachers, administrators, and school communities through competitive metrics associated with high-stakes, standardized test scores;
- reshaping the vision and vocabulary of public schools along the lines of corporate businesses, including the redefinition of school leadership as "management," the recasting of district leadership as "Chief Officers" (i.e., CEOs, COOs, CFOs, etc), the identification of students and parents as "consumers," the redefinition of learning and teaching as "production targets," "performance indicators," "value added," and the like;
- narrowing of the purposes of publication to that of solely meeting the needs of the business community and/or that of the economy (losing sight of other important humanistic, civic, cultural, and environmental goals of public education);
- reliance on democratically unaccountable NGOs, philanthropies, for-profit and non-profit organizations, and corporations for guidance on, and implementation of, public education policy.

It is within this context of corporate education reform—as an extension of the neoliberal state—that we see the rise of new networks of governance surrounding public education. At this point we would like to return to Lipman's (2011) above discussion of the distinction between *government* and *governance*. *Government* is public, and it is structurally connected to democratic forms of accountability. While we recognize the multitude of problems with our current system of democratic government (and question the degree of democracy that even exists at all), the formal mechanism for voting democratically elected representation out of office does exist. Thus, *government* bodies that determine education policy and practice at least have some level of public accountability and are required to maintain some level of transparency to the public through regulation and the public reporting of records. *Governance*, on the other hand, has no mechanism for public accountability and no commitment to transparency, and *network governance* itself diffuses accountability by distributing it across a network of organizations and actors, where no single organization or actor can necessarily be held accountable. Indeed, the foundation of network governance in education policy is largely consistent with the broader neoliberal project: the transfer of power and coordination from bureaucratic structures to informal social networks of private individuals and organizations working to transform public education by constructing new education markets (see Ball and Junemann, 2012).

The Bill & Melinda Gates Foundation (2013) is a good example to briefly highlight what we mean by *governance*. The Gates Foundation has become an immensely powerful player in the restructuring of public education policy and practice in the United States. They have invested hundreds of millions of dollars in a specific set of education reforms including, but not limited to, the Common Core State Standards, charter schools and other "school choice" initiatives, and using high-stakes, standardized tests to evaluate teacher performance. These investments have gone to both the U.S. government, but also to a bevy of non-profit organizations working as policy actors at local, state, and national levels. High-level Gates Foundation employees have been placed in high-level positions in the U.S. Department of Education, and the U.S. Department of Education has worked extensively with many Gates Foundation funded organizations to advance its policy goals (Barkan, 2011, 2012; D. Hursh, 2011; Ravitch, 2013; Saltman, 2011). Indeed, as highlighted in our chapter here, "Other People's Policy: Wealthy Elites and Charter School Reform in Washington State" (see also, Au and Ferrare, 2014), the Gates Foundation, and Gates himself personally, were both directly connected to a campaign to legalize charter schools in the U.S. state of Washington. This provides a good illustration of *governance* because it highlights two key, simultaneously operating processes. First we see the shrinking neoliberal state evacuating its commitment to, and authority and power over, public education, only to be filled by a network of corporate interests associated with the neoliberal project. Second, and concurrently, these corporate interests operate out of a neoliberal common sense by advancing policies guided by free market assumptions, and, as is the case with philanthropies such as the Gates Foundation, prioritizing the funding of organizations and projects in line with a neoliberal policy agenda.

One of the central issues with this type of *governance* by corporations, corporate interests, and non-governmental organizations is that there is absolutely no mechanism for holding them accountable for what they do to public institutions, including public education. Bill Gates Jr. highlights this issue well. Talking about the Gates Foundation's policy agenda for public education during an interview at Harvard in September of 2013, Gates openly admitted that, "It would be great if our education stuff worked, but that we won't know for probably a decade" (Strauss, 2013, n.p.). If the Gates and Gates Foundation funded reforms do not work, and there is not much evidence, if any, that they do work (Ravitch, 2013; Saltman, 2012), what can the public do about it? What is the mechanism for holding Gates and his foundation accountable for any damage that he has done to our children over the last 15 years? The answer is that there is no such mechanism. As Bosworth (2011) so eloquently puts it, "To paraphrase F. Scott Fitzgerald, today's plutocrats are not like you and I; nor do they resemble the politicians we elect. Even when they assume the authority to set public policies, they are, I fear, not sackable" (p. 386). As central players in networks of education policy governance, Bill Gates Jr., the Gates Foundation, and the collection of corporations and organizations shaping and implementing education policy in the United States operate with authority and power over public education, but they have no required transparency or accountability to the public. They are reconstructing public education along the lines of the neoliberal model, with many private entities making massive profits at the expense of public assets, and we have no formal way to recoup our losses and fix what they have done. This is the nature of network governance in the neoliberal state.

Methodologies of Policy Mapping

In this section we introduce the methodologies that will be encountered throughout the chapters in this volume, as well some that are not used but are crucial to understanding policy network analysis in general. While all the chapters have the objective of "mapping" policy networks within the corporate reform movement, the approaches for doing so vary depending on the specific research questions. For example, some of the chapters use formal social network analysis and related multivariate techniques, while others use network ethnography and critical cartography—and in some cases these approaches are combined. Our goal here is to provide a broad overview of social network analysis and then describe the related tools that analysts use to highlight different aspects of policy networks. As we will see, these approaches to network analysis share many of the same basic assumptions and together offer analysts a powerful set of tools to examine the formation, transformation, and effects of policy networks currently shaping schools and education systems around the globe.

Social Network Analysis

The use of theories and methods from social network analysis (SNA) in education research is not a new phenomenon. Sociologists of education, for example, have used these techniques to study ability and peer group structures (Hallinan and Sorensen, 1985), course-taking patterns (Friedkin and Thomas, 1997), classroom resistance (McFarland, 2001), and desegregation and interracial contact (Feld and

Carter, 1998), among other topics. More recently, education researchers have drawn upon social network analysis within the realm of education policy and reform (Daly, 2010; Song and Miskel, 2007). These developments—which include the chapters in this book—have also given rise to policy network analysis (Ball and Junemann, 2012) in which researchers aim to construct the network governance structures through which organizational and individual actors shape educational policies and reform movements (see, e.g., Au and Ferrare, 2014; Kretchmar et al., 2014; Reckhow and Snyder, 2014). The focus on policy networks is increasingly relevant as these network governance structures expand in scope and power.

The power of social network analysis in this context comes from the fact that it gives primacy to social relations and embeds social actors within these networks of relations. This is a decidedly different way of viewing the world than, say, a general linear model that attempts to predict an outcome based on a set of "independent effects." Wasserman and Faust (1994, p. 4) distinguish SNA from other forms of inquiry in the following ways:

1.   Actors and their actions are viewed as interdependent rather than independent, autonomous units;
2.   Relational ties (linkages) between actors are channels for transfer or "flow" of resources (either material or nonmaterial);
3.   Network models focusing on individuals view the network structural environment as providing opportunities for or constraints on individual action;
4.   Network models conceptualize structure (social, economic, political, and so forth) as lasting patterns of relations among actors.

Social network analysis thus embodies many of the same relational assumptions that critical researchers make about education policy and practice. In this sense, critical education researchers can use SNA without compromising their ontological assumptions about the social world—a compromise that often leads many critical analysts to mistakenly eschew formal methods altogether (Ferrare, 2009).

Social network analysis actually refers to an entire family of techniques that make use of mathematical concepts such as those in set theory, graph theory, and matrix algebra. Actors (e.g., individuals, groups, or organizations) within a network are referred to as nodes (or vertices) and relations between actors as ties (or edges). Data collection can take numerous possible forms, such as observations, interviews, questionnaires, or documents, making SNA complementary to methods spanning from ethnography to archival analysis to survey research. The key thing to keep in mind is that the actual data being collected are *relations between actors*. The relations between actors can be directional (called "arcs") or non-directional. In a matrix of directed relations, actor i can direct a relation to actor j ($n_i \rightarrow n_j$), but this does not necessarily mean that the relation is reciprocated (i.e.,

$n_j \rightarrow n_i$). In either case, the relations can be dichotomous (present or not present) or take on a range of values that indicate the strength, intensity, or frequency.

There are multiple kinds of social networks that can be analyzed. Ego-centric approaches to SNA, for instance, are those whose focal point is a single actor (called "ego") and the ties this actor has with others (called "alters"). In contrast, non-ego-centric (often called "sociocentric") methods tend to focus more on the structure of the relations as a whole rather than from the perspective of any one actor. The sociocentric approach is the most commonly used from of SNA in policy network analysis, likely because the purpose is often to piece together the diffused organization of network governance structures. However, in some cases ego-centric analysis may make more sense if the purpose is to understand how organizations' ties shape their policy decisions, for example.

Most of the research using SNA analyzes one-mode networks, which are those that focus on relations among a single set of actors. In contrast, two-mode networks—often called affiliation networks—center on the relationship between a set of actors and a set of events. In an affiliation network, events can take on numerous forms, such as participation in a curriculum program, policy initiative, or affiliation with an organization. In an affiliation matrix, then, actors are not directly connected but rather become affiliated through the events they share in common. Events, too, become affiliated through the actors they share in common. This duality of actors and events (Breiger, 1974) means that the organization of inter-personal and inter-event affiliations are simultaneously distinguishable and mutually constitutive: the positions in one mode constitute the relational units of analysis in the other (and vice-versa) (Mohr and Duquenne, 1997). Affiliation networks can easily be transformed into one-mode networks through matrix multiplication. Through this process one can then analyze the number of events that each actor shares in common, or the number of actors that each event shares in common using standard graph theoretic measures (see below). However, the full mapping of both dualities offers analysts a more thorough picture of the relations since it simultaneously illustrates the number and substance of affiliations.

Formal Approaches to Network Analysis

In addition to graphing relations to illustrate or "map" the structure of networks, there are a variety of available techniques to learn about the properties of networks and the nodes constituting the relations. The range of techniques is vast and thus a full introduction falls outside the scope of this chapter.[1] However, it is worth conceptually introducing a few techniques that are relevant to engaging with the chapters in this book. For example, a basic way to analyze the activities of actors in a network is to assess the number of ties associated with each actor. Such a measure is referred to as the degree of a node. For example, if Organization A is tied to Organizations B and C, then these two ties are said to be "incident" upon Organization A. The degree of a node, then, is simply the number of lines incident on that node. In a directed graph the degree of a node is expressed directionally as indegree and outdegree. The indegree represents the total number of arcs terminating at a node, whereas the outdegree represents the total number of arcs originating at the node. In a funding network, for instance, if Foundation A gives individual grants to 15 different organizations, then the outdegree of Foundation A is 15. In the same network, if Organization A receives 25 foundation grants then the indegree of Organization A is 25. In general, the degree does not provide substantively rich information about the nodes, but it does provide an informative description of how involved different actors are in the network.

Network analysts are often interested in the cohesion of relations between actors. The most popular measure of cohesion is the density (Δ), which describes the proportion of ties in a graph (or subgroup) relative to all possible ties. The density of a graph ranges from a value of 0, if there are no ties present in the graph (called a null graph), up to 1, in which each node is connected to all other nodes in the network (called a complete graph). The density thus allows researchers to assess one aspect of cohesion in a graph and to compare the cohesiveness to other graphs. A graph with a density of 0.500 has a greater proportion of total possible ties present than a graph with a density of 0.333. However, characterizing any graph as dense (or sparse) is always a relative assertion that is contingent upon the context of the network. For example, some policy networks may only have a density of, say, 0.250, but this may actually be quite dense relative to other policy networks.

Other common ways to analyze networks include subgroup analysis of cliques or factions and identifying microcosms or equivalence classes within the larger network (called structural equivalence). Finally, in some cases it is possible to test specific hypotheses about network structure and to include network measures into other types of formal models (see Carrington, Scott, and Wasserman, 2005). While the field of policy network analysis has rarely made use of the latter approaches, there are many possible applications for future work.

There are also a number of multivariate techniques commonly used to analyze network data. Cluster analysis, for example, is a procedure for classifying objects (e.g., actors) into groups based on any number of measures of (dis)similarity (Everitt, Landau, Leese, and Stahl, 2011). The basic procedure is to use an algorithm that iteratively places similar actors (or events) in the same groups while splitting dissimilar actors into different groups. The primary output in cluster analysis is called a dendrogram—a tree-like diagram that illustrates the clusters and decision-steps the algorithm made to attain them. Another common multivariate tool is multidimensional scaling (MDS) (Borg and Groenen, 2005; Kruskal and Wish, 1978). Rather than classifying the actors or objects into mutually exclusive groups, MDS is a technique for graphically representing the degree of similarity or dissimilarity between objects as distances between points in a low dimensional space. Whereas cluster analysis groups objects in an either/or fashion (i.e., an actor is placed into either group A or B), MDS plots objects in terms of "to what degree" distances. Even though a cluster analysis may place four actors in the same group, for instance, MDS may reveal that some of these actors are actually more similar than others. Thus, one advantage of MDS over cluster analysis is that the former does not force objects into groups that may not actually represent the data. In addition, MDS allows analysts to quantitatively assess the fit of the graphical representation, whereas standard forms of cluster analysis do not.

As noted above, many networks take on the form of an affiliation network—relations between a set of actors and a set of events. There are a wide variety of techniques to analyze affiliation networks. In addition to using graph theoretic approaches, a relatively common way of looking at affiliations is through the use of correspondence analysis. Correspondence analysis (Greenacre, 2007) is a powerful tool that can be used to illustrate (dis)similarities between actors and events as distances in a low-dimensional space. This makes CA very similar to MDS, with the main difference being that MDS is typically used for one-mode data whereas CA is typically used with two-mode data. As with standard SNA methods, each of these multivariate techniques provides researchers with the ability to visualize complex sets of relationships.

Networks, Meaning, and Space

Although SNA effectively maps the structure of relations between actors in a network, it is less effective at capturing how culture and agency mediate these relations. Some have argued that SNA "has inadequately theorized the causal role of ideals, beliefs, and values, and of the actors that strive to realize them; as a result, it has neglected the cultural and symbolic moment in the very determination of social action" (Emirbayer and Goodwin, 1994, p. 1446). Others have extended this argument by suggesting that SNA only pays attention to the immediately observable relations between actors and events (Bourdieu and Wacquant, 1992) and thus transform dynamic, multidimensional power relations into flat and static structures (Ball and Junemann, 2012). While these critiques overstate the extent to which SNA is incapable of accounting for meaning and power, they certainly point to a limitation in the way analysts have often operationalized SNA in social research.

Social network analysts and sociologists more generally have responded to these criticisms by focusing extensively on the relations between cultural meanings, power, and network structures (e.g., DiMaggio, 2011; McLean, 2007). Others have developed forms of *network ethnography*, a set of approaches that attempt to bring together ethnographic field methods and social network analysis techniques. We introduce the latter approach here given its use by many of the contributors to this volume. Howard (2002, pp. 561–562) identifies four conceptual dimensions of network ethnography. First, the traditional notion of field sites is relaxed to include the expansive terrains in and through which communities of practice are situated. This turns out to be particularly important for many of the analyses in this volume because they include global flows of power channeled through a wide variety of technologies and media. Second, SNA techniques can be used to identify informants in a less haphazard way (e.g., snowball sampling) by allowing researchers greater control over the process of gathering information. These efforts can, in turn, lead to additional informants that would have otherwise gone unnoticed. Finally, the network ethnography approach makes it easier to examine the flow of meanings through the network over time. As this approach has been extended and adapted to education policy contexts (Ball and Junemann, 2012), analysts have found that network ethnography also allows for greater attention to the power relations that constitute the dynamic flows of material and symbolic resources.

We would like to suggest that network ethnographic approaches are also in a strong position to capture the (often fluid) spatial contexts of education policy networks. The networks analyzed in the following chapters constitute forms of socio-spatial relations that are also situated across different scales, places and territories (Jessop, Brenner, and Jones, 2008). Indeed, sociologists of education have increasingly paid attention to these spatial dimensions of education policy and practice (Ferrare and Apple, 2010; Gulson and Symes, 2007; Lipman, 2011; Robertson, 2010). There are a variety of methodological tools available to examine these intersections, with the most popular coming from the field of Geographic Information Sciences (see Choi, 2009 for applications of GIS in education policy). In this volume the use of GIS is informed by critical cartography (Harley, 1989). Critical cartography is actually a set of tools and theoretical perspectives that focus on the relations of power that shape cartographic representations of space. By recognizing that the work of cartographers is culturally embedded and inherently political, critical cartographers believe they can produce more critical (and thus accurate) cartographic representations of space (Crampton and Krygier, 2006). The application of GIS and critical cartography in education policy is an important complement to the emergence of policy network analysis, as it offers researchers ways to represent how these networks are (re)shaping space through neoliberal projects.

When taken together, social network analysis, related multivariate techniques, network ethnography, and critical cartography offer researchers a wide range of tools to capture the complexity of the education policy networks currently influencing education systems around the world. Of course, the techniques described above merely scratch the surface of what is available. As education policy network analysis moves forward it will be important that methodological toolkits are adapted and expanded accordingly. This process requires a great deal of collective, multidisciplinary effort. As evidenced in the following chapters, this work is already underway.

The Chapters

The chapters in *Mapping Corporate Education Reform: Power and Policy Networks in the Neoliberal State* offer analyses of networks of actors surrounding neoliberal education policy and corporate reform. Making use of social network analysis, in various iterations and forms, these chapters illustrate the ways powerful networks of private/non-public organizations (philanthropies, non-profit organizations, for-profit organizations, corporations, and other non-governmental policy actors) are stitched together to effectively form new, relatively unaccountable, governance structures for education, essentially occupying the authoritative spaces created by the shrinking of the neoliberal state. To be clear, we do not mean to imply that the establishment of spatial occupation for the neoliberal project is simply a passive retreat of the state being replaced by aggressive private forces. We want to emphasize that the retreat of the state, as well as the space then occupied by private interests, are neoliberal aggressions built into the neoliberal model itself. Neoliberal interests in the state intend to reduce its size, reach, and social support, and they also intend for the markets of public assets they create to be occupied by private interests. Combined, the shrinking of the state and the marketization of all things public, are simply a compulsion of neoliberalism more generally (Harvey, 2007). The chapters here ultimately serve as various case studies of this aggressive neoliberal encroachment on the public and government vis-à-vis the formation of new forms of network governance by private interests and organizations. In what follows we provide a brief summary of each chapter that contextualizes how each speaks to the neoliberal state and network governance.

In Chapter Two, "mEducation as a Site of Network Governance," Santori, Ball, and Junemann utilize network ethnography methods to examine governance networks built around mobile education, with specific focus on how free market, entrepreneurial narratives either appropriate or subordinate other educational narratives about equity, access, and upward mobility. Within the context of the neoliberal state, this chapter illustrates how mobile education is being used to marketize public education in ways that make use of discourses of profit and opportunity while blending with international discourses of social justice, human rights, and equity.

In Chapter Three, "Network Restructuring of Global Edu-business: The Case of Pearson's *Efficacy Framework*," Hogan, Sellar, and Lingard combine SNA and network ethnography to map the networks surrounding a global marketing document of the massive, for-profit education corporation Pearson, entitled *Efficacy Framework*. This chapter thus looks at how, in a neoliberal context, a multinational corporation like Pearson has a complex and powerful network of educational influence (what they term as "network capital") around the world.

In Chapter Four, "Mapping the Education Entrepreneurial Network: Teach For America, Charter School Reform, and Corporate Sponsorship," Sondel, Kretchmar, and Ferrare use a wide variety of social network analysis methods to look at the complex network of individuals, organizations, and corporations surrounding policies and decisions connected to Teach For America and charter school reform initiatives in the United States. Within the context of the neoliberal state, this chapter highlights the levels of collusion between non-profit and for-profit organizations, corporations, and government agencies in the creation of mutually beneficial educational policies, and, as is the case elsewhere, these policies concentrate power in the hands of a network of private actors to the exclusion of community members and educators.

In Chapter Five, "International Access Project: A Network Analysis of an Emerging International Curriculum Program in China," Liu uses a network ethnography approach to examine the rise of neoliberalism in China and focuses specifically on the relationship of policy actors surrounding the emergence of a new international curriculum program in China. In doing so Liu highlights how such curriculum programs are not only directly connected to the development of new public-private, for-profit partnerships as a part of neoliberal governance, but also how these programs also serve to benefit the upward mobility schemes of Chinese elites.

In Chapter Six, "Mapping Neoliberal Reform in Chile: Following the Development and Legitimation of the Chilean System of School Quality Measurement (SIMCE)," Campos-Martínez, Pössel, and Inzunza follow the development of high-stakes testing in Chile, making several key historical and contemporary connections between public-private actors in the development and implementation of Chilean System of School Quality Measurement. As noted previously in this introduction, the case of Chile is of historical importance given that the neoliberal experiment at a national level functionally started there, and so their experience is an important example for the rest of the world. Thus, while the implementation of neoliberal education policies is relatively new in countries such as the United States, the authors of this chapter are afforded the chance to illustrate how neoliberal network governance is not only established, but also how it matures over the course of multiple decades.

In Chapter Seven, "Mapping the Discourse of Neoliberal Education Reform: Space, Power, and Access in Chicago's Renaissance 2010 Debate," Bell does a novel analysis of how policy networks of new governance surround the public debate over education policy vis-à-vis the two major newspapers in Chicago during the run-up to and implementation of the Renaissance 2010, corporate education reform plan for Chicago Public Schools. Bell's work draws from a diverse range of methodological tools, including a multivariate analysis of newspaper themes and the representation of these themes over the space of Chicago's neighborhoods through the use of critical cartography and GIS. Lending support to Harvey's (2007) analysis of the ways that the media is used to develop the ideological support for neoliberalism, Bell's chapter illustrates how, within the neoliberal state, media, corporate interests, and the elite functionally collude in an attempt to sway mainstream, public commonsense understandings of a set of neoliberal education reforms.

In Chapter Eight, "Other People's Policy: Wealthy Elites and Charter School Reform in Washington State," we (Au and Ferrare) use a directed graph to look at the network of philanthropies, non-profit organizations, and individual donors connected to a public campaign to legalize charter schools in the U.S. state of Washington by a popular vote of the public. This chapter highlights how a relatively small group of wealthy elites advance their personal education reform agenda using networks of resources that flow from their personal caches of wealth either directly to the campaign to legalize charter schools or indirectly vis-à-vis their affiliated philanthropies' funding of select, pro-charter school, non-profit and advocacy organizations. Politically we highlight how within the neoliberal state, education policy (in this specific case in the state of Washington) is being determined for all children by a small group of elites with no public accountability and who do not send their own children to public schools.

In Chapter Nine, "Gangsta Raps, Power Gaps, and Network Maps: How the Charter School Market Came to New Orleans," Buras uses a network ethnography approach to examine the neoliberal experiment taking place in New Orleans. There the public school system has been dismantled entirely and reconstructed as a "free market" competition among charter schools. In this way Buras' chapter critically analyzes what has happened to the public schools when the neoliberal state has been almost totally shrunken, with the remaining policy space filled by the governance of private interests—a situation that Buras points out has created massive inequities and injustice there.

In Chapter Ten, "Enterprise Education Policy and Embedded Layers of Corporate Influence," Burch and Smith look at how, as a direct result of the No Child Left Behind federal education policy in the U.S., public school districts and states are increasingly turning to digital technology (i.e., online instruction, digital textbooks, hardware, and software) provided by private, for-profit enterprises, as a means to "fix" the achievement of students who perform poorly in schools. As an example of network governance in the neoliberal state, Burch and Smith's chapter illustrates how policymakers, business interests, and state agencies functionally collude to create policies that are mutually beneficial, including the direct benefit of corporate interests, and resulting in increased privatization of public education.

Conclusion

We close this introduction by admitting that in many ways this collection is incomplete, largely because there is a growing amount of formal and informal mapping of corporate education reform being done in a multitude of pockets (see, e.g., Detroitucation, 2013; Osborne, 2014), and much of it does not necessarily make use of SNA to accomplish considerably powerful work analyzing such networks (see, e.g., Scott and Jabbar, 2014). And certainly, as of this writing, the neoliberal state is our current reality here in the US and around most of the world, so there are many, many more critical analyses of the new governance of education by corporate interests that have yet to be done. However, taking our cue from the *Theses on Feuerbach* (Marx, 1978), we want to emphasize that the point here is not just to study and interpret corporate education reform and the new governance through network analyses. The point is to highlight the contradictions such networks present relative to democracy, power, equality, and public institutions in hopes of opening up space to contest and change these policies and practices into systems that meet the needs of the vast majority of the populace, and not just enrich and empower the few.

Note

1   For a thorough introduction to social network analysis see Wasserman and Faust (1994). For more advanced modeling techniques see Carrington, Scott, and Wasserman (2005).

References

Anyon, J. (1997). *Ghetto schooling: A political economy of urban educational reform.* New York: Teachers College Press.

Apple, M. W. (2001). Comparing neo-liberal projects and inequality in education. *Comparative Education, 37*(4), 409–423.

Apple, M. W. (2006). *Educating the "right" way: Markets, standards, god, and inequality* (second ed.). New York: RoutledgeFalmer.

Au, W. (2009). *Unequal by design: High-stakes testing and the standardization of inequality.* New York: Routledge.

Au, W. (2013). What's a nice test like you doing in a place like this?: The edTPA and corporate education reform. *Rethinking Schools, 27*(4). Retrieved August 13, 2014 from www.rethinkingschools.org/archive/27_04/27_04_au.shtml

Au, W., and Ferrare, J. J. (2014). Sponsors of policy: A network analysis of wealthy elites, their affiliated philanthropies, and charter school reform in Washington State. *Teachers College Record, 116*(8). Retrieved July 30, 2014 from www.tcrecord.org/content.asp?contentid=17387

Ball, S. J. (2012). *Global education inc.: New policy networks and the neo-liberal imaginary.* New York: Routledge.

Ball, S. J., and Junemann, C. (2012). *Networks, new governance and education.* Bristol, UK: Policy Press.

Barkan, J. (2011). Got dough?: How billionaires rule our schools. *Dissent, 58*(1), 49–57. doi:10.1353/dss.2011.0023

Barkan, J. (2012). Hired guns on astroturf: How to buy and sell school reform. *Dissent, 59*(2), 49–57.

Bill & Melinda Gates Foundation. (2013). How we work: Awarded grants. Retrieved October 20, 2013 from www.gatesfoundation.org/How-We-Work/Quick-Links/Grants-Database

Borg, I., and Groenen, P. J. F. (2005). *Modern multidimensional scaling: Theory and applications.* New York: Springer.

Bosworth, D. (2011). The cultural contradiction of philanthrocapitalism. *Society*, *48*, 382–388. doi:10.1007/s12115–011–9466-z

Bourdieu, P., and Wacquant, L. J. D. (1992). *An invitation to reflexive sociology*. Chicago: University of Chicago Press.

Breiger, R. (1974). The duality of persons and groups. *Social Forces*, *53*, 181–190.

Burch, P. (2009). *Hidden markets: The new education privatization*. New York: Routledge.

Carrington, P. J., Scott, J., and Wasserman, S. (2005). *Models and methods in social network analysis*. Cambridge: Cambridge University Press.

Choi, D. S. (2009). New possibilities for critical education research: Uses for Geographical Information Systems (GIS). In M. W. Apple, W. Au, and L. A. Gandin (Eds.), *The Routledge international handbook of critical education* (pp. 449–464). New York, NY: Routledge.

Crampton, J. W., and Krygier, J. (2006). An introduction to critical cartography. *ACME: An International E-Journal for Critical Geographies*, *4*(1), 11–33.

Daly, A. J. (Ed.). (2010). *Social network theory and educational change*. Cambridge: Harvard University Press.

Davies, W. (2014). Neoliberalism: A bibliographic review. *Theory, Culture and Society*. doi:10.1177/0263276414546383

Detroitucation (2013). Ever wonder where all the money is going/coming from? Retrieved August 20, 2014 from http://detroitucation.wordpress.com/2013/09/29/ever-wonder-where-all-the-money-is-goingcoming-from/

DiMaggio, P. (2011). Cultural networks. In J. Scott and P. J. Carrington (Eds.), *The SAGE handbook of social network analysis* (pp. 286–300). Thousand Oakes, CA: Sage Publications Ltd.

Emirbayer, M., and Goodwin, J. (1994). Network analysis, culture, and the problem of agency. *American Journal of Sociology*, *99*, 1411–1454.

Everitt, B. S., Landau, S., Leese, M., and Stahl, D. (2011). *Cluster analysis* (fifth ed.). West Sussex, UK: John Wiley & Sons.

Fabricant, M., and Fine, M. (2012). *Charter schools and the corporate makeover of public education*. New York: Teachers College Press.

Fabricant, M., and Fine, M. (2013). *The changing politics of education: Privatization and the dispossessed lives left behind*. Boulder, CO: Paradigm Publishers.

Feld, S., L., and Carter, W. C. (1998). When desgregation reduces interracial contact: A class size paradox for weak ties. *American Journal of Sociology*, *103*(5), 1165–1186.

Ferrare, J. J. (2009). Can critical education research be "quantitative"? In M. W. Apple, W. Au, and L. Gandin (Eds.), *Routledge international handbook of critical education* (pp. 465–481). New York: Routledge.

Ferrare, J. J., and Apple, M. W. (2010). Spatializing critical education: Progress and cautions. *Critical Studies in Education*, *51*(2), 209–222.

Friedkin, N. E., and Thomas, S. L. (1997). Social positions in schooling. *Sociology of Education*, *70*(4), 239–255.

Gee, J. P. (1996). *Social linguistics and literacies: Ideology in discourses* (second ed.). New York: RoutledgeFalmer.

Greenacre, M. (2007). *Correspondence analysis in practice* (second ed.). Boca Raton, FL: Chapman & Hall/CRC.

Gulson, K., and Symes, C. (Eds.). (2007). *Spatial theories of education: Policy and geography matters*. New York: Routledge.

Hallinan, M. T., and Sorensen, A. B. (1985). Ability grouping and student friendships. *American Educational Research Journal*, *22*(4), 485–499.

Harley, J. B. (1989). Deconstructing the map. *Cartographica, 26*(2), 1–20.

Harvey, D. (2004a). *A geographer's perspective on imperialism: Conversations with history*. Berkeley, CA: UC Institute of International Studies.

Harvey, D. (2004b). The "new" imperialism: Accumulation by dispossession. *Socialist Register, 40*, 63–87.

Harvey, D. (2007). Neoliberalism as creative destruction. *Annals of the American Academy of Political and Social Science, 610*, 22–44.

Harvey, D. (2014). *Seventeen contradictions and the end of capitalism*. New York: Oxford University Press.

Howard, P. N. (2002). Network ethnography and the hypermedia organization: New media, new organizations, new methods. *New Media & Society, 4*(4), 550–574.

Hursh, D. (2011). The Gates Foundation's interventions into education, health, and food policies: Technology, power, and the privatization of political problems. In P. E. Kovacs (Ed.), *The Gates Foundation and the future of U.S. "public" schools* (pp. 39–52). New York: Routledge.

Hursh, D. W. (2006). Neoliberalism and the control of teachers, students, and learning: The rise of standards, standardization, and accountability. *Cultural Logic, 4*(1). Retrieved from www.eserver.org/clogic/4–1/hursh.html

Jessop, B., Brenner, N., and Jones, M. (2008). Theorizing sociospatial relations. *Environment and Planning D: Society and Space, 26*, 389–401.

Kliebard, H. M. (2004). *The struggle for the American curriculum, 1893–1958* (third ed.). New York, NY: RoutledgeFalmer.

Kretchmar, K., Sondel, B., and Ferrare, J. J. (2014). Mapping the terrain: Teach For America, charter school reform, and corporate sponsorship. *Journal of Education Policy*. doi:10.1080/02680939.2014.880812

Kruskal, J. B., and Wish, M. (1978). *Multidimensional scaling* (Vol. 11). London: Sage.

Lipman, P. (2011). *The new political economy of urban education: Neoliberalism, race, and the right to the city*. New York: Routledge.

Marx, K. (1978). Theses on Feuerbach. In R. C. Tucker (Ed.), *The Marx-Engels reader* (second ed., pp. 143–145). New York: W. W. Norton.

McFarland, D. A. (2001). Student resistance: How the formal and informal organization of classrooms facilitate everyday forms of student defiance. *American Journal of Sociology, 107*(5), 612–678.

McLean, P. D. (2007). *The art of the network: Startegic interaction and patronage in renaissance florence*. Durham, NC: Duke University Press.

Mohr, J. W., and Duquenne, V. (1997). The duality of culture and practice: Poverty relief in New York City, 1888–1917. *Theory and Society, 26*, 305–356.

Osborne, E. (2014). Visualized—how Bill Gates bought the Common Core. Retrieved August 1, 2014 from www.honestpracticum.com/visualized-how-bill-gates-bought-the-common-core/

Ravitch, D. (2013). *Reign of error: The hoax of the privatization movement and the danger to America's public schools*. New York: Alfred A. Knopf.

Reckhow, S., and Snyder, J. W. (2014). The expanding role of philanthropy in education politics. *Educational Researcher*, 1–10. DOI: 10.3102/0013189X14536607.

Robertson, S. (2010). "Spatialising" the sociology of education: Stand-points, entry-points, vantage-points. In S. J. Ball, M. W. Apple, and L. Gandin (Eds.), *Routledge international handbook of sociology of education* (pp. 15–26). London and New York: Routledge.

Roy, A. (2014). *Capitalism: A ghost story*. Chicago: Haymarket Books.

Saltman, K. J. (2011). From Carnegie to Gates: The Bill and Melinda Gates Foundation and the venture philanthropy agenda for public education. In P. E. Kovacs (Ed.), *The Gates Foundation and the future of U.S. "public" schools* (pp. 1–20). Oxon, UK: Routledge.

Saltman, K. J. (2012). *The failure of corporate school reform*. Boulder, CO: Paradigm Publishers.

Scott, J. T., and Jabbar, H. (2014). The hub and the spokes: Foundations, intermediary organizations, incentivist reforms, and the politics of research evidence. *Educational Policy*, 28(2), 233–257.

Song, M., and Miskel, C. G. (2007). Exploring the structural properties of the state reading policy domain using network visualization technique. *Educational Policy*, 21(4), 589–614.

Strauss, V. (2013). Bill Gates: "It would be great if our education stuff worked but. . . ." Retrieved August 1, 2014, from www.washingtonpost.com/blogs/answer-sheet/wp/2013/09/27/bill-gates-it-would-be-great-if-our-education-stuff-worked-but/

Wasserman, S., and Faust, K. (1994). *Social network analysis: Methods and applications*. New York: Cambridge University Press.

Zeichner, K. M., and Pena-Sandoval, C. (2015). Venture philanthropy and teacher education policy in the U.S.: The role of the New Schools Venture Fund. *Teachers College Record*, 117(6). Retrieved August 5, 2014 from www.tcrecord.org

2

mEDUCATION AS A SITE OF NETWORK GOVERNANCE

Diego Santori, Stephen J. Ball, and Carolina Junemann

Network Governance and Education

As a new kind of governing mechanism, network governance relies "on a dense fabric of lasting ties and networks that provide key resources of expertise, reputation and legitimization" (Grabher, 2004, p. 104). However, policy networks also work through the circulation of more subtle elements like narratives about what counts as a "good" policy, which can determine the course of action of those key resources. Patterson and Monroe (1998, pp. 315–316) argue that "insofar as narratives affect our perceptions of political reality, which in turn affect our actions in response to or in anticipation of political events, narrative plays a critical role in the construction of political behavior." In this paper we examine how enterprise narratives of innovation, entrepreneurship, and scalability intersect, and perhaps appropriate (or at least subordinate), narratives of access, equal opportunity, and social mobility. We do this by looking at a specific instantiation of global governance networks structured around what has been referred as mEducation, or mobile education, with particular attention to key nodal sites that work to fusion and channel these narratives. The GSMA defines mEducation as "the use of individual, portable devices which make use of mobile networks in mainstream education settings, aligning with curriculum objectives or used for high-stakes assessment. mEducation incorporates both learning content and administrative activities" (GSMA mEducation, 2012, p. 3).

The basic premise of this paper is a simple one: the increasing role of mobile technology as a policy solution to expand access to education, enhance teaching effectiveness, and accelerate learning, and the growing interest from the business sector in mEducation as a niche of commercial opportunity and profit, work to blur international development discourses of human rights, equity, and social justice with business discourses of entrepreneurship and leverage.

The paper pays particular attention to the mEducation Alliance, as a space of knowledge sharing, validation and production, highlighting the role of some key players in shaping and to some extent delineating the principles that underpin those practices. The mEducation network (see Figure 2.1 below), we argue, constitutes an "epistemic community" organized around specific interpretations of existing social problems, emerging business niches, and new policy solutions. Here we want to explore both the network animation, as the set of practices that keeps the network alive, and network evolution, as the continuous displacement of its elements that alters the form or density of existing configurations. In order to "identify the actors in these networks, their power and capacities, and the ways through which they exercise their power through association within networks of relationships" (Dicken, Kelly, Olds, and Wai-Chung Yeung, 2001, p. 93), we use the "method" of "network ethnography" (Howard, 2002), a mapping of the form and content of governance relations and processes in a particular field, a variation of what Bevir and Rhodes (2006) call "ethnographic analyses of governance in action." Through a backward mapping of the key relationships and connections linking policy actors, nodes, events, organizations and technologies and, specifically, through the following of specific "cases" or programs of action (Latour, 1993) we aim to offer an account of mEducation as a space of network governance. In particular, we focus our attention on the work of different kinds of spaces of exchange, collaboration, and production (such as online communities

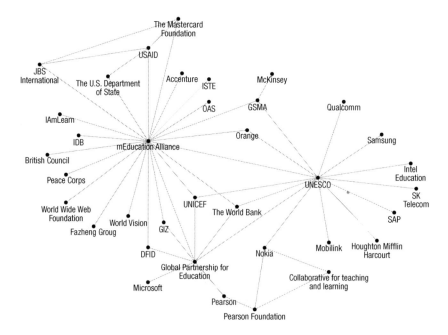

FIGURE 2.1 mEducation policy network

and forums, conferences and symposiums) as points of "meetingness"[1] and as sites of discourse and practice, what McCann and Ward (2011, p. 12) call the "different 'wheres' in and through which policies are moulded and mobilized."

The Ed-Tech Ecosystem

Ed-Tech has come to represent a major site of business opportunities, a multi-billion dollar global market. Indeed, recently (June 2014) the U.S.-based education newspaper *Education Week* published a special report called "Navigating the Ed-Tech Marketplace" (Education Week, 2014b), characterizing the educational technology market as "in a state of frenzied activity" (p. 1). In its opening paragraph, this report offers a thrilling account of its market dynamics, one in which education, technology, and entrepreneurship are mutually dependent:

> Venture capital is flowing into the sector at a torrential pace, fuelled by the belief that start-ups can use new digital tools to transform education— and generate profits. At the same time, established companies are changing the way they do business, shifting from print to digital resources and materials, and merging with or acquiring other companies to help them make that transition.
>
> *(p. 1)*

The market is so vast that websites such as EdSurge have created an Ed-Tech index (EdSurge, 2014), which offers information on 959 products categorized as curriculum, teacher needs, school operations, post-secondary, and "everything else." Indeed, the constant proliferation of new initiatives and products gives the impression of an unfettered market. For instance, the website TechCrunch (2014) claims that, in the U.S. context, education technology-focused start-ups raised over USD 500 million in the first quarter of 2014. On the other hand, Ed-Tech is becoming an increasingly structured space through the work of "globalizing microspaces" that condense and regulate (both tacitly and explicitly) the principles of action and interaction within this growing field. The International Society for Technology in Education (ISTE) is an example of this. Through a series of resources and tools ISTE aims to support "educators and education leaders committed to empowering connected learners in a connected world" (ISTE, 2014). ISTE encompasses a wide range of possibilities for participation such as professional learning networks that enable exchange and collaboration around specific topics, such as "1to1" network (with 2300 members), digital storytelling network (with 1300 members), or virtual environment networks (with 916 members). ISTE is also a space for advocacy, leadership and commerce. The Advocacy Toolkit offers a "personal advocacy checklist" to track and set advocacy goals, as well as a set of templates that include the "digital learning success story" to help Ed-Tech advocates maximize impact by clearly articulating their story, or the "elevator pitch" template, to maximize impact "when you only have a minute or less to make a powerful case for digital learning." The "Lead & Transform" diagnostic tool enables the evaluation of a school or district's progress towards technology integration, providing personalized feedback towards leveraging strengths and identifying opportunities for growth (ISTE, 2014). ISTE also works as an Ed-Tech marketplace, with an online catalogue of services and featured companies. Finally, ISTE has developed its own standards for students, teachers, administrators, coaches, and computer science educators.

Grand Narratives and Little Stories

As a discursive space, Ed-Tech is dominated by grand narratives of innovation, scalability, acceleration, value for money, and systemic change, as well as little stories of individual risk-taking entrepreneurial spirit. Somers (1994, p. 616) argues that the core feature of narrative is that "it renders understanding only by connecting (however unstably) parts to a constructed configuration or a social network of relationships (however incoherent or unrealizable) composed of symbolic, institutional, and material practices." Ed-Tech represents a specific genre within the broader category of entrepreneurship, characterized by the trilogy of vision, risk and success. These stories are intrinsically relational, and they constitute "a joint social production and as such they are interrelated to each other and to the spatial-temporal context in which they are expressed" (Scuzzarello, 2010, p. 17). That is, each individual narrative ascribes meaning from a complex, multilevel interaction with other existing narratives in the web.

GSV Advisors, an education-sector-focused investment bank based in Chicago, represents an interesting illustration of the ways in which the Ed-Tech grand narrative is constructed and circulated. From the outset, they claim that GSV stands for "Global Silicon Valley," suggesting that "Silicon Valley is no longer just a physical place, but also a mindset that has gone viral" (GSV Advisors, 2012a). In line with this thinking, they have published two white papers that are full of images, famous quotes, and figures. Both reports are structured around a fundamental challenge that threatens the collective possibilities of existence of a given community, a challenge to be confronted by a group of risk-takers that are willing to go beyond the limits of imagination. With the image of Berliners celebrating the fall of the wall on the front cover, GSV's white paper titled *Fall of the wall: Capital flows to education innovation* (GSV Advisors, 2012b) claims that "The 'wall' of opposition to investing in education has come down, for now, bringing in a welcome flood of financial and entrepreneurial capital." Under the title *Revolution 2.0: How Education Innovation is Going to Revitalize America and Transform the U.S. Economy* (GSV Advisors, 2012c), Ed-Tech is portrayed as a tidal wave that can bring innovation to unimagined horizons. Narrated in a battle jargon, the report claims that "the time is now," presenting the Ed-Tech revolution as a collective project, a joint adventure, a crusade. Notably, the following quote from Margaret Mead is used in the report to convey the sense of a collective enterprise for the common good: "Never doubt that a small group of thoughtful, committed citizens can change the world; indeed, it's the only thing that ever has."

The process of narration, Scuzzarello (2010, p. 18) argues, always entails a selective process of appropriation and omittance of certain elements, but also of "fitting in" in some discourses. This is evident in GSV's reports, through the appropriation of the rhetorics of the *American Revolution* and the *Fall of the Wall*, as well as the omitting of the failure and bankruptcy of many Ed-Tech initiatives (Hack Education, 2013). In turn, these narratives are intertwined with little stories of "successful" edupreneurs and teachers that circulate through websites, blogs, and magazines. A snapshot of this is captured by the narrative of agony and success of Mr. Hensley, the developer of Intagrade, a dropout-prevention software program. An article titled *Vendors struggle to master the K-12 system*, tells his story:

> Mr. Hensley's company managed to sign up about 30 districts and schools for its dropout-prevention software. But that wasn't enough to keep up with the expenses, or build the company. In 2012, when he flew to an education conference in New York City to look for seed-funding, the company was "pretty close" to running out of money, he recalled.
>
> Then came an unexpected turn: at the conference, he met a representative from the global education company Pearson, which was impressed enough with the product to eventually agree to buy it, two years after Intagrade was launched.
>
> *(Education Week, 2014b, p. 10)*

Narratives "are ongoing processes with dynamic rather than static ties" (Scuzzarello, 2010, p. 17). The notion of dynamic ties suggests simultaneous links to multiple spaces (real or imaginary), as in this narrative of effort, struggle and success, where the conference is presented as a place of transformation. Teachers are also part of these narratives of innovation and success, as noted by Education Week's special report *Getting personal: Teachers, technology and tailored instruction* (2014a), which tells the success story of Neebe, an English teacher who left behind the "analog" instruction model:

> Under Neebe's model, students write their essays during class on a shared Google Document, and she can immediately help students who are confused, stalled, or have questions. She can also explore ideas with them.
>
> The most challenging book she assigns is *The Scarlet Letter*, and last year, Neebe created an interactive iBook to help students struggling with the text. The iBook contains what Neebe calls "video footnotes," which are meant to give context to parts of the novel that are particularly hard to understand. In one of these, for instance, Neebe gives a three-minute

overview of American Romanticism. In another, a former art museum guide gives a four-minute overview of light and color patterns in the text.

(Education Week, 2014a)

Neebe was awarded the "Outstanding Young Educator Award" by the International Society of Technology in Education (ISTE) for demonstrating vision, innovation, action, and transformation using technology to improve learning and teaching (ISTE, 2014). Thus, little stories are integrated into grand narratives of success and opportunity, ultimately reinforcing the figure of the entrepreneur as the promise of indefinite innovation.

U.S. Market

The US represents the largest Ed-Tech market in the world. According to CB Insights, a venture capital database and angel investment database, while the reported overall Ed-Tech investment remained below the USD 100 million in 2012, it surpassed half a million dollars in 2014 via 103 transactions, attracting more venture capital and angel investors than ever before. According to GSV, this increased attention to Ed-Tech as an area of investment was catalyzed by the U.S. regulatory framework, specifically by the demands from recent policy initiatives such as "Race to the Top" and "Common Core Standards."

GSV Advisors notes that the number of disclosed transactions in which companies are raising money primarily in K-12 education and concentrated mainly in Ed-Tech, went from 18 valued at USD 121 million in 2007 to 145 transactions valued at USD 629 million in 2013. Even more, as noted by Education Week (2014b),

> venture-capital firms that once generally avoided the K-12 market are now diving in. In February, Remind 101 Inc., a free mobile-messaging service for teachers, raised USD 15 million in a funding round led by venture-capital company Kleiner Perkins Caufield & Byers; and educational analytics company BrightBytes raised USD 15 million in funding through Bessemer Venture Partners.
>
> *(p. 6)*

However, Ed-Tech is not a homogeneous field. Quite the contrary, it is a dynamic space with differentiated market trends for each subsector. For instance, according to extrapolations from the Software and Information Industry association (SIIA) 2011–2012, the productivity tools segment experienced a recent decline as school districts move towards free software such as Google Apps for Education; professional-development revenues increased over 10 percent, as result of the demands from government and school policies based on student-performance data; Learning Management Systems (LMS), tutoring, and General Educational

Development (GED) services evidenced a significant decline (*Education Week*, 2014b, pp. 16–18). Not surprisingly, testing and assessment remained the largest Ed-Tech segment, with an estimated market over USD 2 billion. If anything, this snapshot of the U.S. Ed-Tech market makes the interdependence between policy and business very apparent, evidencing how profit and regulatory environments are mutually dependent.

A Nodal Point in the Ed-Tech Business—GSV Advisors

GSV Advisors provide merger and advisory and private placement services with a focus on Ed-Tech. With over 20 years in the market, GSV claims to have completed 283 transactions totaling over USD 41.2 billion. For instance, GSV was the exclusive financial advisor for the sale of Lexia to Rosetta Stone in August 2013 for USD 22.5 million, advisor for the sale of Campuslabs to Higher One in August 2012 for USD 85.4 million, and advisor to the sale of The Learning Company for USD 3.3 billion (GSV Advisors, 2012a).

Among other international organizations, GSV is a member of SIIA and ISTE, and supports high-impact not-for-profits such as Teach For America, Knowledge Is Power Program (KIPP) Schools, and the Network for Teaching Entrepreneurship (NFTE). In addition to the white papers mentioned already, GSV Advisors, together with Arizona State University (ASU), run the "Education Innovation Summit", which they refer to as "the Knowledge Economy's Mecca of conversation and activism devoted to accelerating learning innovation around the world" (GSV Media, 2014). The 2014 edition was sponsored by 50 companies and organizations including Bill & Melinda Gates Foundation, Pearson, Microsoft, Dell, AT&T, and McGraw Hill Education. The summit included keynote speeches from Netflix CEO Reed Hastings and even celebrities such as NBA legend and global social entrepreneur Earvin Magic Johnson, interviews with major figures such as the U.S. Secretary of Commerce Penny Pritzker, speeches from former Governor of Florida Jeb Bush, Donald Graham, founder of Graham Holdings, lead director of Facebook, and former Chairman and CEO of the Washington Post Company, and presentations from other 190 influential speakers from the "global Ed-Tech ecosystem." Following McCann (2010, p. 23) these speeches are "particular types of storytelling, involving strategic namings and framing, inserted into a specific context where actors are predisposed to a certain range of policy opinions."

Based on the notion of Return on Investment (RoI), GSV advocates Return on Education (RoE) as a key test of an education company's potential, which basically means "driving down costs while increasing access and producing better outcomes" (GSV Advisors, 2012c, p. 62). Notably, GSV argues that by adopting RoE, the terms "for-profit" and "not-for-profit" become irrelevant, "as they represent corporate structures and thus have no bearing on the effectiveness of a particular program or product" (p. 298). As noted in previous work (Ball, 2012,

p. 67), events such as conferences are also "sites of persuasion," in this case where business narratives are "continually enacted, performed and practiced" (McCann, 2010, p. 27). Through the RoE Innovation Awards, the GSV–ASU summit works as a platform for the circulation and proliferation of specific views about the role of education in a democratic society.

The Emergence of mEducation

mEducation represents a case in point for the study of network governance in education, particularly because unlike traditional systems of education delivery, the "m" component is generally outside the domain of the state. mEducation is presented in reports, websites and conferences as a business solution to constraints of time and space imposed by the school on education delivery enabling learning anytime, anywhere, and represents the path towards real-time access and independence, seamless monitoring, customization, and collaboration. As noted by the mobile association Groupe Speciale Mobile Association (GSMA), mEducation is different from eLearning in its "ability to unlock the user from a fixed infrastructure and limited distribution" (GSMA Development Fund, 2010, p. 6). This means that, almost by definition, mEducation involves cross-sector cooperation (device manufacturer, mobile operator, education system). In what follows we explore the role of two key nodal sites (GSMA and UNESCO) in delineating the "globalizing microspace" of mEducation.

Delineating the Field—Landscaping

A joint report by McKinsey & Company and GSMA claims that mEducation is poised to become a USD 70 billion market by 2020. This estimated growth, the report highlights, is based on interrelated trends such as increased availability and penetration of smart portable devices; a digital native and technology-literate generation fast emerging; and increasing popularity of education apps (15–17 percent of titles at the major App/eBook/Audio stores are education-based, where Education is the second most popular download category behind Games). Notably, based on customer metrics from Strategy Analytics, a U.S.-based market research and consultancy firm, the McKinsey-GSMA (2012) report highlights:

> 25 million education-linked apps were downloaded in 2009 and 270 million in 2011—a more than tenfold increase. The growth in free education apps has been significantly higher than the overall market growth. Paid education apps have also grown to 36 million downloads in 2011, representing a total revenue of USD 120 million—a sharp rise over the 4.5 million paid downloads in 2009 worth USD 15 million.

(p. 12)

In turn, governments are investing in mobile learning in order expand access and improve learning outcomes, with at least 15 countries currently investing in deployments of mobile devices for schools at national or state level. Taken together, these trends create a "fertile environment" (McKinsey & Company, and GSMA, 2012, p. 5) for the growth of mEducation products and solutions:

- educational e-books and courses accessed through portable devices,
- learning management systems (LMS) and authoring tools,
- game or simulation-based learning tools,
- collaboration tools,
- adaptive assessment services,
- test preparation support,
- distance tutoring and homework support.

Many of these solutions have turned into significant business deals, such as Providence Equity Partners acquiring BlackBoard Inc. (an education software company that developed BlackBoard Learn, a virtual learning environment and course management system) in 2011 for around USD 1.64 billion; the sale of a 90 percent stake in Wireless Generation (mobile assessment software) to News Corporation in 2010 for approximately USD 360 million; and Research in Motion's acquisition of Chalk Media (the developer of Mobile Chalkboard, a software to create, manage and track mobile content including courses and training materials) in 2008 in an all-cash deal of USD 18.7 million (*Education Week*, 2014b, p. 24; McKinsey & Company, and GSMA, 2012). The McKinsey-GSMA report particularly addresses Mobile Network Operators (MNOs) in relation to the business opportunity that mEducation represents. Interestingly, it discusses strategic options for capturing a share in the education market that range from simply providing connectivity, to more sophisticated products that include technical enablers such as IT, network, content and data management services, or end-to-end mEducation services, which promise the highest revenues. Indeed, some tele-communications operators have already stepped into the end-to-end mEducation business. For instance, Telefónica has created its own dedicated education company, Telefónica Learning Services (TLS), which offers a wide range of products for individual students, schools, and companies, with recent expansion overseas (Brazil, Chile, Colombia, and Peru). TLS's flagship service is WePack, an integrated solution that includes hardware (Vexia tablets for all students), management and administration, maintenance and insurance, wireless internet in the classroom, and access to Telefónica's educational platform WeClass, which provides content and teacher training. This service is charged to the school on a per-student monthly fee (Telefónica Learning Services S.A., 2013).

Another example of MNOs providing learning solutions is T Smart Learning (SK Telecom, 2013), a tablet-based smart education platform launched by SK Telecom. In partnership with 12 Edu-businesses, the Korean mobile service provider offers access to content per subject as well as coursework support. Apart from a wide range of support tools (i.e., smart notes, edu-games, etc.) this mobile learning platform presents some innovative features such as text messages to keep students motivated, as well as real-time access to students' academic performance for parents.

GSMA

GSMA has developed a wide range of reports that outline the principles, scope, and challenges of mEducation. The Mobile Education Landscape Report (GSMA, 2011) focuses on the mEducation market, outlining its size and potential, as well as key players and products, and their impact on the wider ecosystem. The New Business Models report (GSMA mEducation, 2012) explores the different strategies applied by mobile operators to address the market needs of key user segments, including B2B (business-to-business), B2C (business-to-customer), B2B2X (where "X" can be a corporation, a school, or a customer). Notably, the report highlights the urgent need for MNOs to influence the policy-making process: "Mobile operators risk being marginalized if they do not engage with policy makers and administrators in the education sector to promote a positive, 'top-down' vision for the adoption and use of mobile learning in the classroom and beyond" (p. 2). *The Mobile Proposition for Education* (GSMA Mobile Education, 2011) outlines the key scenarios for mobile education, including vocational education and training, school learning environment, out-of-classroom education and collaboration, professional learning and development, and special needs. GSMA also produced a series of Mobile Education country reports, which include France, Japan, Spain, the United Kingdom, and the United States, and provide context-specific insights in relation to compulsory, vocational, and higher education. Finally, through a series of case studies, the *mLearning: A Platform for Educational Opportunities at the Base of the Pyramid*, by the GSMA Development Fund, discusses challenges and opportunities of mLearning in developing countries. It is asserted that, while eventually enhancing learning opportunities, these initiatives also represent a huge opportunity in terms of access to new markets and investment opportunities, as well as the possibility to experiment —that is trying out products and services in a low-stake environment. In fact, under the subtitle "mLearning is a Business, not just CSR Activity," GSMA Development Fund (2010) notes:

> There is greater and more immediate value in vocational forms of mLearning where the end user is paying for the service. Health education, language lessons and general life skills are seen by mobile customers as valuable and worth paying for. Many MNOs have CSR activities surrounding education, for example donating funds and resources to help build schools or sponsoring scholarships. Whilst this type of activity often falls in line with company's

strategic social responsibilities and is an altruistic contribution to society, MNOs should consider the benefits of their own networks. By merely conducting "business as usual," implementing and growing their network coverage, they are increasing the opportunities for those in rural and ultra regions to "get connected" and use mLearning services, thus increasing customer base and revenues.

(p. 30)

Again here the convergence of policy goals, such as increasing participation in education and addressing urban/rural and gender inequalities with business interests, is very evident.

UNESCO

The pressing demands from the Millennium Development Goals (MDG) and Education for All (EFA) to expand access to education in developing countries set a conducive environment for different forms of collaboration. In contexts of extreme material and cultural deprivation, education is increasingly delivered through a mix of "strategic alliances, joint working arrangements, networks, part-nerships, and many other forms of collaboration across sectoral and organizational boundaries" (Williams, 2002, p. 103). Within the context of international devel-opment, mEducation represents a "silver bullet," a policy solution to reach those children that cannot attend school because parents require them to work and bring income into the household; provide content in local languages in countries where the language used in schools is different from that used at home; support girls dropping out of school due to violence, sexual abuse or poor sanitation; empower schools and students in rural communities providing updated learn-ing resources adapted to their local context; provide pupil teachers with training and continuing professional development; and overcome issues such as teacher absenteeism and classroom overcrowding due to teacher shortage (GSMA Development Fund, 2010).

In consonance with these claims, in 2010 UNESCO launched its Mobile Learning initiative, with the aim to promote the use of mobile technologies to further the objectives of Education For All. Through an initial three-year agreement, the communications and information technology multinational Nokia has committed to a USD 5–10 million investment in order to support the emerging field of mEducation. This involves conducting research to identify possible applications of mobile technology, with particular attention to the use of mobile technologies to support teacher training and capacity-building, as well as school analytics and management. The agreement also seeks the development of new mobile applications with educational potential. All this mapping, research and experimentation are to be disseminated through events, guidelines, and landscape reports for teachers and policy makers.

Through a working paper series on mobile learning, UNESCO discusses the policy implications of mEducation by analyzing ongoing initiatives from the field. The landscape report *The future of mobile learning* (UNESCO, 2013a) discusses the state of mobile learning, with emphasis on the potential that mLearning initiatives have in order to meet the EFA goals, as well as its limitations. The *Policy guidelines for mobile learning* (UNESCO, 2013b) outlines the condition of possibility for an mEducation environment that will include: supporting the provision of robust and affordable mobile networks within and across communities; advocating for "m-rate" subsidies to promote mobile access to the internet for education purposes; the creation of incentives for developers to build content specifically for mobile devices; and encouraging the development of platforms or software that allow classroom teachers to create or tailor mobile content. Furthermore, region-focused reports discuss the context-specific implications of mobile education for Africa and the Middle East, Asia, Europe, Latin America, and North America. For instance the *Turning on mobile learning in Africa and the Middle East* (UNESCO, 2012) report showcases the MoMath project in South Africa developed by Nokia as a model of inclusivity through multistakeholder partnerships.

Since 2011, UNESCO has hosted the Mobile Learning Week, an annual conference on mobile technologies and education that brings together different stakeholders to share how affordable and widespread mobile technologies can advance Education for All goals. Nokia, SK Telecom, SAP, and Intel Education are partners in this initiative, which in 2014 was sponsored by Qualcomm, Houghton Mifflin Harcourt, and Fazheng Group/Beijing Royal School. But the Mobile Learning Week is more than just a space of knowledge sharing and networking, it is also a space of policy making. Apart from the keynotes, workshops, sessions, and discussions, UNESCO's Mobile Learning Week runs a senior education policy makers' forum, organized in partnership with GSMA. This invitation-only meeting of high-level government officials aims to discuss issues relating to mobile learning and policy. Notably, the 2013 report reads,

> policy makers said that they need training and guidance, with support from the mobile industry, given that many mobile learning initiatives are largely without precedent in the field of ICT in Education. Towards this end, future UNESCO and GSMA-led mobile learning policy workshops may be offered.
>
> *(UNESCO and GSMA, 2013, p. 2)*

This represents an interesting move in terms of forms of governance through the "informal authority" networks, where selected policy makers are invited to join an issue network and receive training from an organization like GSMA that "represents the interests of mobile operators worldwide" (GSMA, 2014).

As part of this initiative, UNESCO also runs country-specific mobile learning field projects, including in Nigeria, Mexico, Pakistan, and Senegal. Using different approaches to support teaching and learning, these projects seek to expand the knowledge-base of mobile learning. For instance, in 2009 the mobile operator Mobilink partnered with UNESCO and Bunyad (a local NGO) to develop the "SMS based literacy" program, which initially targeted 250 females in a rural area of southern Punjab province to improve their literacy skills. Bunyad provided teacher training on how to teach reading and writing using mobile phones, and participant girls were provided with a low-cost mobile phone and prepaid connection.

In 2013 Mobilink was awarded the GSMA Global Mobile award in the category "Best Mobile Education or Learning Product or Service," and subsequently expanded, extending its outreach across Punjab, Khyber Pakhtunkhwa, Federally Administered Tribal Areas and Sindh through a new agreement between UNESCO and Mobilink. To some extent, perhaps, this illustrates the extent to which some networks are a "tautological space," where the same initiatives and innovations circulate through mutual reference and recognition. Or as Mundy (2010) puts it, "mutually reinforcing forms of authority."

UNESCO and Samsung electronics have recently (2014) announced their first global partnership. This alliance will bring together UNESCO's Mobile Learning initiative and Samsung's Smart School, a mobile education solution that aims to enhance the classroom learning environment through features such as screen-sharing (with instant sharing of screen content on the e-board to students' personal devices), real-time attendance and participation tracker, and real-time question and answer (which enables students to write a question on their device that will then appear on their classmates' screens as well as on the e-board).

Overall, these two key nodal sites GSMA and UNESCO offer numerous synergies, as evidenced by their joint initiatives and reciprocal recognition through awards and reference in institutional documents and reports.[2] This convergence in the issues and approaches to mEducation, in turn, raises questions in relation to possibility of other players, including national and local governments, to participate and shape both global as well as local agendas.

The mEducation Alliance

In order to illustrate the convergence of the business and international development sectors into increasingly integrated spaces, the final focus of our analysis is on the Mobiles for Education (mEducation) Alliance. According to its mission statement, the aims of mEducation Alliance (2012) are "reducing barriers to access appropriate, scalable, and low-cost mobile technologies to help improve learning outcomes in formal and non-formal education across all levels, especially in low-resource and developing country contexts."

The mEducation Alliance's (2012) commitment to "serve a convening function for practitioners, funders and leaders of the public and private sectors, to promote cooperation and coordination of efforts and knowledge in order to spur the innovation, affordability, and accessibility of mobile technologies for improved learning outcomes," is reflected by its diverse steering committee, which includes multilateral organizations such as The World Bank, UNICEF, UNESCO, Inter-American Development Bank; bilateral organizations including British Council, Department for International Development, Organization of American States, Peace Corps, the U.S. Department of State, United States Agency for International Development, Deutsche Gesellschaft für Internationale Zusammenarbeit (GIZ); international organizations such as Global Partnership for Education, International Association for Mobile Learning (IAmLearn), International Society for Technology in Education (ISTE), International Telecommunication Union (ITU), World Vision, World Wide Web Foundation; and business organizations such as Groupe Speciale Mobile Association (GSMA), and The MasterCard Foundation. Drawing on some of our previous work (Ball, 2012), the mEducation Alliance could be considered a transnational advocacy network (TAN). TANs are "communicative structures" organized around the "shared values of their members." As such, they mobilize information, resources, stories, and symbols, bringing pressure to bear on political actors and organizations.

Communities of Practice

The mEducation Alliance aims not just to bring different stakeholders together but to "form communities of practice" around specific interest areas. Working groups are both spaces for *knowledge sharing*, based on experiences of success and failure of ongoing projects, *knowledge validation*, by practitioners on the ground, and *knowledge production*, through the development of landscape reports. Each working group has its own participants, sponsors and partners, group links and discussions, which we discuss below.

The Mobile Education for Numeracy (mNumeracy) working group was commissioned by Bundesministerium für wirtschaftliche Zusammenarbeit und Entwicklung (BMZ) and implemented by Deutsche Gesellschaft für Internationale Zusammenarbeit (GIZ) and Global Partnership for Education (GPE), with the aim of collecting evidence on the effectiveness, efficiency, scaling-up possibilities and sustainability of mobile education for numeracy, and with a special focus on measuring learning outcomes in numeracy using mobile technologies.

Together with Education Development Center, Inc. (EDC), the Mobiles for Reading (mReading) working group was also launched in 2013. In line with practices of knowledge sharing, the International Reading Association hosted the second mReading working group meeting to discuss recent evaluation data from the Global Literacy Professional Development Network (GLPDN)[3] project. In addition, the United States Agency for International Development (USAID) together with the mEducation Alliance and the All Children Reading: A Grand Challenge for Development have recently commissioned the report *Mobiles for Reading: A Landscape Research Review* (2014). This report, developed by the UNESCO Chair in Learning and Literacy, focuses on 44 existing projects to explore the use of mobile ICTs designed to support and accelerate reading and comprehension.

As a result of a collaborative initiative between The MasterCard Foundation, USAID, and JBS International, the Mobiles for Youth Workforce Development (mYWD) working group was launched in 2012 with the aim of exploring how mobile technologies can increase access to training and employability for young people. This working group has produced four learning series, which focus on issues such as scale and sustainability or specific topics such as gender. Again, the collective interest of this group resulted in a landscape review (MasterCard Foundation, USAID, & mEducation Alliance, 2013), which identified 80 initiatives, organizations, projects, products, and services, and approximately 275 publicly available documents describing efforts that use mobiles to support mYWD. Taken together, these communities of practice constitute spaces where policy ideas are "shaped and given momentum in the telling of stories during meetings" (McCann, 2010, p. 32).

Spaces of Imagination, Commitment, and Challenge Setting

As part of its activities, since 2011 the mEducation Alliance has run an international symposium. The latest symposium (2013) was themed "commit fair for project scaling" simultaneously offering a space for meetingness (Urry, 2003) and a space for imagination. With the aim to "bring together leading project implementers and funders to promote and forge new partnerships," the mEducation Alliance launched an open call for proposals that were subsequently reviewed and scored by a planning committee. Through this competitive process, 17 projects were selected to present to a "panel of investors" that would ask questions and provide feedback. In these microspaces, PowerPoints are presented, documents are circulated, videos shown, experiences recounted, "research" is reported, and policy success celebrated in processes of "contingent, cumulative and emergent knowledge production" (McCann, 2010, p. 36).

The symposium, however, represents not just a space for grant-seeking from different projects from the field, but also a space "to create innovative strategies for education development through brainstorming and collaboration" (mEducation Alliance, 2012). As noted by the following tweet (overleaf) from one of the participants, fun and idea generation came together at mEdu2013.

Mignon Hardie
@mignonhardie

🐦 Follow

#mEdu2013 Networking session to work out what non tech things we'd do on a desert island... #ideageneration #fun

3:52 PM - 15 Oct 2013

1 RETWEET

↩ 🔁 ★

One of the most visible outcomes of the symposium is the announcement of commitments to the field of mEducation, where policy narratives are "assembled into a set of 'actionable' ideas" (McCann, 2010, p. 31). Some of the commitments announced at the symposium included Accenture Development Partnerships' commitment to provide business and mentoring support to mEducation projects. Also, the multinational telecommunications corporation Orange selected six projects presented at the symposium to be sponsored through Orange Labs. By devoting a total of 120 days of employee time, Orange will provide specialized technical assistance to the following mEducation initiatives:

- Real-time Access + Utilization of Children's Learning Data (Columbia Earth Institute);
- SMILE (Seeds of Empowerment);
- LEARNET (Natoma Group);
- Yes Youth Can! Western Mobile Market Place (Winrock International and Mobile Movement);
- Professional Learning for Educators Series (PLES)-Mathematics (Aga Khan Academy); and
- Integrating Mobile Learning Solutions for Syrian Refugees (UNESCO).

These policy microspaces, we argue, are pre-eminently spaces of exchange and excitement where trust is built, commitments are made, and deals done, and policy imaginaries are given shape and substance (Ball, 2012, p. 68).

Conclusion

mEducation brings together business narratives of risk, innovation, and commercial opportunity; social enterprise narratives of impact and systemic change through scalable solutions; and international development narratives of social inclusion and equity through education. Our analysis of the Ed-Tech sector in general and the emergence of mEducation as a distinct market niche and policy solution highlight the role of specific organizations in the landscaping of this dynamically evolving space. Seeking to pluralize political authority, these TANs provide a network of relations for the diffusion of knowledge and information, and mobilize change in the public perception of social problems. The mEducation Alliance offers a case in point to explore governance in action through practices of knowledge sharing, validation, and production. In particular, the working groups of mNumeracy, mLiteracy and mYWD represent complex spaces that enable spontaneous participation through forums, meetings, and workshops where participants from the field share problems, solutions, and resources, and at the same time they are highly regulated spaces, that can only operate under the sponsorship of well-established organizations with defined interests and vision. Further, while the exchange and collaborative input from members works to consolidate the presence of mEducation as a visible policy and business area, the possibilities of contribution and control over the syntheses that are circulated and reproduced by transnational and advocacy networks remains very limited and superficial. From our analysis of working groups and "Pitch Fest sessions" it could be argued that these networks of governance represent a "space of contradiction," where the possibilities of co-creation and delimitation of this dynamic space mainly depend on their ability to reinforce the overall strength of the network.

TANs, note Cavett-Goodwin (2008), work "underneath, above, and around the state" with different degrees of impact depending on the strength and depth of their networks and the vulnerability of the target state or organization (Ball, 2012). Traditional lines and demarcations—public and private, market and state—are being breached and blended, and in many ways those categories are no longer analytically useful for policy analysis. In sum, what we want to suggest here is that the landscape and modalities of educational governance are changing. There is no absolute change but rather a shift in the mix of policy players, the emergence of new sites and spaces of policy, and new developing synergies between policy and business imaginaries. As a result, there is a concomitant increase in the opacity of policy making (Ball, 2012). There is a complex mix in all of this between big global agencies, big multinationals, and many small governments struggling with intractable social problems. In the search for scalability and leverage participation and input are asymmetrical. The blurring between social justice discourses and those of profit opportunity—and the possibility to "do good and have their profit, too" (Strom, 2006)—enables business not simply to benefit from policy, but to become key actors in policy construction and educational governance. This raises fundamental questions about democratic participation and the responsibility of governments and other public institutions in the provision of social services and civil rights (Ball and Olmedo, 2011). More generally, for national governments—especially those of small and fragile states—all of this portends a reduction in their capacity to steer their education systems.

Clearly, what is evident here is that key education policy decisions are now being made in new places by different people and organizations. The policy process is becoming more opaque and participation or dialogue more difficult for those outside the networks we have outlined above. This raises questions about democratic engagement and about the focus of policy analysis. In both respects new methods and responses are necessary. Those who seek to achieve more democratic models of policy making need to organize themselves in ways that are internationally extensive and locally adaptable. Critical researchers need to bring to bear what Beck calls a "cosmopolitan sociology." This is, he says, a necessary condition for grasping the dynamics of an increasingly cosmopolitan reality. Over and against this, he argues that "national sociology" is beset by "a failure to recognize—let alone research—the extent to which existing transnational modes of living, transmigrants, global elites, supranational organizations and dynamics determine the relations within and between nation-state repositories of power" (Beck, 2005, p. 23). "National sociology" is beset by the fallacy of what he calls "Methodological nationalism," that is "the standpoint of social scientific observers who implicitly or explicitly undertake research using concepts and categories associated with the nation." This chapter is part of our attempt to move from the latter to the former.

Note

1 Meetingness, according to Urry, is the occasional face-to-face encounters that are central to the functioning of networks "in order both to 'establish' and to 'cement' at least temporarily those weak ties" (2003, p. 161).
2 There are 13 references to GSMA in the UNESCO (2013) report *The Future of Mobile Learning: Implications for policy makers and planners.*
3 Launched in 2009 in partnership with Nokia, the Pearson Foundation and the Collaborative for Teaching and Learning (CTL), GLPDN provides customized and interactive mentoring and self-training support through the Nokia Education Delivery (NED) system. Using handheld mobile devices provided by Nokia, teachers download training materials and videos of effective practices and complete emailed/text messaged self-study activities as part of a school-based study group.

References

Ball, S. J. (2012). *Global Education Inc.: New policy networks and the neo-liberal imaginary.* London: Routledge.
Ball, S. J., and Olmedo, A. (2011). Global social capitalism: Using enterprise to solve the problems of the world. *Citizenship, Social and Economics Education, 10*(2 and 3), 83–90.
Beck, U. (2005). *Power in the global age: a new global political economy.* Cambridge: Polity Press.
Bevir, M., and Rhodes, R. A. W. (2006). *Governance stories.* London: Routledge.
Cavett-Goodwin, D. (2008). Forces constructing consent for the neoliberal project. Retrieved July 31, 2014 from http://culturalshifts.com/archives/206
Dicken, P., Kelly, P. F., Olds, K., and Wai-Chung Yeung, H. (2001). Chains and networks, territories and scales: Towards a relational framework for analysing the global economy. *Global Networks, 1*(2), 89–112. doi: 10.1111/1471-0374.00007

EdSurge. (2014). The EdSurge Edtech Index. Retrieved July 20, 2014, from www.edsurge. com/products/—!/

Education Week. (2014a). Award-Winning Educator Taps Technology to Layer Instruction. *Getting personal: Teachers, technology and tailored education.* Retrieved July 31, 2014 from www.edweek.org/tm/collections/package/getting-personal/index.html?intc=thed

Education Week. (2014b). Navigating the Ed-Tech marketplace. *Special report on K-12 educational technology.* Retrieved July 29, 2014 from http://ew.edweek.org/nxtbooks/ epe/ew_06112014_v2/index.php--/0

Grabher, G. (2004). Learning in projects, remembering in networks? Communality, sociality, and connectivity in project ecologies. *European Urban and Regional Studies, 11*(2), 103–123.

GSMA. (2011). *Mobile education landscape report.* Retrieved July 28, 2014 from www.gsma. com/connectedliving/wp-content/uploads/2012/03/landscape110811interactive.pdf.

GSMA. (2014). Retrieved July 25, 2014 from www.gsma.com/

GSMA Development Fund. (2010). *mLearning: a platform for educational opportunities at the base of the pyramid.* Retrieved July 25, 2014 from www.gsma.com/mobilefordevelop ment/wp-content/uploads/2012/04/mlearningaplatformforeducationalopportunities atthebaseofthepyramid

GSMA mEducation. (2012). *mEducation new business models: Innovation in practice.* Retrieved July 29, 2014 from www.gsma.com/connectedliving/wp-content/uploads/2012/ 10/GSMA_NewBusinessModels_10_12.pdf

GSMA Mobile Education. (2011). *The mobile proposition for education.* Retrieved July 31, 2014 from www.sktelecom.com/en/press/detail.do?idx=966

GSV Advisors. (2012a). Retrieved July 22, 2014 from http://gsvadvisors.com/

GSV Advisors. (2012b). *Fall of the wall: capital flows to education innovation.* Retrieved July 23, 2014 from http://gsvadvisors.com/wordpress/wp-content/themes/gsvadvisors/ GSV Advisors_Fall of the Wall_2012–06–28.pdf

GSV Advisors. (2012c). *Revolution 2.0: How education innovation is going to revitalize America and transform the U.S. economy.* Retrieved July 24, 2014 from http://gsvadvisors.com/ wordpress/wp-content/themes/gsvadvisors/American Revolution 2.0.pdf

GSV Media. (2014). *ASU+GSV Summit.* Retrieved July 18, 2014 from http://asugsv summit.com/

Hack Education. (2013). *Top Ed-Tech Trends of 2013: The Business of Ed-Tech.* Retrieved July 25, 2014 from http://hackeducation.com/2013/12/23/top-ed-tech-trends-2013- business/

Howard, P. N. (2002). Network ethnography and the hypermedia organization: New media, new organizations, new methods. *New Media & Society, 4*(4), 550–574. doi: 10.1177/146144402321466813

ISTE. (2014). Retrieved July 20, 2014 from www.iste.org/

Latour, B. (1993). *We have never been modern.* Cambridge, MA: Harvard University Press.

MasterCard Foundation, USAID, and mEducation Alliance. (2013). *Landscape Review: Mobiles for Youth Workforce Development.* Retrieved July 25, 2014 from www.meducation alliance.org/sites/default/files/landscape_review_final_web.pdf

McCann, E. (2010). Urban policy mobilities and global circuits of knowledge: Toward a research agenda. *Annals of the Association of American Geographers, 101*(1), 107–130. doi: 10.1080/00045608.2010.520219

McCann, E., and Ward, K. (Eds.). (2011). *Mobile urbanism: Cities and policymaking in the global age.* Minneapolis: University of Minnesota Press.

McKinsey & Company, and GSMA. (2012). *Transforming learning through mEducation.* Retrieved July 31, 2014 from www.gsma.com/connectedliving/wp-content/uploads/2012/04/gsmamckinseytransforminglearningthroughmeducation.pdf

mEducation Alliance. (2012). Retrieved June 26, 2014 from www.meducationalliance.org/

Mundy, K. (2010). "Education for All" and the global governors. In M. Finnemore, D. Avant & S. Sell (Eds.), *Who governs the globe?* (pp. 333–355). Cambridge: Cambridge University Press.

Patterson, M., and Monroe, K. R. (1998). Narrative in political science. *Annual Review of Political Science, 1,* 315–331.

Samsung. (2014). *Samsung and UNESCO Announce First Global Partnership.* Retrieved July 28, 2014 from www.samsung.com/ae/news/localnews/2014/samsung-and-unesco-announce-first-global-partnership

Scuzzarello, S. (2010). *Caring multiculturalism: local immigrant policies and narratives of integration in Malmo, Birmingham and Bologna.* Lund: Department of Political Science, Lund University.

SK Telecom. (2013). *SK Telecom launches innovative mobile learning platform named T Smart Learning.* Retrieved July 8, 2014 from www.sktelecom.com/en/press/detail.do?idx=966

Somers, M. (1994). The narrative constitution of identity: A relational and network approach. *Theory and Society, 23*(5), 605–649. doi: 10.1007/bf00992905

Strom, S. (2006). *What's Wrong With Profit?* Retrieved July 24, 2014 from www.nytimes.com/2006/11/13/us/13strom.html?pagewanted=print&_r=0

TechCrunch. (2014). *Education Technology Startups Raised Over Half A Billion Dollars in Q1.* Retrieved July 24, 2014 from http://techcrunch.com/2014/03/26/education-technology-startups-raised-nearly-half-a-billion-dollars-in-q1/

Telefónica Learning Services S.A. (2013). *Telefónica launches Wepack-Weclass, a pioneer system to integrate ICT in education.* Retrieved July 10, 2014 from www.telefonicalearningservices.com/noticia?articleid=228216

UNESCO. (2012). Turning on mobile learning in Africa and the Middle East: Illustrative innitiatives and policy implications. *Working paper series on mobile learning.* Retrieved July 29, 2014 from http://unesdoc.unesco.org/images/0021/002163/216359e.pdf

UNESCO. (2013a). *The future of mobile learning: implications for policy makers and planners.* Retrieved July 30, 2014 from http://unesdoc.unesco.org/images/0021/002196/219637e.pdf

UNESCO. (2013b). *Policy guidelines for mobile learning.* Retrieved July 25, 2014 from http://unesdoc.unesco.org/images/0021/002196/219641e.pdf?utm_source=Mobile+Learning+Week+2013_v3_CfP&utm_campaign=8885b82361-UNESCO_Mobile_Learning3_28_2013&utm_medium=email

UNESCO and GSMA. (2013). *UNESCO–GSMA senior education policy makers' forum report.* Retrieved August 1, 2014 from www.unesco.org/new/fileadmin/MULTIMEDIA/HQ/ED/images/UNESCO_GSMA_SPMF_Report_2013.pdf

Urry, J. (2003). *Global complexity.* Cambridge: Polity.

USAID, and mEducation Alliance. (2014). *Mobiles for reading: A landscape research review.* Retrieved July 25, 2014 from www.meducationalliance.org/sites/default/files/usaid_wagner_report_finalforweb_14jun25_1.pdf

Williams, P. (2002). The competent boundary spanner. *Public Administration, 80*(1), 103–124. doi: 10.1111/1467-9299.00296

3

NETWORK RESTRUCTURING OF GLOBAL EDU-BUSINESS

The Case of Pearson's *Efficacy Framework*

Anna Hogan, Sam Sellar, and Bob Lingard

Introduction

Edu-businesses have become influential policy actors in education today. Their enhanced significance is linked to the emergence of new modes of network governance, both nationally and globally, that have emerged with state restructuring and associated changes in processes of education policy production. In this chapter, we focus on Pearson, a leading global edu-business, which has shifted the focus of its business from education inputs (e.g., textbooks) towards measuring educational outcomes (e.g., testing). More specifically, we will consider the recruitment of Sir Michael Barber, former senior public servant in the Blair UK government, as a strategy for expanding Pearson's *network capital* (Urry, 2007), which is being used to drive the restructuring of the business and its global repositioning. Barber is a 'boundary spanner' (Williams, 2002), who moves across the public and private sectors, an increasingly common phenomenon today with network governance and the partial privatization of policy and policy networks (Mahony, Hextall, and Menter, 2004).

Utilizing network ethnography (Howard, 2002; Ball and Junemann, 2012), we map the networks associated with Pearson's *Efficacy Framework*, a business and accountability strategy created to ensure that Pearson's services and products are having "a measurable and proven impact on learners' lives" (Pearson, 2014). The network diagrams that we present in this chapter were constructed using Gephi open-source software. These diagrams were informed by the three interrelated activities of network ethnography: 1) internet searches; 2) interviews; and 3) the use of these searches and interviews to construct network diagrams (Ball and Junemann, 2012). Specifically, we analyzed corporate documents relating to Pearson's *Efficacy Framework* and the reworking of their business strategy, conducted three interviews with representatives from Pearson, and used a variety of Internet searches to map the networks presented here. We acknowledge Ball's (2012, p.144) point that network maps of this kind freeze flows and flatten asymmetries of power. We thus suggest that these networks be viewed as descriptive devices rather than analytical representations. However, our analysis here foregrounds the importance of network connections in the restructuring of Pearson's edu-business model and the diagrams clearly illustrate the connectivity to a range of policy actors that was made available to the company with the appointment of Barber.

Networking: Pearson's New Business Strategy and the Role of Sir Michael Barber

In 2011, Pearson appointed Sir Michael Barber as the company's Chief Education Advisor. The press release announcing this development proclaimed Barber's authority as an education expert, given his previous roles as a public servant for the UK government, as a partner at McKinsey & Company, and as Head of McKinsey's global education practice, where he coauthored the two influential reports: *How the world's most improved school systems keep getting better* (Mourshed, Chijioke, and Barber, 2010) and *How the world's best-performing schools come out on top* (Barber and Mourshed, 2007). Barber's new role was to,

> lead Pearson's worldwide program of research into education policy and efficacy, advise on and support the development of products and services that build on the research findings, and play a particular role in Pearson's strategy for education in the poorest sectors of the world, particularly in fast-growing developing economies.
>
> *(Pearson, 2011, para. 2)*

As then Pearson CEO Marjorie Scardino said about the appointment of Barber:

> Michael Barber has deep experience in and an irrepressible passion for education. So does Pearson—now actively engaged in advancing learning in more than 70 countries. And both of us want to make education more effective for more people because we believe that makes societies more effective for more people.
>
> *(Pearson, 2011, para. 5)*

The appointment of Barber to Pearson is not only indicative of new hybrid career structures of policy actors who span public, private and philanthropic domains and are linked to neo-liberal policy settings and new state modalities (Ball and Junemann, 2012), but also suggests the importance of such boundary spanners for edu-businesses such as Pearson, which are seeking to refashion their role as an organizational policy actor in education. This role can be expanded, modified and legitimated by the mobilities of people like Barber and the network capital to which they provide access (Urry, 2007). Barber also brings to an edu-business such as Pearson intimate knowledge of policy production processes inside state structures, as well as earlier experience as a university academic.

Urry (2007, p. 197) defines network capital as "the capacity to engender and sustain social relations with those people who are not necessarily proximate and which generates emotional, financial and practical benefit (although this will often entail various objects and technologies or the means of networking)". The ability to network is not evenly distributed and requires specific resources. Position in a network, and ultimately power, is dependent on mobilities of different kinds. Mobilities are not necessarily about travel, but rather the movement of people, ideas, objects and information, what Appadurai (1996) referred to as "flows." Indeed, Urry (2007) argues that the new and increasingly diverse range of mobilities, and their sheer scale, speed and transnationality, has led to the emergence of a "mobility complex," a field in Bourdieu's sense, that is reconstituting the nature of power relations above and beyond the effects of cultural and economic capitals, by refiguring social relations through a range of new phenomena:

> the scale of movement around the world, the diversity of mobility systems now in play, the especial significance of the self-expanding automobility system . . . the elaborate interconnections of physical movement and communications, the development of mobility domains that by-pass national societies, the significance of movement to contemporary governmentality and an increased importance of multiple mobilities for people's social and emotional lives.
>
> *(Urry 2007, p. 195)*

Network capital also "is now an essential prerequisite for 'living in the rich north of contemporary capitalism'" (Urry, 2007, p. 196) and people clearly develop a "taste" for mobility and networking. Here we can see the third of Bourdieu's interrelated concepts of field, capital and habitus in play, when conceiving of a distinctive form of network capital: habitus is inflected by "multiple mobilities [that] set up new kinds of distinction of taste, between the modes of movement, the classes of traveler, the places moved to, the embodied experiences of movement, the character of those also moving and so on" (Urry 2007, p. 196). Network capital thus requires the physical supports for networking—the infrastructure that enables mobility and connectivity—as well as the embodied competencies of individuals and groups to gain advantage from these supports to different degrees—a certain disposition, in Bourdieu's sense, for networking.

Boundary spanners like Barber, for whom "networking is the predominant *modus operandi*" (Williams 2002, p. 117), have high levels of network capital associated with their movement across public/private sectors and other related mobilities. It is not, however, their movement itself that is important here. Rather, as Urry (2012, p. 27) observes, movement is important insofar as it enables people to become more connected with one another:

> The concept of network capital brings out that underlying mobilities do nothing in themselves. What are key are the social consequences of such mobilities, namely, to be able to engender and sustain social relations with those people (and to visit specific places) who are mostly not physically proximate, that is, to form and sustain networks often at-a-distance. So network capital points to the real and potential social relations that mobilities afford.

Boundary spanners tend to have high network capital because they are proficient at creating inter- and intra-organizational social connections, including between the public and the private sector. Here power becomes a case of who you know, not what you know (Elliot and Urry, 2010).

In an interview with one of Pearson's executives, and in the context of discussing Pearson's *Efficacy Framework*, the importance of Barber's networks for some of the company's latest initiatives was made clear:

> To be honest a lot of these people are Michael's acquaintances from the decades of work he's been doing in education. That was our first port of call. We just went through Michael's address book and said, let's reach out to these people.

By appointing Barber as Chief Education Advisor, Pearson gained access to the network capital embedded in his person and his social connections. This is evident from the network diagram overleaf (Figure 3.1). Here we can observe those people who contributed to Pearson's *Efficacy Framework* documents, and while we do not discuss *who* these people are until later in this chapter, what is equally important here are the connections themselves. The connections in this figure represent Barber's social ties, where he has been successful at using his networks. These were generated through years in the education industry, as evidenced in the diagram by people he has worked with previously, coauthored publications with or collaborated with in various education projects to generate a network that connects high-profile policy actors across philanthropy, business, government, international organizations and the academy.

Thus, in emphasizing the connectivity of network capital we are following Urry (2007) in distinguishing this form of capital from social capital. According to Bourdieu (1986, p. 248), social capital is the "aggregate of the actual or potential resources that are linked to possession of a durable network of more or less

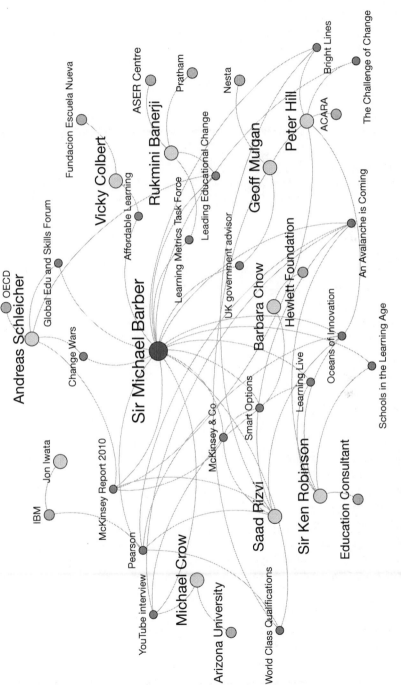

FIGURE 3.1 Sir Michael Barber's network of relations

institutionalized relationships of mutual acquaintance and recognition." In these terms, as explained by Bourdieu and Wacquant (1992), social capital is constituted from the sum of the resources (both economic and cultural) produced and acquired through social structure. This concept of social capital encourages a view of networks from the perspective of the embodied resources that are connected, and with the potential to transmogrify into economic capital. Inkpen and Tsang (2005) point out that a consensus has emerged within network literature that social capital represents the "resources embedded within, available through and derived from the network of relationships possessed by an individual or organization" (p.151).

Network capital provides a different perspective, emphasizing the connections themselves, rather than the resources connected. Urry (2007, p. 200) argues that social capital, particularly Putnam's (2000) emphasis on propinquitous community, is insufficient to describe the social dynamics at work in the production of network capital, because

> it presumes that only small scale communities can generate face-to-face proximities and relations of trust. By contrast, the . . . concept of network capital brings out how co-presence and trust can be generated at a distance, and thus presupposes extensive and predictable travel and communications and the emergence of a distinct new field of "mobilities."

Network capital is generated through mobilities, can be produced at a distance and is self-catalyzing—the production of connections is central to its value and it creates opportunities to create more connections. In contrast, social capital tends to emphasize relations established in a particular place and the benefits to an individual of the resources to which these relations provide access—the production of connections is instrumental here, rather than an end in itself. The distinction between the two forms of capital is thus a matter of perspective on social networks.

Importantly for our analysis here, "network capital is not to be viewed as an attribute of individual subjects . . . [It] is a product of the relationality of individuals with others and with the affordances of the 'environment'" (Urry 2007, p. 198). Huggins (2010, p. 522) distinguishes between the potential value of network capital for organizations, as opposed to social capital that tends to advantage individuals:

> the source of network capital is rooted in economic rationality, whereby firms invest in establishing calculative networks to access the knowledge they require. The source of social capital is based on social rationality, whereby individuals invest in social networks to access embedded resources relating to sociability and social expectations.

While Barber brings to Pearson his own social capital, the effect of this appointment is to provide Pearson with access to network capital; that is, to increase the organizational power to network and the organization's power within networks. Indeed, the second network diagram (Figure 3.2) included overleaf represents the ways in which Pearson has been able to benefit from the network Barber has established. Each of the organizations, represented by the individuals with whom Barber is connected, work with or employ Pearson for various products and services.

The appointment of Barber has contributed to Pearson's transformation from a media holding company to an edu-business by helping to establish a networked environment in which the organization can be positioned as a legitimate policy actor. Instead of this transformation being seen as one motivated purely by profit, Barber, as "a leading authority on education systems and education reform" (Pearson, 2011) with connections to a range of government and academic actors in education policy globally, is able to help constitute an assemblage in which Pearson might become seen as a morally authoritative agency in educational matters.

Our argument here is that Pearson has undergone a transformation of its business that has been made possible, in part, through the acquisition of network capital. It seems likely that such transformations will continue as more companies—print-publishing and media businesses in particular—recognize the potential profitability of the education industry and seek to establish a field in which they can be reconstituted and recognized as edu-businesses. For example, News Corporation has acquired former New York City Department of Education Commissioner, Joel Klein to head their education division, Amplify. Such movements of boundary spanners, and access to the social connections they are able to generate, potentially increase legitimacy and therefore influence and power for these organizations in education markets, and thereby enhance their potential success in relation to organizations with less network capital. For example, Barber, as a former bureaucrat, can help to communicate the relevance and currency of Pearson's activities to government officials, and this likely serves to promote the perceived legitimacy and authority of using Pearson for government contracts and services (see also Burch and Smith, this volume). Barber is also a former academic with connections into that world as well, another element of his contribution to Pearson's network capital.

However, Barber's role at Pearson contributes to the reformulation of its business strategy in multiple ways. As Pearson (2011) stated in the press release announcing his appointment, Barber will "lead Pearson's worldwide programme of research into education policy and efficacy." Thus, Pearson's acquisition of Barber has been part of the constitution of the type of edu-business they desire to be; that is, one that is not only a successful supplier of products and services, but one that helps to shape and inform global policy processes (Pearson plc, 2012). In the following sections of the chapter we analyze the recent development of Pearson's *Efficacy*

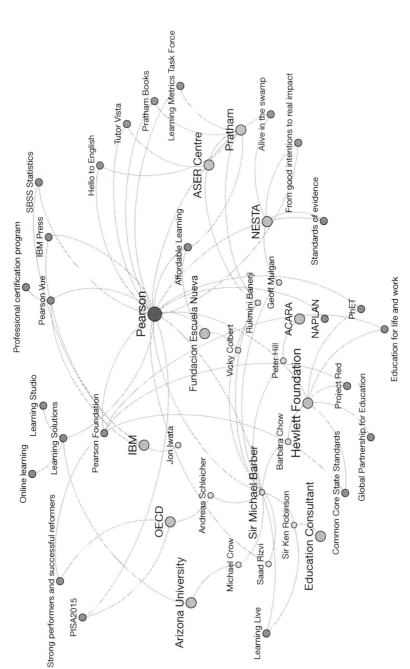

FIGURE 3.2 Pearson's network cultivated from Barber's relations

Framework, which Barber is responsible for developing. We argue that through this particular initiative, Pearson has not only reconstituted its business model, but is increasing its potential to refigure education policy processes globally.

Mapping the Network of the *Efficacy Framework*

> Learning is a life-changing opportunity—and a great education should have a measurable, proven impact on learners' lives. That's what Pearson's efficacy programme and tools are all about.
>
> *(Pearson, 2014)*

In November 2013, Pearson released their *Efficacy Framework*, which included two publications, *Asking more: The path to efficacy* and *The incomplete guide to delivering learner outcomes,* as well as an associated website and access to their efficacy tool for global review. By 2018, Pearson has committed to report on audited learning outcome measures and targets, alongside its financial accounts. As the associated press release explains:

> The company's ambition is to ensure that its work is driven by an ever-clearer understanding of how it can maximize and measure its impact on learning outcomes, drawing on the lessons of the healthcare industry to invest in research and development and build new partnerships that will address the most pressing unmet needs in education . . . Efficacy now moves from a pilot program in Pearson to the centerpiece of its global education strategy.
>
> *(Pearson, 2013, para. 3)*

In essence, Pearson's efficacy strategy can be understood as a key technique of neoliberal management, where performative mechanisms are employed to ensure an organization's improvement and effectiveness (Lyotard, 1984; Rose, 1999). However, in this case the framework is also tied to a desire for Pearson to "do good" through its education products and services.

Pearson explain that the term "efficacy" was adopted from the pharmaceutical industry (a case of the medicalization of educational research) and is defined as: "A measureable impact on improving people's lives through learning" (p.12). The *Incomplete Guide* (Barber and Rizvi, 2013a) states:

> Note that, with this definition, it is the learning outcome that we are pursuing. Passing a test or an exam is good, but it is not an end in itself: what we really want to see is the benefit of doing so in someone's life . . . We realize that by including the ultimate outcome in the definition, we are setting a high bar for what we mean by efficacy. We are inspired by the medical profession,

but aim even higher. Often in medicine there are high rates of readmission and recurrence, and some doctors are incentivized by procedures performed rather than outcomes achieved. We want to hold ourselves to a standard based not on the potential of our products, but on the ultimate outcome for the learner, on how an individual's life is measurably improved.

(pp. 12–13)

Thus, for Pearson, efficacy means that their education products and services come with an evidence-based guarantee of improving outcomes—much like a prescribed drug from your local GP is expected to cure what ails you. In this sense, efficacy is a public accountability mechanism of a particular kind, as suggested by a representative of Pearson:

It's not just about: Oh trust us. We're Pearson. We're an education company. It becomes very much about, well trust us, because you've got the evidence. Really, everything that we do should be evidence-based, so you're actually able to demonstrate to whoever it is you're going to be working with that this is actually something that should work well for you.

When an edu-business is as successful as Pearson, with its dominant market position and considerable global influence (Ball, 2012), one may raise the question: Why are these accountability processes necessary? In answering this question, a Pearson representative identified the need for the company to provide evidence in regard to the efficacy of its products and services:

The more you do, the bigger the target becomes on your back to be honest, and you just need to be aware of that. You need to be sensitive to it, because with that level of influence comes an awful lot of responsibility, which is in some respects, where the *Efficacy Framework* comes in for us. If we're going to have this level of responsibility, then we need to get it right.

In these terms, Pearson's *Efficacy Framework* could, in part, be considered a reaction to public criticism. In the wake of globalization, the spread of neo-liberalism, financial crises and the growth of inequality (Piketty, 2014), multi-national corporations have faced increasing amounts of public criticism from various groups. In the case of education, there seems to be a fear that for-profit edu-businesses like Pearson might undermine the sovereignty of national education policy practices, contribute to a democratic deficit and, in the process, contribute to undesirable consequences associated with the increasing privatization of the provision of public "goods." This is picked up in the way opponents of Pearson have changed the company motto of "Always Learning" to "Always Earning" in their protest slogans.

The popular and influential education policy actor, Diane Ravitch, who was the former Assistant Secretary of Education in President George W. Bush's administration, has been particularly outspoken about what she sees as the "Pearsonization" of American students and schools. In a recent blog post titled "The United States of Pearson" (2012) she writes:

> It is widely recognized by everyone other than the publishing giant Pearson that its tentacles have grown too long and too aggressive. It is difficult to remember what part of American education has not been invaded by Pearson's corporate grasp. It receives billions of dollars to test millions of students . . . With the U.S. Department of Education now pressing schools to test children in second grade, first grade, kindergarten—and possibly earlier— . . . the picture grows clear. Pearson will control every aspect of our education system.

Indeed, many critiques levelled at corporations like Pearson speak of their unfettered power and their lack of public accountability. However, as Holzer (2010) points out, while they may appear to be a mighty octopus with far-reaching tentacles, the closer you get, the more you see a nervous creature that shies away from public attention. Holzer argues that it is near impossible for corporations to avoid the "goldfish bowl" of public scrutiny and they are thus forced to respond to the public perception and evaluation of their actions and activities.

In this context we are seeing the promotion of new conceptualizations of Corporate Social Responsibility (CSR). In the past CSR may have been considered a matter of philanthropy, where corporations invested some of their profits back into the community to make a positive contribution to society. This is still one element of CSR for Pearson, and its philanthropic arm, the Pearson Foundation, works with partners to promote "literacy, learning and great teaching" (Pearson Foundation, 2014). However, CSR is also a discourse that has been adopted to support the broader activities of Pearson. Through their *Efficacy Framework*, Pearson is seeking to communicate with external stakeholders by anticipating how their actions are being evaluated by the public and positioning themselves as accountable and responsible for the outcomes of their services and products. As Holzer (2010) observes, the company is making substantial efforts to portray itself as a good "corporate citizen." Interview data from another Pearson representative support this narrative:

> I think for us, with the *Incomplete Guide* we initially were thinking a different line of approach and that might be a future publication which was, if you look at the history of capitalism and traditional large operations, it's over the last few years that there has been really a lot of distress against these large institutions . . .

Consumers have lost confidence in these large institutions and what Pearson is saying is that, as a large institution, but also any other large institution, for it to really gain back customer trust it has to be a more responsible corporation. It has to be accountable for not just the financial returns but also the outcomes it delivers . . .

In the past you see a lot of CSR initiatives which often large corporations do a lot of bad stuff but then they have the CSR arm that does some good marketing and just donates money and what we are saying is that a responsible corporation can't function like that. CSR can't be like just a side show, it has to be a core part of the mission of the company.

This presents a slightly different understanding of the "new philanthropy" and "social capitalism," which Ball (2012, p.66), Ball and Junemann (2012) and Olmedo (2013) have analyzed, where the work of philanthropic organizations, such as the Pearson Foundation, are morally strategic components in new education policy processes. It is clear that with Pearson the notion of corporate responsibility now transcends its philanthropic activities and is being integrated into their everyday business activities. This is a phenomenon described by Bishop and Green (2008, p.177) as "philanthrocapitalism," in which CSR is being driven by the belief that doing good can be profitable, or is at least able to boost the corporation's reputation. Thus, Pearson's *Efficacy Framework* reflects an appreciation that continuing success, or power in education policy networks, is dependent on playing by "the rules of the game," where "power is not something that can be acquired, seized or shared" (Foucault, 1979, p. 94), but is something embedded in social relations, in this case, between Pearson and the "critical" public. Here, Pearson's two efficacy documents—*The Incomplete Guide* and *Asking More*—are particularly important in understanding how they are seeking to "play the game."

"The Incomplete Guide to Delivering Learning Outcomes"

The Incomplete Guide, as explained by Barber and Rizvi (2013a, p.9), "is incomplete because it is just one view of the complex world of learning, and we are aware that we have only just begun." They continue:

We are writing this guide now partly because we want to be transparent about our approach, but partly also to test our thinking on what is clearly a major issue not just for us but for educators generally . . . For this reason, our main purpose in publishing this paper (and inviting people outside Pearson to use and test the framework online) is to invite comment and dialogue from all those that might be interested . . . Together, perhaps we can make this guide complete.

Barber and Rizvi go on to provide an outline of Pearson's efficacy strategy and the document is composed of three main sections. The first describes the factors involved in efficacy, which are identified as the "factors at play when learning is supposed to happen" (p.13). These include:

1.   The student(s) with his/her/their incumbent level of motivation;
2.   The teacher and/or technology with his/her/its capacity to make an impact and;
3.   The interaction or relationship between them.

The document suggests that, when combining these factors, "if this mix is right, learning should happen" (p.13).

The second section describes Pearson's efficacy reviews, which are designed to assess the degree to which its products and services contribute to, and support, these factors. As the *Incomplete Guide* explains, there are four interrelated phases of an efficacy review, including: guiding questions about the intended outcomes of the product or the efficacy goals; the evidence that supports whether a product is achieving these goals or not; the plan to ensure efficacy goals are delivered; and the capacity both of internal Pearson employees and their customers to deliver the product. We can see in these steps echoes of traditional rational approaches to, or prescriptions for, public sector policy making (Hogwood and Gunn, 1984) and the hand of Sir Michael Barber. The third section of the *Incomplete Guide* outlines what Pearson has learnt from the 100 efficacy reviews, undertaken in over 15 different countries, which had been completed at the time of writing *The Incomplete Guide*. Ultimately, Pearson identifies ten lessons from these reviews:

1. Set clear efficacy goals
2. Develop products underpinned by evidence
3. Build and use effective data systems
4. Employ iterative processes
5. Take an open approach
6. Understand the learners' desired outcomes
7. Train your customers to use your product
8. Shape the debate with influential stakeholders
9. Give your people the incentive to focus on outcomes
10. Start now.

Arguably, it is the eighth point here that is most interesting for our analysis. A Pearson representative expanded on how the company aims to shape debate with influential stakeholders:

> I think traditionally or in the past we lived in a world where education policy was often shaped behind really closed doors at all levels, like at the

school level, at the higher education level. But we are now entering this interesting space where anyone with a good idea is able to really be influential and we're also entering this age where we are more connected with the end learner.

What we're saying, that it's important for anyone who's passionate about education to be able to participate in the dialog around what's important, to be able to share ideas with people and shape the debate.

The point of that is, it's a lesson for us at Pearson where we want to be more engaged with stakeholders, and both learn from them, but also influence the education debate to more focus on education outcomes and not just inputs but it's also to let anyone who's interested in education to have a voice and more actively communicate what their perspective is.

Inviting this type of open dialogue is an interesting step for an edu-business that has in the past faced considerable criticism about its educational activities. Again, this was a question posed to Pearson:

What's interesting is ever since we did the launch we have gotten a lot more interest from both the supporters of Pearson and the critics of Pearson. Our approach to that and I've actually gone out and spoken to many of the traditional critics of Pearson and said, "Look, we're really serious about this. I'm opening up the doors to you. You can come join us. You can go see an efficacy review. You can read our company's bonus policy that says, 'The CEO will be incentive based on the delivery of his efficacy work.'"

I've been trying to actively engage the supporters but also the critics and saying, "Look, why don't you help inform our opinion" because I think there are a range of critics of Pearson. There are some that are thoughtful critics, but then there is also a group of people who think anything that is for-profit and tied into education always has to be wrong, which I think is an extremist perspective. We have to deal with critics across the spectrum and our answer to that now is we are really confident what we are doing and we are welcoming the traditional critics to come and see what we are doing, critique it and then form their opinions.

As the Pearson representative suggests, engagement around these issues is about networking, where particular critics can be brought into the network. As suggested, if "thoughtful" critics are engaged in debate, it is then easier to position those outside of the network as "extreme." Thus, connection here equals legitimacy, both for Pearson in the fact that they have extended their network to include (particular) critics and for those disconnected from the network and are thus positioned "illegitimate" because "extreme." Indeed, Pearson's second document, *Asking More*, is important in this sense because it sets the agenda for the legitimacy of this "open door" dialogue.

"Asking More: The Path to Efficacy"

Asking More (Barber and Rizvi, 2013b) is a publication that collates the essays of nine influential education policy actors. As the document explains, it "brings together a small sample of the many individuals who are driving high-quality learning and a relentless focus on outcomes" (p. 3). It is suggested that "reading their contributions together, three particular insights resonate with, and will drive further, the agenda we have set ourselves at Pearson" (p. 4):

1. The importance of a clear purpose and goal;
2. The impact of acting with urgency, and working tirelessly to drive change; and
3. The necessity today to build the sophistication of our measurement for tomorrow.

The contributors to *Asking More* are high-profile individuals who represent the different sectors of government, business, and education and, together, their contributions discuss a set of varied issues from geographically disparate places. These individuals and their organizations are represented in the network diagram below (Figure 3.3 overleaf). As a brief overview, the contributors and their areas of contribution are as follows:

- Barbara Chow—Program Director of the Hewlett Foundation's education program. Chow argues that "deeper learning" can be promoted through better standards and better tests that require students to apply what they have learnt to real life situations.
- Geoff Mulgan—Chief Executive of Nesta. Mulgan argues that "appealing policies" are often implemented despite the lessons of experience and evidence that they do not work. He suggests that a revolution in education and evidence is long overdue and four players in particular have a role: governments who need a visible commitment to evidence; businesses that adopt greater accountability measures for their products and services; international bodies like the OECD that generate evidence and; the public in their role as direct purchasers of education and influencers of schools and governments.
- Jon Iwata—Senior Vice President, Marketing and Communications, IBM. Iwata describes the emergence of "big data" and the advancements of intelligent computing, which together mean that "every system today is becoming a learning system" (p. 26).
- Andreas Schleicher—Acting Director for Education and Skills and the Secretary General's Special Advisor on Education Policy, OECD. Schleicher shows how an "independent, internationally-benchmarked data set like PISA

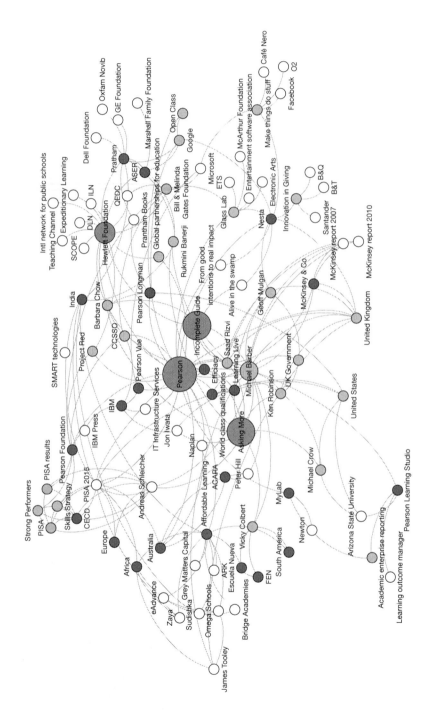

FIGURE 3.3 Pearson's "Efficacy Framework" network

can provide insight for national governments, drive up expectations and crucially, be put to practical use" as a tool for reform (p. 31).

- Vicky Colbert—Founder and Director of Fundación Escuela Nueva (FEN) and coauthor of the Escuela Nueva (EN) educational model. Colbert argues that, from her experience working in Columbia and many other countries, she has learnt a critical lesson: educational outcomes cannot be achieved through the will of governments alone. Instead, Colbert argues that "public-private partnerships and the role of civil society are indispensable for quality and sustainability in educational institutions" (p. 40).

- Rukmini Banerji—Director, Aser Centre and leadership team member at Pratham. Banerji discusses her work in developing and scaling the Aser process in India and other emerging markets. She suggests that these large-scale assessments are increasingly important in demonstrating system-wide improvement and, equally, can highlight to governments the need for improvement.

- Professor Michael Crow—President, Arizona State University. Crow describes his vision for the "New American University," which is designed around eight principles: leverage our place; transform society; value entrepreneurship; conduct use-inspired research; enable student success; fuse intellectual disciplines; be socially embedded and; engage globally. He suggests that technology and digital learning can engage new learners and shape educational programmes around individual student needs.

- Sir Ken Robinson—Education advisor, strategist and author. Robinson asks the question: Can you measure creativity? He defines this as "the process of having original ideas that have value" (p. 58) and suggests that creativity is important for everyone. Thus, Robinson argues that creativity can be taught and assessed.

- Peter Hill—former Chief Executive of ACARA. Hill highlights the importance and power of assessment for improving teaching and learning, but also asks how we can reform assessment techniques for the twenty-first century. He suggests that the answers lie in harnessing new digital technologies.

Overall, the topics discussed here relate to assessment, data, accountability and digital technologies, which arguably are the current product strengths of Pearson. These contributors and their topics were discussed with interviewees, and one representative explained:

> We basically went to some authors and we went to some others as well and said; "we're announcing our focus on efficacy and the need to focus on outcomes. If you want to, what is your perspective on that? How do you think it relates to the work you've been doing and what do you think the importance of that is?" That's how we approached that. As a result, we have this assortment of essays, not all of them are connected to each other, or directly connected to the Pearson journey, but we wanted a nice

range of perspectives that could go alongside and establish the context for Pearson's work.

If we consider the network diagram, we already know from our discussions above that the connections between the people who contributed to *Asking More* are, in part, representative of Barber's social relationships. For example, consider Geoff Mulgan: while he is currently the Chief Executive of Nesta, he previously worked for the UK government at the same time as Barber, as the Director of Policy under Tony Blair, Director of the Prime Minister's Strategy Unit and Chief Advisor to Gordon Brown MP in the early 1990s.

These contributors are not only high profile, but also representative of a range of educational organizations that include for-profit edu-businesses, philanthropic organizations, government, institutes and higher education. As explained by a Pearson representative, the invitations extended to these contributors were the result of a strategic decision:

> Yeah, we definitely wanted a range of voices just because we thought it would be really interesting to get some, a viable idea of perspectives. It was definitely a strategic decision. For example, initially we thought that we are getting a lot of perspectives from educational institutions but then we said let's try to get IBM's perspective as well because, they're not a traditional educational institution but they are really deeply embedded into this idea of data, and the importance of data and how it could apply in learning. It was definitely a strategic decision. We started with a longer list, obviously some people don't have the time to contribute to these things, so we ended up with this list in the end but we did try to get a range of perspectives.

One particularly noticeable element of this network is the geographical diversity of the contributors, the diversity of organizations they represent, as well as the mix of education work and activities in which they are involved. While most represent North America, Europe and Australia, there are also connections to South America, India and Africa. Unsurprisingly, these are the geographical regions that Pearson has targeted as their "growth markets" with the burgeoning middle class numbers that are set to invest greatly in education. A Pearson representative confirmed that this geographical diversity was also a criterion for selecting contributors:

> It was absolutely intended because we wanted to get a global perspective. I think often with these kinds of things it ends up being very centric around the US, UK or Australia, or either being for emerging markets, or really US centric. So we were really conscious, and said that we needed to get a range of perspectives globally.

Asking More could be considered an advertisement for Pearson's *Efficacy Framework*. Through the various contributors it is able to generate a form of authority and legitimacy for the efficacy initiative and fuel the assumption that Pearson is not solely focused on selling inputs into education. Rather, the document positions Pearson as genuinely engaged in understanding the complexity of contemporary education issues globally, in order to pursue better student outcomes by working with others.

It is clear from the network diagram and discussions with Pearson representatives that contributors were strategically selected based on their organizations, their areas of educational expertise and their geographical location. Given this, it would be difficult to argue that the philosophical and political positions of the contributors are neutral and balanced overall. Indeed, most of the essays are characterized by the promotion of neoliberal imaginaries of education and education quality driven by testing, data and digital technologies. Yet, quite obviously, it is not the intention of this document to provide a critical perspective; rather, it purposefully assembles high-profile policy actors to affect the legitimacy of Pearson in global education policy processes. It not only plays the game; it could be considered a game changer.

Implications: Edu-businesses as Powerful Global Policy Actors

Ball (2012, p.93) has argued persuasively that education policy analysis today has to extend beyond the nation state to take in the global and the new spaces of national/global imbrications. Lingard and Sellar (2013) have argued a similar case. There is a need to acknowledge the role of international organizations, as well as state actors in policy processes, but the major point is that such analysis today must consider the growing role of edu-businesses in all aspects of the policy cycle. In this chapter and through our network diagrams, we have shown how Pearson is reconstituting itself in this way and using network capital across various sectors of the social—governments, higher education, business, international organizations—to strengthen and legitimate its role in all aspects of the education policy cycle, from agenda setting, through policy production and implementation to evaluation. The recruitment of boundary spanners such as Sir Michael Barber brings access to their social capital, but more importantly utilizes this capital to strengthen the network capital—their connections—available to the company and can help to legitimate their position in relation to policy processes. Network capital has value based on connections between individuals and "the affordances of the 'environment'" (Urry, 2007). In recruiting Barber, Pearson can build a network environment in which they are connected to a range of policy actors across economic and academic fields. These connections potentially modify the affordances of their environment and the positioning of the company within or in relation to these fields.

What we see in the network diagrams is a blurring of boundaries between Pearson as corporation and Pearson as a network of interests and objectives spread beyond corporate boundaries and into spaces of policy, academic research and philanthropic discourses. As Elliot and Urry (2010, p. 61) observe, "high network capital allows significant participation in meetings," and as Grek (2013) has shown, it is through meetings that policy ideas travel and influence the policy cycle. Meetings are also affectively charged encounters that enable relations of trust to develop. There is a feedback loop involved in networking, whereby the establishment of connections leads to face-to-face encounters that strengthen ties and facilitate more opportunities for connection and influence. Further, one is known by the company one keeps, and the opportunity to participate in meetings and other events that have a focus on education beyond Pearson's immediate commercial interests, casts the company in a different light.

We have shown that Pearson is utilizing a strategy of CSR to legitimate their policy work as part of the broader phenomenon of the privatization of the policy producing community (Mahony et al., 2004). For example, by opening up dialogue with the company's critics and developing mechanisms for generating evidence for the efficacy of the company's products and services, Pearson can be seen as positioning itself in networks of peer review and debate, which draw on practices from the academic field. Network capital is thus an important ingredient in Pearson's corporate restructuring to position the company as an entity apparently responsible for the public good and with a role to play in public policy.

In relation to our network diagrams, we stress that they are descriptive, rather than providing analytical insights into the nature of connections between nodes; that is, they freeze flows, mobilities, developments, on-going change, and emphasize a horizontal perspective, "a flat ontology" (Ball, 2012, p. 5), at the expense of vertical perspectives on power relations and asymmetries. Our analysis, in contrast, has aimed to move beyond description of horizontal connections to raise questions about the asymmetries of power involved in these developments, which are linked to and expressive of the move to new modes of governance in education (Ball and Junemann, 2012). We emphasize the influential role of Pearson in these developments (see Ball, 2012, pp. 124–128) and their success in rebadging the business as it utilizes these new modes of governance for profit making, while representing themselves as good corporate citizens, an exemplar of the emergent philanthrocapitalism.

References

Appadurai, A. (1996). *Modernity at large.* Minneapolis: University of Minnesota Press.
Ball, S. J. (2012). *Global education Inc. New policy networks and the neo-liberal social imaginary.* Oxon: Routledge.
Ball, S. J. and Junemann, C. (2012). *Networks, new governance and education.* Bristol: The Policy Press.

Barber, M. and Mourshed, M. (2007). *How the world's best-performing schools come out on top*. London: McKinsey & Company. Retrieved June 29, 2014 from http://mckinseyon society.com/how-the-worlds-best-performing-schools-come-out-on-top/

Barber, M. and Rizvi, S. (2013a). *The incomplete guide to delivering learning outcomes*. California: Pearson

Barber, M. and Rizvi, S. (2013b). *Asking more: The path to efficacy*. California: Pearson.

Bishop, M. and Green, M. (2008). *Philanthrocapitalism: How giving can save the world*. London: Black Publishers Ltd.

Bourdieu, P. (1986). The forms of capital. In J. Richardson (Ed.) *Handbook of theory and research for the sociology of education* (pp. 241–248). Westport, CT: Greenwood.

Bourdieu, P., and Wacquant, L. J. D. (1992). *An invitation to reflexive sociology*. Cambridge: Polity Press.

Elliot, A. and Urry, J. (2010). *Mobile lives*. Oxon: Routledge.

Foucault, M. (1979). *Discipline and punish: The birth of prison*. London: Penguin Books.

Grek, S. (2013). Expert moves: International comparative testing and the rise of expertocracy. *Journal of Education Policy, 28*(5), 695–709.

Hogwood, B. and Gunn, L. (1984). *Policy analysis for the real world*. Oxford: Oxford University Press.

Holzer, B. (2010). *Moralizing the corporation: Transnational activism and corporate accountability*. Cheltenham: Edward Elgar Publishing.

Howard, P. N. (2002). Network ethnography and the hypermedia organization: New media, new organizations, new methods. *New Media & Society, 4*(4), 550–574.

Huggins, R. (2010). Network resources and knowledge alliances: Sociological perspectives on inter-firm networks as innovation facilitators. *International Journal of Sociology and Social Policy, 30*(9), 515–531.

Inkpen, A. and Tasng, E. (2005). Social capital, networks and knowledge transfer. *The Academy of Management Review, 30*(1), 145–165.

Lingard, B. and Sellar, S. (2013). Globalization, edu-business and network governance: The policy sociology of Stephen J. Ball and rethinking education policy analysis. *London Review of Education, 11*(3), 265–280.

Lyotard, J.-F. (1984). *The postmodern condition: A report on knowledge*. Minneapolis: University of Minnesota Press.

Mahony, P., Hextall, I. and Menter, I. (2004). 'Building dams in Jordan, assessing teachers in England': A case study in edu-business. *Globalisation, Societies and Education, 2*(2), 227–296.

Mourshed, M., Chijioke, C., and Barber, M. (2010). *How the world's most improved schools systems keep getting better*. London: McKinsey & Company. Retrieved June 29, 2014 from http://mckinseyonsociety.com/downloads/reports/Education/How-the-Worlds-Most-Improved-School-Systems-Keep-Getting-Better_Download-version_Final.pdf

Olmedo, A. (2013). From England with love . . . ARK, heterarchies and global 'philanthropic governance'. *Journal of Education Policy*, 575–597. doi: 10.1080/02680939. 2013.859302

Pearson. (2011). Sir Michael Barber to join Pearson as Chief Education Advisor. Retrieved June 29, 2014 from www.pearsoned.com/sir-michael-barber-join-pearson-chief-education-advisor/#.U6JilsZ38-Y

Pearson. (2013). Pearson commits to measure and report impact on learning outcomes. Retrieved June 29, 2014 from www.pearson.com/news/2013/november/pearson-commits-tomeasureandreportimpactonlearningoutcomes.html?article=true

Pearson. (2014). Pearson Efficacy. Retrieved June 29, 2014 from http://efficacy.pearson.com

Pearson Foundation. (2014). Pearson Foundation. Retrieved June 29, 2014 from www.pearsonfoundation.org

Pearson plc. (2012). Annual report and accounts 2012. Retrieved June 29, 2014 from www.pearson.com/content/dam/pearsoncorporate/files/cosec/2013/15939_PearsonAR12.pdf.

Piketty, T. (2014). *Capital in the twenty-first century*. Cambridge: The Belknap Press of Harvard University Press.

Putnam, R. D. (2000). *Bowling alone*. New York: Simon & Schuster.

Urry, J. (2007). *Mobilities*. Cambridge: Polity Press.

Urry, J. (2012). Social networks, mobile lives and social inequalities. *Journal of Transport Geography*, *21*, 24–30.

Ravitch, D. (2012). The United States of Pearson? Retrieved June 29, 2014 from http://dianeravitch.net/2012/05/07/the-united-states-of-pearson-2/

Rose, N. (1999). *Powers of freedom: Reframing political thought*. New York: Cambridge University Press.

Williams, P. (2002). The competent boundary spanner. *Public Administration*, *80*(1), 103–124.

4

MAPPING THE EDUCATION ENTREPRENEURIAL NETWORK

Teach For America, Charter School Reform, and Corporate Sponsorship[1]

Beth Sondel,[2] Kerry Kretchmar, and Joseph J. Ferrare

Introduction

In this paper we illustrate the relationships between Teach For America (TFA) and federal charter school reform to interrogate how policy decisions are shaped by networks of individuals, organizations, and private corporations. This research is grounded in our fundamental beliefs that a functional democracy relies on consistent assessment of how, by whom, and to whose benefit policy decisions are made. Thus, we seek to provide evidence that TFA is a central node in a network promoting the growth of charter schools that amplifies the voices of sponsored organizations and individuals, while potentially disenfranchising the voices of community members and educational professionals.

Each year, TFA places over 4,000 recent college graduates, the vast majority of whom have not studied education, in classrooms in low-income communities. TFA teachers are trained in a five-week summer institute before being hired as teachers of record for two years by school districts. TFA founder Wendy Kopp started the organization with the stated dual missions to fill teaching shortages in urban and rural districts and develop leaders for a movement to close the growing "achievement gap."

Most research on TFA focuses on its effectiveness and impact as a teacher preparation program (Heilig and Jez, 2010). Some argue that TFA effectively prepares teachers to have immediate and significant positive effects on their student performance (Decker, Mayer, and Glazerman, 2004; Xu, Hannaway, and Taylor, 2011) while others challenge this research methodology (Kovacs and Slate-Young, 2013) and otherwise show that TFA's short training insufficiently prepares corps members and that the two-year commitment further deprofessionalizes teaching (Darling-Hammond, 1994; Darling-Hammond and Youngs, 2002). However, extant research has not empirically addressed the second aspect of Kopp's mission. Teach For America plays a central role in a network of leaders and organizations that support, manage, and promote free market philosophy as a guide for reform. This network is situated within the larger context of contemporary shifts towards market-based ideology in educational policy that have taken shape in the past decade (Apple, 2006; Ravitch, 2010). In this paper, we map a nexus of individuals and organizations constituting an education entrepreneur network to illustrate how TFA's movement to close the achievement gap is also fundamentally a movement towards corporate sponsorship, choice, and competition. While the network advances multiple agendas, including the deregulation of teacher education, promotion of accountability policies, and dismantling of teacher unions, our analysis focuses specifically on TFA's relationship to charter reform. Although critical scholars have effectively critiqued market-based practices and often implicated TFA, our analysis adds empirical evidence that demonstrates the complexity of the organization's fundamental role in charter school reform.

In the following, we use policy network analysis to create a visual representation of TFA's key role in developing and connecting personnel, political support, and financial backing for charter reform. Next we examine how the networks unfold at a local level by zooming in on a case study of New Orleans, which has served as an experimental laboratory for charter-district reform, at the helm of which is TFA. By mapping out these connections, we hope to provide a foundation for further investigation of how this network affects policies.

Perspective and Background

In February of 2011, TFA celebrated their twentieth anniversary by holding a summit in Washington DC, at which their connection to market-based policies was made evident. Kaya Henderson, interim chancellor of DC and TFA alumnus, stood in front of the 11,000 TFA corps members and alumni in the room and announced that:

> Twenty years ago, Wendy Kopp started an organization, and that organization became a call to action, and that call to action became a movement, and that movement is changing this country . . . We need you in our charter schools, our superintendents office, writing our policies, and the list goes on . . . This is the revolution we've been waiting for.

Former chancellor of the New York Department of Education, Joel Klein and well-known market-based reformer John Schnur agreed that this was "our Egypt moment" and that those of us in the room sat at the helm of our modern Civil Rights Movement. Throughout the weekend, TFA alumni and educational leaders testified that charter schools are the panacea, frequently citing the high percentage of charters in New Orleans and Washington DC as educational success stories to replicate. TFA claims to be an apolitical organization, yet they are explicit in their desire to drive systemic change through neoliberal educational policies.

Since the 1970s, countries throughout the world, including the United States, have experienced the proliferation of neoliberalism—through policies, through the ways we talk about and understand society, and through the ways we govern (Harvey, 2005). Neoliberalism prioritizes freedom and individualism over the collective, and defines freedom and individualism in commercial and consumer terms. Neoliberal policies promote the free market, personal responsibility, choice and private enterprise, and view government as ineffective and bureaucratic. In language, it sounds like "public is bad, private is good" rhetoric. In action, neoliberalism favors increased privatization and deregulation and decreased state intervention, coupled with the defunding of public services, such as higher education, libraries, and healthcare (Apple, 2006; Ball, 2007; Burch, 2009; Harvey, 2005; Hursh, 2005). In brief, neoliberalism is an increased commitment to the promotion of unbridled capitalism, under the premise that the free market should govern businesses and society.

Shifts towards neoliberalism are evident in many spheres of life, but have had an especially profound impact on education, as evidenced by neoliberal policies such as mayoral control in many large cities, the No Child Left Behind Act (NCLB) and its reauthorization, Race to the Top, merit-pay initiatives for teachers, a boom in value-added research systems for school districts, and dramatic increases in the number of charter schools (Apple, 2006; Ball, 2007; Burch, 2009; Giroux, 2009; Ravitch, 2010). These policies have been enacted because the nation has become convinced that our schools are failing due to limited options, management failure, lack of accountability, the heavy weight of bureaucracy, and uncooperative teachers' unions and that this threatens our economic stability and international standing (Apple, 2006; Ball, 2007; Saltman, 2009a). This makes policies that promote deregulation, accountability, and systems of choice the inevitable solution.

The focus on bureaucratic problems and managerial solutions, rather than resource neglect and racist public policy, for example, obfuscates the structural, systemic, and historical root causes of an increasingly stratified society. This divorce of education and economic analysis is often used by educational reforms to convince the general public that we do not have to alleviate poverty to work towards equity. Even as public schools are stripped of resources, they are simultaneously blamed for their diminishing services and responsibility is abdicated further away from the government and onto schools, families, and the individual (Apple, 2006; Lipman, 2011). Further, systems of choice and accountability have been critiqued for disenfranchising community members by shifting decision-making power from democratically elected bodies to appointed boards and positions (Chambers, 2006). This is particularly true in urban districts where communities of color struggle to maintain democratic participation when forced to interface and negotiate with large, corporate-backed initiatives and the governing boards of charter management organizations, which are often constituted of business elites (Buras and Urban South Grassroots Research Collective, 2013; Lipman, 2011).

One of the most pervasive examples of neoliberal reform is evident in charter district policies. While charter schools were originally developed by progressive educators in the 1990s, corporate elites and politicians from both major U.S. parties have taken them up as an opportunity to merge public education with market-based assumptions: when individuals are given the freedom of choice, competition will evolve and drive the overall improvement of services (Dingerson, Peterson, Miner, & Walters, S., 2008; Wells, Slayton, & Scott, 2002). Charter reform embodies neoliberal ideology insofar as it 1) serves to blur the lines between the public and private sector by allowing charter management organizations (CMOs) and school leaders to run and treat schools like for-profit companies, 2) provides venues to test business practices in the public sphere, 3) creates opportunity for capital expansion and the outsourcing of services to private companies, and 4) legitimizes the private sector as viable providers of public services in the process (Dingerson, Peterson, Miner, and Walters, 2008; Wells, Slayton, and Scott, 2002; Wells, Lopez, Scott, and Holme, 1999).

Venture philanthropists have also emerged as strong proponents of charter school reform. Philanthropists have a long history of significant influence in education (Scott, 2009), and with current funding scarcity urban districts rely on philanthropic support. Thus, billionaires (most notably Bill Gates Jr., Sam Walton, and Eli Broad) are able to leverage their financial and symbolic power. Many have backgrounds in the corporate sphere, and thus to varying degrees apply concepts from venture capital finance and business management to education (Lipman, 2011; Ravitch, 2010; Saltman, 2010; Scott, 2009). Applying a venture capital model, educational philanthropists have funded the infrastructure of the education entrepreneur network, which has shifted economic and cultural control from public to private interests and, in turn, undermined public democracy (Saltman, 2010). As we outline below, the education entrepreneur network, in which TFA plays a central role, helps to ensure that philanthropic money is funneled preferentially toward market-based policies.

Privatization, and more specifically charter school reform, has become the primary charge of urban educational reformers, abetted by school closures and takeovers under No Child Left Behind and Race to the Top (Ravitch, 2010). As is the case with public schools, the quality of individual charters is varied. A national analysis of more than 70 percent of the students in charters found that only 17 percent are performing better than traditional public schools on standardized tests, while 37 percent are performing worse (Center for Research on Education Outcomes, 2009). This suggests that charter schools are not the panacea of educational reform (Payne and Knowles, 2009). Charter schools may provide options for families neglected by traditional public schools, provide individual students with pathways to higher education, or allow for flexibility in staffing and curriculum, which potentially enables schools to respond directly to the needs of communities and students (Payne and Knowles, 2009).

Conversely, charter schools siphon funding away from already strapped districts, push out and otherwise neglect to serve the needs of English Language Learners, the homeless, and special education students, and have higher rates of racial and economic segregation than traditional public schools (Frankenberg, Siegel-Hawley, and Wang, 2010; United States Governmental Accountability Office, 2012). Additionally, systems of choice tend to privilege those with the resources to navigate application processes and enrollment requirements. While charter schools take diverse forms, the education entrepreneur network is focused on "no-excuses" charter schools in urban and rural areas that target low-income students, oftentimes by extending the school year and school day, developing an exacting focus on improving standardized test scores, and enculturating students in middle-class mores (Thernstrom and Thernstrom, 2003).

Charter schools have implications beyond their direct effects on individuals and communities, as they play a pivotal role in a privatization agenda promoting choice, competition, and deregulation as solutions for urban education reform (Apple, 2006). Research has already demonstrated that the overbearing accountability systems that accompany privatizing education create an exacting focus on raising students' test scores. This results in curricula tailored towards testing preparation and away from individual and cultural relevance; decreased opportunities for developing critical thinking skills; pedagogy heavily weighed towards direct as opposed to child-centered instruction; and diminished relationships between teachers and students, particularly for low-income students and students of color (Lipman, 2004; McNeil, 2000; Valenzuela, 2005). This intense focus may potentially raise test scores, but may also define and limit the type of education students in low-income communities receive.

Promoters of charter schools are not explicit in their efforts to privatize, in fact they tend to characterize themselves as public. For example, the Knowledge is Power Program (KIPP) refers to itself as KIPP Public Charter Schools and defines itself on their website as: a national network of free, open-enrollment, college preparatory *public schools*. Charters are public, according to the National Alliance for Public Charter Schools, insofar as they are tuition free and open to every student, non-sectarian, publicly funded, and held accountable to state and federal academic standards (NAPCS, 2013). Yet charter schools challenge the notion of education as a public good on many accounts and, as we have discussed above and will demonstrate below, serve as a key example of the recent shift to more nuanced, "back door" forms of privatization (Burch, 2009).

Policy Network Analysis

As educational reform movements become more complex and organizationally inter-connected, it behooves critical scholars to develop new theoretical and methodological tools capable of piecing together these relationships. As such, we have examined the education entrepreneur network through the lens of critical policy scholarship. This framework was developed as a counter-hegemonic response to traditional policy science, which limits analyses to the "technical and immediately realizeable" inside-the-system understandings of and solutions for urban education (Grace, 1984, p. 32). Conversely, critical scholars deny that an increase in test scores alone evidence an improvement in educational systems and additionally situate policies within social, economic, political, and cultural contexts (Lipman, 2011). By looking at the relationships between policies and the contexts they respond to and enable, critical scholars bring to the fore the specific interests and relations of power-shaping educational policy processes (Grace, 1984; Lipman, 2011).

To examine the relationship between TFA and charter school reform we use policy network analysis (Ball, 2012; Grabher and Powell, 2005). In the past decade there has been a fundamental shift in governance away from elected hierarchical systems towards networks of resources, expertise, and reputation (Grabher and Powell, 2005). Rhodes (1995, p. 9) defines "network" as the body of inter-dependent actors and organizations engaged in the provision and exchange of informational, monetary, and human resources. These networks increasingly act as "shadow states," in which unelected, decentralized bodies exercise profound influence on public policy without public accountability (Ball, 2012; Lipman, 2011; Saltman, 2009b; Scott, 2009).

To better understand how and by whom governance happens, researchers have begun to use policy network analysis to investigate network formations and interactions. Tracing these out, Ball argues, is the first step toward understanding how they function in policy-making processes (Ball, 2012). For example, Ball has used policy network analysis to map out how education policy is being reformed and re-worked on a global scale. He discusses how philanthropists, entrepreneurs, and politicians have created networks through the commodification and accumulation of educational programs, resources, and systems and through this network has emerged a shared globalized vision for "best practices," which are built on the assumptions of neoliberalism. In this tradition, our analysis illustrates how TFA has developed a network that acts as a "shadow state" to influence charter school policy.

Methodology

In this paper we utilize graphing techniques from social network analysis to map the flow of material and nonmaterial resources through the patterns of relational ties between TFA and other individuals and organizations. To construct the different dimensions of the network we use a combination of simple directed and undirected graphs to illustrate the presence and/or strength of network ties (see Chapter 1 in this volume for a detailed discussion of SNA methods). For example, to illustrate the structure of ties between TFA and a variety of individual and organizational actors (see Figure 4.2 on page 75) we graph an actor-by-actor matrix that specifies whether a tie between actors i and j is present or not. In this graph the lines indicate the simple presence or absence of ties without any reference to strength or direction of the relations. In other applications, however, we do account for the strength and/or direction of ties between actors. For example, the graph in Figure 4.1 illustrates the strength of ties between TFA and organizations founded by, in partnership with, or staffed at high levels by TFA alumni. Additionally, in Figure 4.3 (see page 79) we use a directed graph to map the flow of financial resources from venture philanthropists to TFA-affiliated organizations.

Data sources

In an effort to develop a comprehensive understanding of the formal connections in the network, we drew from multiple data sources, including the two most recent TFA annual reports and alumni reports, as well as publicity and marketing materials. We also analyzed TFA's application for the Investing in Innovation grant competition and the two most recent IRS 990s of primary funders, which documents financial exchanges between philanthropists and non-profit organizations.

To identify connections to TFA (Figure 4.1) we looked for one or more of the following:

- organizations that were founded by TFA alumni;
- organizations that have formal, documented partnerships with TFA, including charter management organizations (CMOs) at which TFA places corps members;
- organizations with one or more TFA alumni in senior level positions.

Using the programs UCINET (Borgatti, Everett, and Freeman, 2002) and Netdraw (Borgatti, 2002), we graphed the valued relations between TFA and the organizations using the scale from 1–3, where a 1 indicates the presence of any of the three conditions bulleted above, a 2 indicates any two of the conditions, and a 3 indicates all three. In the resulting graph each line depicts the strength of connections between TFA and the organizations based upon our pre-specified criteria. Three levels of thickness weight the lines linking TFA to the organizations in the graph, in proportion to the magnitude of the relationship, with the thickest lines corresponding to all three conditions. Further, the type of line specifies the way the organization is connected to TFA. We recognize that—depending upon the measurement—the strength of the three forms of connection may be quantitatively different. However, our primary objective is to illustrate connections and to note that some organizations are connected through more forms of relationships than others.

For the second network graph we highlight a select group of TFA alumni easily identifiable as leaders and proponents of charter school agendas. This is not an exhaustive list of powerful alumni or connections. In this sense our estimation of TFA's reach is likely conservative. Nevertheless, these select individuals illustrate the crucial role of TFA alumni in expanding and sustaining the network. To identify connections between these leaders and other organizations (Figure 4.2), we looked for one or more of the following empirically verifiable relations:

- Individuals were connected to organizations if they had founded, led, or been employed by the organization, served on their advisory or governance board, or were awarded a fellowship by the organization.
- Organizations were connected to districts or other organizations if they had documented partnerships. Some organizations are connected by large regional or national partnerships, while others by a school partnership, or by a collaborative project.

Unlike the valued graph in Figure 4.1, the lines connecting pairs of individual and organizational actors in Figure 4.2 show the presence and structure of ties without reference to the strength of those ties. The relative positions of the nodes are also informative. Intuitively, nodes with (relatively) central positions have greater prominence than those positioned peripherally. Using an iterative algorithmic procedure called *spring embedding* the nodes are moved to locations in the graph that minimize the variation in line length. However, the distances between nodes should not be interpreted directly in the same way as in, say, multidimensional scaling. Ultimately it is the lines that depict the strength, presence, and/or direction of relationships between nodes in a graph.

In Figure 4.3, we followed the money. To track the shared financial networks that are critical to organizations depicted in Figures 4.1 and 4.2, we examined the 990s of the Gates, Walton, and Broad foundations, three of the largest funders of TFA (Barkan, 2011). The initial matrix consists of the set of recipient organizations and the set of transmitting funders, where the relations represent the total amount of money donated from the latter to the former (i.e., a directed graph). Next, we categorized each contribution into five categories: 1=less than $100K, 2=$100K–$499K, 3=$500K–$999K, 4=$1M–$4.99M, and 5=$5M or more. These categories constitute weights corresponding to five levels of line thickness connecting the organizations and venture philanthropists.

Results

Figure 4.1 illustrates how TFA, a self-proclaimed human capital organization (TFA, 2012), serves key organizations that promote charter school reform. This network includes numerous CMOs (KIPP, Uncommon Schools, Achievement First); organizations that train charter school leaders and founders (New Leaders For New Schools, Building Excellent Schools); philanthropic organizations that train district leaders in market-based practices (Broad Center for the Management of

School Systems, Aspen Institute-New Schools Venture Fund); charter reform advocacy groups (Excellence for Educators, New Schools for New Orleans); and data management organizations (The Achievement Network).

Figure 4.1 represents 12 of 28 non-profit, national CMOs that manage ten or more charter schools, or 51 percent of the total charter schools that are managed by large non-profit CMOs. Additionally, Figure 4.1 represents 25 percent of the charter schools managed by large for-profit CMOs, including ImagineSchools, the nation's largest for-profit CMO (Miron, Urschel, Yat Aguilar, and Dailey, 2011). However, this contextualization of the network has limitations. It utilizes the most recent CMO data from 2010–2011, although CMO numbers increase significantly each year. In 2010–2011, KIPP managed 102 charter schools. In March 2013, they managed 125 schools. Additionally, these statistics do not account for CMOs that manage fewer than ten schools, or many newer CMOs in Figure 4.1 that currently have 2–8 charters with intentions to expand (SCI Academy, Renew Schools, Explore Schools, Crescent City Schools).

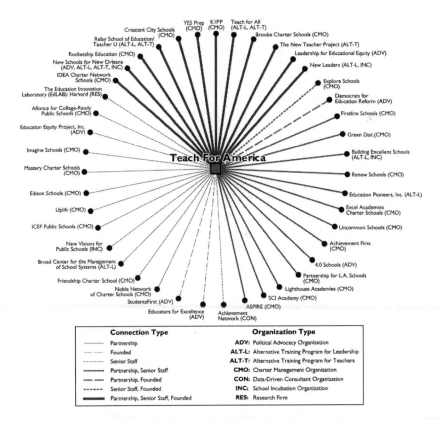

FIGURE 4.1 Graph of TFA's organizational ties (tie strength ranges from 1–3)

TFA's website asserts that, "To achieve system-wide change, we need transformational leadership at every level." Their goals include developing alumni to serve as leaders at school, district, community, advocacy, and political levels (TFA, 2012). Figure 4.1 suggests that TFA alumni are working in each of these capacities in the charter school sectors.

Perhaps the richest example of the intricate connections between TFA and charter reform is evident in TFA's relationship to CMOs that subscribe to the "no excuses" model. As illustrated in Figure 4.1, many "no excuses" CMOs, such as KIPP, YES Prep, and IDEA were founded by TFA alumni. Other such charters have partnerships with TFA and are heavily staffed at all levels by TFA affiliates (Stone and Tierney, 2010). The increasing thickness of lines connecting TFA and organizations denotes multiple aspects to their connections. For example, the thickest line (weight of 3) links TFA and KIPP because the organizations are connected along numerous dimensions—KIPP was founded by TFA alumni, has a partnership with TFA, and 50 percent of KIPP school leaders (TFA, 2012) and 33 percent of KIPP's staff nationwide (KIPP, 2014) are TFA alumni. The shared personnel between TFA and "no excuses" CMOs is in part a result of TFA's increasing placement of corps members in charter schools. For example, over half of the New York City TFA corps members teach in charters. Further, these "no excuses" CMOs and leadership training programs specifically target TFA affiliates in their recruitment efforts (TFA, 2012).

The graph in Figure 4.2 situates TFA within a more complex network environment, one in which additional organizational and individual actors serve as critical medium through which partnerships are formed and personnel are distributed. An easy way to evaluate the prominence of individual actors in an undirected network is to look at the *degree* of each actor, which is simply the number of lines incident upon a given node. For instance, while TFA is the most prominent actor in the network (degree of 36), other organizations such as KIPP (16), The New Teacher Project (15), and New Leaders (11) also occupy central positions due to their relative prominence in the network. Moving out from the central core are key districts where these central actors have solidified their reach, including the New York Department of Education (9), Newark Public Schools (6), Louisiana Recovery School District (6), and District of Columbia Public School District (6).

Moving out further from the core organizations and districts we begin to see the scope of influence of notable TFA alumni who have developed, led, and connected central actors and regions in this network through their educational entrepreneurship. These individuals are connected to many of the organizations highlighted in Figure 4.1 and are typically linked to at least two other organizations within the network (see Table 4.1). Thus, while it is organizations that are often conceptualized as the entities that connect individuals, Figure 4.2 illustrates another dimension of the network that provides insights into the ways individuals serve as crucial vectors that connect organizations. Some of these organizations

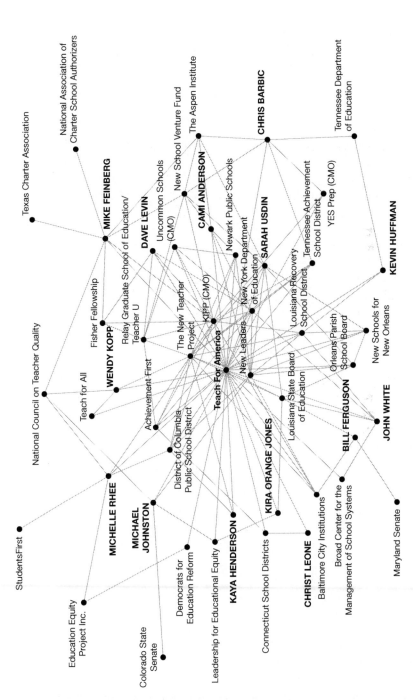

FIGURE 4.2 Graph of ties between key organizational and individual actors

Labels in figure:

StudentsFirst

National Council on Teacher Quality

Texas Charter Association

National Association of Charter School Authorizers

MIKE FEINBERG

New School Venture Fund

The Aspen Institute

CHRIS BARBIC

Tennessee Department of Education

Fisher Fellowship

DAVE LEVIN

Uncommon Schools (CMO)

CAMI ANDERSON

Newark Public Schools

WENDY KOPP

Relay Graduate School of Education/Teacher U

KIPP (CMO)

New York Department of Education

SARAH USDIN

Tennessee Achievement School District

YES Prep (CMO)

Teach for All

Achievement First

The New Teacher Project

New Leaders

Louisiana Recovery School District

KEVIN HUFFMAN

Education Equity Project Inc.

Teach for America

Orleans Parish School Board

New Schools for New Orleans

MICHELLE RHEE

District of Columbia Public School District

Louisiana State Board of Education

BILL FERGUSON

JOHN WHITE

MICHAEL JOHNSTON

Democrats for Education Reform

KIRA ORANGE JONES

Colorado State Senate

Leadership for Educational Equity

KAYA HENDERSON

Connecticut School Districts

CHRIST LEONE

Baltimore City Institutions

Broad Center for the Management of School Systems

Maryland Senate

TABLE 4.1 Organizational affiliations of TFA alumnus

TFA alumni	Affiliations
Cami Anderson	Aspen/New Leaders Venture Fund—Fellow in Entrepreneurial Leader in Public Education Program
	New Leaders—Former Chief Programs Officer
	New York City Department of Education—Former Superintendent of Alternative High Schools and Programs
	Newark Public Schools—Superintendent
	Teach For America—Former Executive Director, New York
Chris Barbic	Aspen/New Leaders Venture Fund—Fellow in Entrepreneurial Leader in Public Education Program
	Tennessee Achievement School District—Superintendent
	YES Prep—Founder and CEO
Mike Feinberg	Aspen/New Leaders Venture Fund—Fellow in Entrepreneurial Leader in Public Education Program
	KIPP—Co-Founder and Superintendent of KIPP, Houston
	National Association of Charter School Authorizers—Advisory Board Member
	National Council on Teacher Quality—Advisory Board Member
	Texas Charter School Association—Board of Directors Member
Bill Ferguson	Baltimore City Institutions—Community Liaison on Education, Assistant to the CEO of Public Schools
	Maryland Senate—Senate Member
Kaya Henderson	DC Public Schools—Former Deputy Chancellor, Current Chancellor
	The New Teacher Project—Vice President for Strategic Partnerships
	Teach For America—Former Recruiter, National Admissions Director, Former Executive Director, DC
Kevin Huffman	Teach For America—General Counsel, Senior Vice President of Growth, Strategy, and Development, Executive Vice President of Public Affairs
	Tennessee Department of Education—Commissioner
Michael Johnston	Democrats for Education Reform—Advisory Committee
	Leadership for Educational Equity—Supported Candidate
	National Council on Teacher Quality—Advisory Board Member
	New Leaders—Policy Advisor
	Presidential Candidate Barack Obama—Education Advisor

continued . . .

TABLE 4.1 Continued

TFA Alumni	Affiliations
Wendy Kopp	National Council on Teacher Quality—Advisory Board Member
	Teach For All—CEO and Founder
	Teach For America—CEO and Founder
Chris Leone	Bloomfield Connecticut—Chief Operating Officer
	Hartford, Connecticut—Former Director of the Regional School Choice Office Torrington, Connecticut—Former Superintendent of Schools
Dave Levin	KIPP—Co-founder, Former Superintendent of KIPP NYC, Leader of KIPP Teaching and Learning Labs
	Relay Graduate School—Board of Trustee Member
	Teacher University—Co-founder
Kira Orange-Jones	Aspen/New Leaders Venture Fund—Fellow in Entrepreneurial Leader in Public Education Program
	Leadership for Educational Equity—Supported Candidate
	Louisiana Board of Elementary and Secondary Education—Elected Member
	Teach For America—Executive Director, Greater New Orleans
Michelle Rhee	DC Public Schools—Former Chancellor
	Education Equity Project—Founding Member
	National Council on Teacher Quality—Advisory Board Member
	New Teacher Project—Founder and Former CEO
	Students First—Founder and CEO
Sarah Usdin	Aspen/New Leaders Venture Fund—Fellow in Entrepreneurial Leader in Public Education Program
	New Schools for New Orleans—Founder and Former CEO
	New Teacher Project—Former Executive director
	Orleans Parish School Board—Elected Board Member
	Teach For America—Former Executive Director, South Louisiana
John White	Broad Superintendents Academy—Alumnus
	Louisiana Recovery School District—Former Superintendent
	Louisiana State Board of Education—State Superintendent
	New York Department of Education—Former Deputy Chancellor of Talent, Labor, and Innovation, Former Deputy Chief Operating Officer, CEO of the Portfolio Division
	Teach For America—Former Executive Director, Chicago and New Jersey

are not illustrated in Figure 4.1, but are included in Figure 4.2 due to their important relation to charter school reform. This is a demonstration of the ways in which the network expands beyond formal partnerships with TFA or with organizations that are founded or led by alumni, and thus illustrates the broadening reach of the education entrepreneur network.

Consider Michelle Rhee as an example of how one individual TFA alumnus moves through organizations, connects constituents, and expands the network to promote a market-based agenda. After completing her TFA commitment, Rhee founded The New Teacher Project, which trains teachers in a program modeled after TFA's training, consults with districts on hiring and staffing issues, and partners with TFA to credential some corps members. During Rhee's tenure as the Chancellor of District of Columbia schools, she significantly increased the number of charters in the district. Currently, Rhee is founder of the political action and lobbying organization StudentsFirst, which, among other agenda items, promotes expanding parental choice and dramatically limiting the power and role of teachers' unions, which are seen as barriers to the growth of charters. Rhee increases her impact as a frequent guest speaker at The Aspen Institute, a self-proclaimed nonpartisan organization seeking to inform philanthropists on which policy initiatives to support and fund. She is also a member of the Educational Equity Project, a coalition of leaders, who advocate for expanding charters through position papers, public forums, and lobbying.

In addition to their connections with CMOs, districts, and non-profit organizations, TFA alumni occupy a growing number of positions as superintendents and elected officials. For example, TFA alumni have been appointed as the State Superintendent of Louisiana and Commissioner of the Tennessee Department of Education, as well as superintendents in the Newark Public School District, District of Columbia Public Schools, and Tennessee Achievement School District. Many of these district leaders have been vocal proponents of the expansion of charters, such as Michelle Rhee and Kaya Henderson in the District of Columbia, and Chris Barbic, in the Tennessee Achievement School District.

TFA is committed to preparing political leaders. Leadership for Educational Equity (LEE), started by TFA alumni, supports the campaigns of TFA alumni to become "levers for long-term systemic change". Unsurprisingly, thus far their candidates have primarily supported school choice agendas. Figure 4.2 and Table 4.1 highlight key political leaders, such as Maryland State Senator Bill Ferguson and Colorado State Senator Michael Johnston, who have advocated for charter reform in their elected positions.

Venture Philanthropy and Corporate Sponsorship

In addition to shared personnel, expertise, and information, many of the organizations depicted in Figures 4.1 and 4.2 are backed by similar sponsorship. For example, Broad, Walton, and Gates all contribute significant amounts of money

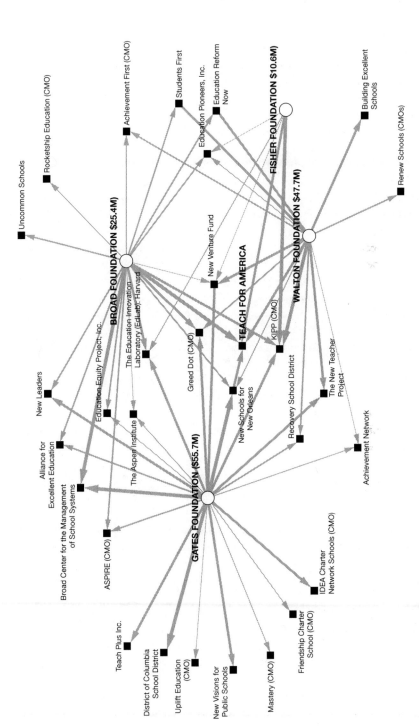

FIGURE 4.3 Directed graph of organizations and key funders

to TFA, KIPP, New Schools for New Orleans, Democrats for Education Reform, and Excellence for Educators, among others. As demonstrated in Figure 4.3, four of TFA's largest funders are the Walton, Gates, Fisher, and Broad foundations, all of which have supported market-based agendas (Barkan, 2011; Saltman, 2010). These philanthropists not only give significant amounts of money to TFA and other members of the network, they have also developed direct service and training programs for CMO and charter school leaders. The Fishers, for example, work in partnership with Dave Levin and Mike Feinburg (TFA alumni) and the Haas School of Business, which trains KIPP school leaders; in 2010–2011 85 percent of Fisher Fellows were TFA alumni (Matthews, 2009). The Broad Foundation had an urban superintendent fellowship responsible for training 43 percent of superintendents in large urban districts across the US in 2011 (Barkan, 2011).

Figure 4.3 demonstrates how TFA and the organizations within its network are heavily supported by venture philanthropists advocating for market-based reform. The Gates Foundation, for example, frames their approach to educational reform in economic terms and has significantly contributed to public school initiatives, but despite being "public" these contributions have often (although not exclusively) been in support of market-based initiatives. Broad's mission, on the other hand, is exclusively market-based, as the Foundation argues for the need to create "alternative pathways that reinvent American education and provide far better learning opportunities." In the same way that TFA asserts that educational change requires leaders at all levels, Gates, Broad, Walton, and Fisher support organizations that further market-based reforms from multiple angles (Saltman, 2010).

The network graphs (Figures 4.1, 4.2, and 4.3) begin to portray the importance of TFA in the education entrepreneur network through the organization's wide scope of connections to CMOs, political advocacy and lobbying groups, venture philanthropists, and individual leaders who have promoted choice. As an example intended to illustrate how this network can shift power and affect policy, we examine the education entrepreneur network's influence in New Orleans. We have chosen New Orleans as an extreme and politically important case, though we do not want to overlook the presence of this network in a growing number of urban districts.

New Orleans

Post-Katrina New Orleans, redeveloped as an experimental laboratory for market-based reform, provides a stark example of how the education entrepreneur network is integral to the privatization project (Buras, 2011; Saltman, 2009b). In the wake of the storm, with much of the voting population displaced, a number of rapid-fire legislative decisions lifted the cap on charters, altered the criteria defining an "academically unacceptable" school that qualified for state takeover, and changed the chartering process to diminish school and community-based participation. This policy put an additional 107 schools under the aegis of the state-run Recovery School District (RSD) (Garda, 2011). Without per-pupil funding, Orleans Parish School Board fired 7,500 predominantly African American school personnel with the stated purpose of avoiding bankruptcy, effectively obliterating locally elected school board control and the local teachers' union. In the rebuilding efforts, the federal government provided 47 million dollars for the development of charter schools with no comparable support given to redevelop traditionally run public schools. The Broad, Gates, Fisher, and Walton foundations, among others, provided over $17.5 million dollars to support these efforts (Saltman, 2009b). As state-run schools reopened many had no choice but to do so as charters, while others were handed over to national CMOs (Buras, 2011). Currently, over 80 percent of students in New Orleans are in charters, with projections for annual increase (Cowen Institute, 2013).

As development of the New Orleans school system continues, the education entrepreneur network plays an ongoing, imperative role (Buras, 2011; 2014; Lipman, 2011). Immediately after the storm, TFA "made a significant commitment to Louisiana—more than tripling the size of [their] corps and alumni base to supply the talent needed to fuel the market-driven reform efforts that are producing dramatic achievement gains" (TFA, 2012). Further, Sarah Usdin, a TFA alumnus, former TFA regional Executive Director, and founder of New Schools for New Orleans (NSNO), was charged with filling the staffing void created by the mass termination of veteran teachers. NSNO relied heavily on partnerships with New Leaders for New Schools and TFA, and their development of TeachNOLA, a program modeled after TFA to develop personnel. While the vast majority of veteran teachers have still not been offered their jobs back, TFA has continued to grow in each year, made possible largely by continual philanthropic support from Walton, Gates, and Broad (Saltman, 2009b; TFA, 2012). Greater New Orleans has the highest concentration of TFA corps members and alumni in the nation, constituting approximately 30 percent of the total teachers in the city, with over 370 first- and second-year TFA teachers, and over 400 alumni in schools, including 27 school leaders (TFA, 2012).

Multiple CMOs in New Orleans were founded by and are heavily staffed by TFA affiliates (Firstline Schools, Crescent City Schools, Renew Schools, Sci Academy), some by upwards of 80 percent (Sondel, 2013). KIPP NOLA is one of the largest, with nine schools and plans for further expansion (KIPP, 2014). Beyond these nine schools, KIPP has had a significant impact on district policy. Paul Vallas, former superintendent of the RSD, hired KIPP staff to model and design district policies. KIPP NOLA also provided leadership and start-up training for NSNO's principal incubation program, which has trained 23 school leaders (NSNO, 2012). Seven of the nine KIPP school leaders and over 60 percent of their instructional staff are TFA corps members and alumni (Sondel, 2013).

The educational leadership governing New Orleans is also comprised of many TFA alumni, including State Superintendent John White, State Board of

Elementary and Secondary Education (BESE) member Kira Orange Jones, and Orleans Parish School Board member Sarah Usdin. White, a TFA alumnus, was also a former TFA Executive Director and Broad Fellow. He was recruited to serve as the Superintendent of the RSD in New Orleans and he appointed, of his top four officials, two TFA alumni and one leader from the KIPP network (Vanacore, 2011). After six months, White was appointed State Superintendent of Louisiana, an appointment made possible in part by the election of Kira Orange Jones. Throughout her campaign and after her election, Orange Jones continued to serve as the Executive Director of TFA-Greater New Orleans. Orange Jones' campaign was spearheaded by Leaders for Educational Equity, the aforementioned organization developed to support the election of TFA alumni. Orange Jones and Usdin relied on campaign budgets that were heavily sponsored by venture philanthropists and far exceeded those of their opponents (Cavanagh, 2012; Cunningham-Cook, 2012).

With the support of White and Orange Jones, Governor Bobby Jindal passed an education proposal that, among other mandates, further expanded the number of charters statewide and fast-tracked the charter approval process. Not only are members of the network promoting charter schools from multiple angles, they have also been tasked with the evaluation of said reforms. Organizations such as NSNO have collected data on the reforms and have reported New Orleans as an unequivocal success story and a model for urban districts nationwide. In a recent report, NSNO advises urban educational leaders to expand CMOs and rely on TFA for "human capital" needs (Brinson, Hassel, and Kingsland, 2012). New Orleans serves as an important example of how the education entrepreneur network exerts influence over policies and educational practices in a local context.

Conclusion

Looking at Figures 4.1, 4.2, and 4.3, it is evident that TFA sits at the forefront of a powerful network of interdependent organizations, foundations, and individual leaders that play pivotal roles in the growth of charter school reform. By depicting the scope of connections within the education entrepreneur network, we have demonstrated that TFA is not only an important actor in charter school reform, but also a preeminent incubator for personnel who go on to staff existing organizations, and for leaders who work to expand the network. It is increasingly clear that TFA's movement "to end educational inequity" has become market-based and charter-reform-driven. In addition to clarifying the relations within the network, we hope to provide a foundation for future research on how TFA corps members are politicized and how ideology, rhetoric, and pedagogy are promoted within the network. Given the rapid expansion of charters driven in part by the strategic and highly funded network we have outlined in analyzing these reforms, it is important to ask how decisions are being made, by whom, and to whose benefit. While the education entrepreneur network is intricately connected, extremely powerful, and rhetorically committed to equity and justice, the impact of their promoted policies on students and communities must be evaluated with a critical eye before we trust in them to make such important decisions for the children of our nation.

Notes

1   Reprinted with permission by Taylor & Francis from Kretchmar, K., Sondel, B., and Ferrare, J. J. (2014). Mapping the terrain: Teach For America, charter school reform, and corporate sponsorship. *Journal of Education Policy, 29*(6), 742–759.
2   Beth Sondel and Kerry Kretchmar contributed equally to this work.

References

Apple, M. W. (2006). *Educating the right way: Markets, standards, god, and inequality* (second ed.). New York: Routledge.

Ball, S. J. (2007). *Education PLC: Understanding private sector participation in public sector education.* London: Taylor & Francis.

Ball, S. J. (2012). *Policy networks and new governance.* New York, NY: Taylor & Francis.

Barkan, J. (2011). Got dough? How billionaires rule our schools. *Dissent, 1*(58), 49–57.

Borgatti, S. P. (2002). *Netdraw network visualization.* Harvard, MA: Analytic Technologies.

Borgatti, S. P., Everett, M. G., and Freeman, L. C. (2002). *UCINET for Windows: Software for social network analysis.* Harvard, MA: Analytic Technologies.

Brinson, D., Hassel, B., and Kingsland, N. (2012). *New Orleans-style education reform: A guide for cities. Lessons learned 2004–2010.* Retrieved May 14, 2013 from: www.newschoolsfor neworleans.org/documents/03012012NOLAstylereform.pdf

Buras, K. (2011). Race, charter schools, and conscious capitalism: On the spatial politics of whiteness as property (and the unconscionable assault on Black New Orleans). *Harvard Education Review, 81*(2), 296–331.

Buras, K. L. (2014). *Charter schools, race, and urban space: Where the market meets grassroots resistance.* New York: Routledge.

Buras, K. L. and Urban South Grassroots Research Collective. (2013). New Orleans education reform: a guide for cities or a warning for communities? (Grassroots lessons learned, 2005–2012). *Berkeley Review of Education, 4*(1), 123–160.

Burch, P. (2009). *Hidden markets: The new education privatization.* New York: Routledge.

Cavanagh, S. (2012) Jackpot of cash from outsiders helped insurgent in LA board race. *Ed Week.* Retrieved May 14, 2013 from www.edweek.org/ew/articles/2012/05/23/32adv-victor_ep.h31.html

Center for Research on Education Outcomes (CREDO). (2009). *Multiple choice: Charter school performance in 16 states.* Stanford University. Retrieved May 14, 2013 from http://credo.stanford.edu

Chambers, S. (2006). *Mayors and schools: Minority voices and democratic tensions in urban education.* Philadelphia, PA: Temple University Press.

Cowen Institute. (2013). *The state of public education in New Orleans.* New Orleans: Author.

Cunningham-Cook, M. (2012). Why do some of America's wealthiest individuals have fingers in Lousiana's education system? *The Nation.* Retrieved May 14, 2013 from www.thenation.com/article/170649/why-do-some-americas-wealthiest-individuals-have-fingers-louisianas-education-system

Daly, A. J. (2010). *Social network theory and educational change*. Cambridge, MA: Harvard Educational Press.

Darling-Hammond, L. (1994). Who will speak for the children? How "Teach For America" hurts urban schools and children. *Phi Delta Kappan, 76*(1), 21–34.

Darling-Hammond, L., and P. Youngs. (2002). Defining "highly qualified teachers": What does "scientifically-based" research actually tell us?" *Educational Researcher, 31*(9), 13–25.

Decker, P. T., Mayer, D. P., and Glazerman, S. (2004). *The effects of Teach for America on students: Findings from a national evaluation*. University of Wisconsin–Madison, Institute for Research on Poverty.

Dingerson, L., Peterson, B., Miner, B., and Walters, S. (Eds.). (2008). Keeping the promise?: The debate over charter schools. Milwaukee, WI: Rethinking Schools.

Frankenberg, E., Siegel-Hawley, G., and Wang, J. (2010). *Choice without equity: Charter school segregation and the need for civil rights standards*. Los Angeles: Civil Rights Project/Proyecto Derechos Civiles, UCLA.

Garda Jnr, R. A. (2011). The politics of education reform: Lessons from New Orleans. *Journal of Law & Education, 40*, 57–215.

Giroux, H. (2009). Obama's Dilemma: Postpartisan Politics and the Crisis of American Education. *Harvard Educational Review* (summer 2009), *79*(2), 250.

Grabher, G. and Powell, W. (2005) *Networks: Critical studies in economic institutions. Volume 1*. Camberley, United Kingdom: Edward Elgar Publishing.

Grace, G. (1984). Urban education: Policy science or critical scholarship. *Education and the City: Theory, history and contemporary practice* (pp. 3–59). New York: Routledge.

Harvey, D. (2005). *A brief history of neoliberalism*. USA: Oxford University Press.

Heilig, J. and Jez, S. (2010). *Teach For America: A review of the evidence*. Boulder, CO: National Educational Policy Center.

Hursh, D. (2005). Neo-liberalism, markets and accountability: Transforming education and undermining democracy in the United States and England. *Policy Futures in Education, 3*(1), 3–15.

KIPP. (2014). *Frequently asked questions*. Retrieved on May 14, 2013 from www.kipp.org/faq

Kovacs, P., and Slate-Young, E. (2013). *Performance versus promises: An evaluation of Teach for America's research page: Executive summary*. University of Alabama Education Policy Center. Retrieved April 5, 2013 from http://uaedpolicy.weebly.com/uploads/6/1/7/1/6171842/tfa-2_1.pdf

Lipman, P. (2004). *High stakes education: Inequality, globalization, and urban school reform*. New York: Routledge.

Lipman, P. (2011). *The new political economy of urban education*. New York: Routledge.

Matthews, J. (2009). *Work hard. Be nice*. New York: Algonquin Books.

McNeil, L. (2000). *Contradictions of school reform: Educational costs of standardized testing*. New York: Routledge.

Miron, G., Urschel, J. L., Yat Aguilar, M. A., and Dailey, B. (2011). *Profiles of for-profit and nonprofit education management organizations: Thirteenth annual report—2010–2011*. Boulder, CO: National Education Policy Center. Retrieved April 5, 2013 from http://nepc.colorado.edu/publication/EMO-profiles-10–11.

National Alliance for Public Charter Schools (NAPCS) (2013). *What are public charter schools?* Retrieved April 25, 2013 from www.publiccharters.org/About-Charter-Schools/What-are-Charter-Schools003F.aspx

New Schools for New Orleans (NSNO). (2012). *New Schools for New Orleans key partners.* Retrieved May 14, 2013 from http://newschoolsforneworleans.org/aboutus_key partners.php

Payne, C., and Knowles, T. (2009). Promise and peril: Charter schools, urban school reform, and the Obama administration. *Harvard Educational Review, 79*(2), 227–239.

Ravitch, D. (2010). *The death and life of the great American school system: How testing and choice are undermining education.* New York: Basic Books.

Rhodes, R. (1995). *The New Governance: governing without government.* London: RSA and ESRC.

Saltman, K. (2009a). Corporatization and the control of schools. In M. Apple, W. Au, and L. Gandin (Eds.), *The Routledge international handbook of critical education.* New York: Routledge.

Saltman, K. (2009b). The rise of venture philanthropy and the ongoing neoliberal assault on public education: The Eli and Edythe Broad foundation. *Workplace: A Journal for Academic Labor, 16,* 53–72.

Saltman, K. J. (2010). *The gift of education: Public education and venture philanthropy.* New York: Palgrave Macmillan.

Scott, J. (2009). The politics of venture philanthropy in charter school policy and advocacy. *Educational Policy, 23*(1), 106–136.

Sondel, B. (2013). *Raising citizens or raising test scores: Curriculum and ideology in post-Katrina charter schools. (Doctoral Dissertation).* Madison, WI: University of Wisconsin.

Stone, N. and Tierney, T. (2010). *The chronicle of philanthropy: "Donors must include attention to accountability with their gifts."* November 1, 2010. Retrieved November 3, 2014 from http://philanthropy.com/article/Donors-Must-Impose-High/125138/.

Teach For America (TFA). (2012). Teach For America website. Retrieved May 14, 2013 from www.teachforamerica.org

Thernstrom, A. and Thernstrom S. (2003). *No excuses: Closing the racial gap in learning.* New York: Simon & Schuster.

United States Governmental Accountability Office. (2012). *Charter schools: Additional federal attention needed to help protect access for students with disabilities.* Report to congressional requesters. June.

Valenzuela, A. (2005). *Leaving children behind: How "Texas-style" accountability fails Latino youth.* Albany: State University of New York.

Vanacore, A. (2011). Recovery school district leader selects four top aides. In *The Times Picayune.* August 23, 2011. Retrieved December 5, 2012 from www.nola.com/education/index.ssf/2011/08/recovery_school_district_leade.html

Wells, A. S., Lopez, A., Scott, J., and Holme, J. J. (1999). Charter schools as postmodern paradox: Rethinking social stratification in an age of deregulated school choice. *Harvard Educational Review, 69*(2), 172–205.

Wells, A. S., Slayton, J., and Scott, J. (2002). Defining democracy in the neoliberal age: Charter school reform and educational consumption. *American Educational Research Journal, 39*(2), 337.

Xu, Z., Hannaway, J., and Taylor, C. (2011) Making a difference? The effects of Teach For America in high school. *Journal of Policy Analysis and Management, 30*(3), 447–469.

5

INTERNATIONAL ACCESS PROJECT

A Network Analysis of an Emerging International Curriculum Program in China

Shuning Liu

Introduction

> Education should face modernization, face the world, and face the future.
>
> *(Deng Xiaoping, 1983—see Shi, 2013)*

Since Deng Xiaoping made this claim in the early 1980s, the Chinese government has carried out a series of educational reforms to improve the modernization and internationalization of its education system. Education for economic development has become the dominant discourse that guides educational reforms in contemporary China, as it does in many other countries (Apple, 2006; Ball, 2013; Mok, Wong, and Zhang, 2009). Among the trajectory of the reforms, three interrelated sets of education reforms deserve special attention in order to understand the rise of the neoliberal approach to reform Chinese education. The first is the reform of decentralization and financial diversification initially issued in 1985 and restated in 1993,[1] which emphasizes that the central government devolves financial responsibility and management of education to local governments. This education reform calls for local governments and state schools to utilize multiple channels to improve their education services and resource provision (Cheng, 1997; Liu and Dunne, 2009; Ngok, 2007; Tsang, 1996). Such school autonomy reforms encourage state schools with quality educational resources to generate additional revenues through expanding their educational services to meet social needs. This reform led to the marketization of education in China (Mok, 2009; Mok et al., 2009).

The second key reform is called the New Curriculum Reform of basic education.[2] Initiated in 1999 and fully implemented in grades 1—12 until 2007, this curriculum reform was expected to transform Chinese education from *yingshi jiaoyu* (examination-oriented education) to *sushi jiaoyu* (commonly translated as "quality education") (Guan and Meng, 2007; Zhong, 2006). The New Curriculum Reform emphasizes improving the global competence of the Chinese population in the face of challenges arising from the knowledge-based economy. It is manifest that the Chinese government links the nurturing of *rencai* (human capital) to the building of a competent nation-state as a response to the requirement of international economic competition (Ball, 2013; Crabb, 2010; Hannum, 1999; Law, 2014). However, the New Curriculum Reform has encountered many "bottlenecks," which make the Chinese government seek solutions via external forces. In particular, the State places hopes for the introduction of high-quality foreign educational resources through new school-running modes.

This brings to our attention the third important education reform—the Chinese-Foreign Cooperation in Running Schools (CFCRS) policy, in particular, a new development of the policy. Since the new versions of regulations were promulgated in 2003 and enhanced in 2004 (Ministry of Education of the People's Republic of China (MOE), 2003, 2004), the practices of CFCRS have enabled Chinese universities to explore new talent-cultivating patterns (Chen and Xie, 2010; Zhang, 2003). By around 2008, the Chinese government had gradually approved Chinese-Foreign Cooperation in Running Schools—High School Programs, which are commonly called International High School Curriculum Programs. These programs were newly created by Chinese elite public high schools in big cities through supposedly cooperating with foreign education institutions. The new international programs imported various foreign curricula, such as General Certificate of Education Advanced Level (A-Level), Advanced Placement (AP), and Global Assessment Certificate (GAC), and integrated them with the Chinese national high school curriculum for preparing Chinese students for the foreign college application process (Huang, 2012; Liu, F., 2013; Zhou, 2013; Zhu, 2013). The unique institutional structure of the CFCRS policy brings private education companies into the development of international programs for profit making. To a large extent, the interventions of these private institutions into Chinese public education reforms are tacit business practices. According to *Beijing's Mirror Evening News*, there have been about 90 such high school programs approved by the government up to 2014. The State sees these new programs as a promising way to improve the internationalization and modernization of the Chinese education system, to promote the Quality Education reform, and to foster students who will gain international perspectives and cross-cultural understanding for Chinese economic development (MOE, 2010).

Despite the rhetorical goals, it is worth examining the practices of the newly-established high school programs influenced by the CFCRS policy in order to disclose the relations with for-profit businesses. This research investigates the International Access Project (IAP, pseudonym) international high school curriculum program, one of the emerging international curricular programs in China. Using network ethnography methods (Ball and Junemann, 2012; Howard, 2002), my research explores the organization and practices of the new curriculum program. This study focuses on mapping out the networks of the social actors who are involved in the IAP program development and examining the interactions and power relations of these social actors in the network relationships. The purpose of this study is to make the tacit relationships between the social actors involved in the for-profit CFCRS high school programs visible. In doing so, this study contributes to a deep understanding of the neoliberal character and implications of the policy and practices of the CFCRS high school programs.

The Convergence of Chinese Education Markets and Global Education Markets

Since the late 1970s, China has undergone dramatic social changes associated with its market-oriented economic reforms. Rapid growth of the national economy has led to urban-rural and regional economic disparities and created great social stratification and class difference (Harvey, 2005; Li, Li, and Sun, 2004; Yan and Chang, 2009). The rising middle and upper classes, who mostly concentrate in urban China, utilize their various forms of capital to secure quality education and social mobility for their children (Bourdieu, 1984; Wu, 2014). Elite public high schools are favored by these new social classes because they are traditionally ideal paths to elite Chinese universities (Shao and Zhang, 2013; Wang, 2011; You, 2007).[3] In the post-compulsory education sector, however, the merit-based student enrollment measured by test scores still plays an important role in determining students' educational mobility and life chances (Hannum, An, and Cherng, 2011; Liu, Y., 2013).[4] In the face of restricted access to quality educational resources, the new social classes demand a market in education for them to diversify their choices.

Thanks to China's entry into the World Trade Organization (WTO) in 2001, the global education market has opened up opportunities for wealthy Chinese students to access top global higher education institutions, especially those in the United States. Going to study in U.S. colleges and universities has become the preferred choice of increasing numbers of wealthy Chinese families (Zhou, 2013). The trend of global higher education and high demand of quality educational resources from new Chinese social classes has created a potentially huge market for education business. The neoliberal approach to trade in educational services embedded in the General Agreement on Trade in Services (GATS) provides an opportunity for Chinese high schools to enter into that global education market (Ding, Yue, and Sun, 2009; Lao, 2002; Robertson, Bonal, and Dale, 2002).[5] The impact of GATS on policy making for Chinese high school education can be seen in the *National Guidelines for Medium-and Long-term Educational Reform and Development 2010–2020* (MOE, 2010), abbreviated as "the

Guidelines." This new education policy puts the internationalization of high school education on the agenda. It highlights the importance of diversifying Chinese high schools, the school-running system, and the modes of education. It also encourages elite public schools to expand their high-quality education resources to meet the needs of students with differing potential. The Guidelines marked a new development in the internationalization and modernization of the Chinese education system as a response to the pressure from global education policies. This can be viewed as what Ball (2012) calls "policy convergence," which paves a way to create a new conduit linking local education markets to global education markets. The emergence of CFCRS high school programs is a manifestation of the interactions of local and global policies. Therefore, these new programs become key sites to explore the linkages between the "local" and "the global."

By offering an alternative pathway for Chinese students to college education, the emerging CFCRS high school programs have a potentially huge market, which can be seen in a recent social and educational phenomenon. In the last five years, a rapidly growing number of urban Chinese high school students who want to apply to universities in the United States have chosen newly-established international curriculum programs in China. These programs help Chinese students prepare for their U.S. college application process by exposing them to an internationalized curriculum—an integration of the Chinese national curriculum with various imported foreign curricula (Huang, 2012; Wang, 2012). Officially, these international curriculum programs are public. But students who choose these new programs have to pay high tuition. The tuition ranges from about 60,000 to 120,000 yuan each year, which is far more expensive than that of any state high school whose yearly tuition is approximately 2,000 yuan. The tuition-charging "public" programs exclude disadvantaged students and create unequal access to international education. These issues make the emerging curriculum programs contentious sites in need of in-depth and critical analysis.

Conceptual Framework

This study is informed by Stephen Ball's concept of network governance. In his recent book, *Global Education Inc.: New Policy Networks and the Neoliberal Imaginary*, Ball (2012) highlights that we now live in a neoliberal globalization age, where individual choices and self-interests are valued over the public good and market mechanisms are widely used to reform public institutions for ensuring individual freedoms. The global spread of this neoliberal ideology has transformed the role of the state in coping with educational problems from "government" characterized by hierarchy and independence to "governance" defined by mutuality, networks, and interdependence. This shift implies new methods of governing society, which are called "network governance" (Ball, 2012; Ball and Junemann, 2012). As Ball (2012) points out, network governance represents new global developments in education policy and education reforms. Drawing on the ideas of Williams

(2002) and Rhodes (1997), Ball explains that network governance means that governments attempt to solve education policy problems by adopting networking, partnership, collaboration, joint working arrangements, and other forms of managerial strategies. Such an approach has involved a wide variety of social actors in education service delivery and education reforms, which not only legitimates new participants, but also constitutes "new kinds of policy communities, usually based upon shared conceptions of social problems and their solutions" (Ball and Junemann, 2012, p. 12). Ball (2012) suggests that we pay special attention to new forms of the participation of private sectors in education in order to understand the increasing role of education business in neoliberalizing the public sector education. As Ball and Junemann (2012) remind us, the network-based forms of governing are often mixed with bureaucracies and markets, which implies a new organizational form that Ball (2012) calls "heterarchies." In this sense, research on the new trend and development of education governance helps us understand changing power relations in education, as well as the "changes in the form and modalities of the state" (Ball, 2012, p. 1). Employing this conceptual framework, my study looks closely at the involvement of private actors in delivering education services and their interactions with public sectors through the CFCRS policy.

Social Network Analysis and Network Ethnography

Social Network Analysis (SNA) focuses on analyzing and representing relationships between social actors. It has recently been recognized as a powerful methodological tool for critical education research (Au and Ferrare, 2014; Ball, 2012; Ferrare and Apple, 2010; Gulson and Symes, 2007; Robertson, 2010). SNA is consistent with a critical socio-spatial theory, which emphasizes that space is socially produced; spaces are social relations stretched out; and space constitutes and is constituted through power relations in social transactions (Robertson, 2010, p. 15–18; Ferrare and Apple, 2010). More importantly, applying a critical lens to a SNA approach entails focusing on power relations embedded in social network relationships (Ball, 2012; Ferrare and Apple, 2010). This book chapter uses network ethnography, which refers to "the process of using ethnographic field methods on cases and field sites selected using social network analysis" (Howard, 2002, p. 561). Through incorporating an ethnographic approach into social network analysis, network ethnography provides "a mapping of the form and content of policy relations in a particular field" and "offers a broader and richer access to the 'social' in social networks than has been the case using just terrestrial data" (Ball, 2012, p. 5). As a variant of SNA, network ethnography aims to provide the "thick description" of a network and focuses on examining power relations embedded in the network made up of different social actors (Ball and Junemann, 2012; Wittel, 2000). It is an appropriate research approach to explore "'new' forms and relationships of governing" (Ball and Junemann, 2012, p. 2). As shown in the graph (see Figure 5.1 on page 99), this study illustrates the network relations between social actors surrounding the development of the IAP program under study. In the graph, circles represent curricular programs as events. Rectangles represent social organizations as actors who participated and were involved in developing curricular programs. The network diagram constructed based on research data helps trace where the Chinese and foreign parts of the international-ized curriculum come from. It also visually demonstrates the affiliations and interactions between social actors who are involved in the new joint international program. This will be discussed shortly.

Data Sources

This study draws on a larger research project conducted from 2011 to 2014, which focuses on investigating educational experiences of Chinese high school students who choose to study abroad. There are four main types of data sources used in this chapter, including high-profile news sources in China, webpages, policy documents, and fieldwork conducted in 2013 in the Sunny High (pseudonym of an elite state high school) IAP International Curriculum Program in Moon City (pseudonym) in China. The news sources comprise of some mainstream newspapers covering the news about IAP international high school programs. Data from fieldwork consists of field notes, advertisement videos about the IAP program, and semi-structured interviews with four school administrators from the Sunny High School as well as one executive administrator and two teachers from an educational consultancy company called China Bridge (pseudonym) International Education Services Co., Ltd. Webpages include those from the field school, related educational companies, and other involved organizations. Policy documents were gathered from the Chinese government websites, such as the MOE and Moon (pseudonym) Municipal Bureau of Education. The network of Sunny High IAP international high school curriculum program has been constructed using the above data. The network is subject to detailed analysis in this present study.

IAP International High School Programs

The IAP international high school program was, in effect, designed by China Bridge International Education Services Co., Ltd. in collaboration with ACT Education Solutions, Limited. Both China Bridge and ACT Education Solutions are for-profit education companies. The former is a Chinese firm located in Moon City, a cosmopolitan city in China, while the latter is an American company located in Iowa City in the United States. The mission of the IAP program is "devoted to high school international education in China." Specifically, it aims to "innovate high school curriculum by bringing students early access to first-rate international education." However, given the fact that its service targets are those Chinese high school students who want to study abroad, the practical goal of the IAP program is to help students prepare for the world's elite universities, "where they hone their talents and strive to become tomorrow's leaders, entrepreneurs and innovators."

The general framework of the program consists of two sets of curriculum systems: Chinese national high school curriculum and the Global Assessment Certificate (GAC) program. The former has been designated through the aforementioned New Curriculum Reform, while the latter as a foreign curriculum is owned by ACT Education Solutions. Based on the importation of the GAC program from ACT Education Solutions, China Bridge invited educational experts and consultants from Chinese universities and educational institutions to discuss how to localize the GAC program for the needs of Chinese students. As a result, this Chinese education company put GAC together with the Chinese national high school curriculum and gave the combined product a new name called the International Access Project (IAP). The rationale of combining these two curricula is to "provide students a solid foundation for learning that combines the best elements of both Chinese and western courses." One of the most interesting parts of the IAP program is that it must be activated through collaborating with partner schools who are eligible to run high schools, get a government permit to run a IAP program, recruit Chinese students, teach Chinese curriculum, and so on. A unique program-running mode is also worth attention. China Bridge, who owns IAP, always seeks partnerships with Chinese elite public high schools as clarified in the company's advertisement—"Prestigious high schools, leading to world top universities"; "Entering prestigious high schools, stepping into the world's top-ranked universities." Since the IAP program was run in 2005, China Bridge has had almost 30 network schools in 20 big Chinese cities. According to the company website, there have been over 5,000 students enrolled in the program throughout China. Given a steady increase in the number of student enrollment, China Bridge expects that there will be 10,000 students attending the IAP program by 2015.

The Sunny High IAP International Curriculum Program is one of the IAP programs in China. It is located in Moon City. This international program was established in 2008 and currently has about 450 Chinese students. It is not only the biggest program among IAP programs, but among the largest of all government-approved "public" international high school curriculum programs in China.

Findings and Discussion

In this section, I will discuss some important findings on a range of organizational actors involved in the development of the Sunny High IAP program, particularly focusing on the activities, purposes, and interests of these participants. Using the graph, I will also describe the relationships of these social actors in order to uncover the characteristics of network governance reflected on the new development and practices of the CFCRS Policy.

Who Are Chinese and Foreign Cooperators?

According to the CFCRS policy, any international high school program should have Chinese and foreign education institutions as collaborators who work together around teaching activities for Chinese students. The government file recording the approval of the Sunny High IAP program application shows that Sunny High and Jefferson (pseudonym) Independence High School in the United States are partner schools. Sunny High is an elite public high school directly administered by the MOE. Because it is located in Moon City, the school is also in the charge of Moon Municipal Commission of Education. School principals of Sunny High were often invited by MOE to discuss high school education reforms, which not only allowed the school leaders to participate in the process of policy making but also enabled them to gain insider information about education policy directions. Given its close relation to MOE, Sunny High is often given privilege (such as material and policy supports) to implement educational reforms. This school acts as an experimental site and is expected to play a leading role in exploring effective school reforms, which makes the study of the emerging Sunny High international program more significant in understanding the character of Chinese educational reforms.

Jefferson Independence High School is a private school located in Washington State and is listed as an official foreign collaborator. According to the American school website, it is "a Washington State approved and nationally accredited independent school," serving homeschoolers, unschoolers, and other independent learners. Jefferson Independence High School provides very flexible education services to students and families, including "global distance learning" and "homeschool and unschooling recognition and support." This American private school is responsible for issuing official Washington State high school diplomas to the students graduating from the Sunny High IAP program. However, Chinese school administrators, teachers, or students in the program knew less about this foreign school and had less interactions with it. Sunny High knew about the American school through China Bridge. In interpreting the roles of the official foreign partner school and China Bridge, the Vice Principal of the Sunny High IAP program Mr. Bian explained,[6] "China Bridge did what the partner school in the United States was supposed to do ... Frankly speaking, Jefferson Independence High School is only for solving the problem of how to get the government approval of our international program."

Mr. Bian's statement above points out that despite the official foreign collaborator, Sunny High actually collaborated with China Bridge, who represented the foreign part of the joint IAP program. This evidence demonstrates that "little-p policies" were "formed and enacted within localities and institutions" for the particular interests of social actors (Ball, 2013, p. 8). Specifically, Sunny High, China Bridge, and Jefferson Independence High School participated in the remaking process of the CFCRS big-P Policy in order to legitimate the Sunny High IAP program. China Bridge took an active role in the process.

China Bridge: The Central Actor in the Network

China Bridge is a key organization in facilitating the establishment and development of Sunny High IAP program. Its representative role was demonstrated in two ways, according to Mr. Wang, the principal of Sunny High. On the one hand, China Bridge helped with making connections between Sunny High and Jefferson Independence High School in dealing with the partnership required by the CFCRS Policy, as just described above. On the other hand, the Chinese company has connections with the foreign curriculum providers of the IAP program. Specifically, China Bridge not only imported the GAC program from the US through cooperating with ACT Education Solutions, but also facilitated the connectivity of two different curriculum systems by connecting and activating the IAP program through the partnership with Chinese elite public schools. As demonstrated in the name of the International Access Project (IAP), China Bridge constructed the project, which helps international education services come into China, aids Chinese students to go abroad, and assists Chinese elite public schools to become international.

As mentioned before, China Bridge imported GAC and put it together with Chinese curriculum to create a new product—IAP. The company regards IAP as its own brand and is ambitious to make it into the most influential brand in the field of the internationalization of Chinese basic education. It appears that China Bridge has an ownership of IAP. However, when exploring where GAC—the core curriculum of IAP—comes from, several foreign organizations come to our attention. In what follows, the central role of China Bridge is discussed by paying attention to the flow of the GAC program.

The Flow of the GAC Program and the Commodification of Curriculum

Global Assessment Certificate (GAC) is a university preparation program, which was originally developed by Campus Group International Education Services, Inc. (CGIES) in 1995. CGIES is a subsidiary of a private education company called Australian Company Campus Group Holdings (CGH) established in Sydney, Australia in 1994. As one of the two main divisions of CGH, CGIES is also a for-profit company. Like its parent company, CGIES views international students from Asian countries who want to study at English-speaking universities as its target customers. The company focuses on preparing such students for admission into higher education by providing a targeted GAC program that focuses on improving academic and linguistic skills. In addition, building the partnership with "pathway universities" that recognize GAC is another strategy adopted by CGIES in providing international students with a "seamless path into universities." According to The Observatory on Borderless Higher Education (2005), CGIES has agreements with approximately 110 "pathway universities," mostly concentrating in Australia, US, UK, and Canada.

Although GAC has increasingly become an internationally recognized university preparation program under the efforts of CGIES, the GAC program made less money than CGH expected. As a result, in 2005, CGH decided to sell CGIES with its products, including GAC, to American College Test (ACT) Inc. The well-known ACT Inc. is a non-profit organization based in the United States. Through the acquisition of CGIES, ACT Inc. created a new for-profit subsidary, which is named ACT Education Solutions. This new company is in charge of the educational programs that CGIES previously owned. The GAC program is one of the main programs that ACT Education Solutions currently runs. Through selling and buying activities, the GAC program was handed over to ACT Education Solutions. This action taken by ACT Inc. signals that this U.S. assessment giant intends to expand its traditional provision of educational services for U.S. citizens into global education services for international students. This intention can be seen in the arrangement of GAC modules. Like ACT as a curriculum-based test, the compulsory modules of GAC include Academic English (listening, speaking, reading, and writing), Mathematics, Computing, Business, Science, Social Studies, and Study Skills. In consideration of the needs of international students, the elective modules highlight test preparation skills, including the International English Language Testing System (IELTS), the Test of English as a Foreign Language (TOEFL) preparation, and ACT preparation Skills. This means that as part of the GAC program all students can take the ACT assessment. The bundling relation between ACT and GAC was highlighted when China Bridge marketed its IAP program. The cooperation between China Bridge and ACT Education Solutions allowed the GAC–ACT bundle to be imported and sold into the Chinese education market. Consequently, the Sunny High IAP program became an ACT test center. However, only those students who enrolled in the IAP program can take the ACT assessment in the test center because they pay tuition fees that allow them to use the GAC curriculum. This issue touches on the requirement and distribution of expensive tuition that students pay for their choice of the IAP program.

Below is a quote from my interview with Principal Wang in which he addresses why the "public" international curriculum program charges high tuition:

SL: As you mentioned, such international high school programs do charge tuition. How do you interpret that the international programs created by Chinese public school require students to pay tuition fees?

Wang: Because . . . uh, this thing . . . because compared with other students . . . these students want . . . how can I say this? . . . they want . . . want to study foreign curriculum. Foreign curriculum is . . . is not provided by the State. Chinese High School Curriculum doesn't offer foreign curriculum. In addition, the cost (of foreign curriculum) is VERY HIGH . . . VERY HIGH. So I need to charge some fees.

SL: What do you mean "cost"? What does the cost include?

Wang: At first, curricular fees. You use foreign curriculum. All foreign curricula require fee payment. Must pay curricular fees!

SL: Really?

Wang: Yes. Of course!

SL: Pay to whom?

Wang: Pay to those who design the curriculum.

SL: Who? Who are they? . . .

Wang: ACT Inc. that I mentioned before.

SL: Ok. They designed . . .

Wang: They designed. It is they that designed the (GAC) curriculum.

SL: Do we pay money to them (ACT Inc.)?

Wang: I don't know to whom the money was paid. We have the agency (China Bridge) to deal with these things.

SL: OK. It (China Bridge) is the agency.

Wang: details . . . I am not clear about the details. But we DO need curricular . . . curricular fees.

SL: Oh! This is a new thing!

Wang: If you use A-Level curriculum, you also need to pay curricular fees.

SL: Oh. Oh.

Wang: If you don't pay, who will allow you to use their curriculum?

SL: No wonder that the cost is high.

Wang: Of course! In addition, foreign teachers . . . the cost of hiring foreign teachers is expensive. The State cannot pay such fees for you . . . cannot pay such fees for meeting the needs of THESE students. The State doesn't have the capacity (to pay fees for those students who need to use foreign curriculum). So the students must sponsor tuition fees. Right? They don't offer free teaching to you. They are not volunteers.

The commodification of curriculum is clearly revealed by the flow of the GAC program and by Principal Wang's emphasis on the cost of using the foreign curriculum. His taken-for-granted attitude towards the payment for the use of foreign curriculum reflects the popular spread of the idea of commodifying education. In addition, his lack of knowledge about who receives the funds for curricular fees further highlights the important, yet invisible, role of China Bridge as a for-profit agency in the network of various institutions involved.

Where does China Bridge Come from? The Privatization of Chinese Public Institutions

Given the central role of China Bridge in the network, it is worth digging into this education firm itself in order to understand power relations between involved social actors. The data show that China Bridge often emphasized its MOE-related background when marketing the IAP program. This is not just a marketing strategy, but also reflects its relations with background institutions. China Bridge is a for-profit International Education Services firm created by China Center for International Education Exchange (CCIEE). CCIEE is an education consultancy company established in 2001, which is affiliated with China Education Association for International Exchange (CEAIE). CCIEE is an independent corporate entity. But it is positioned as a "joint-stock partnership" enterprise and it belongs to "collective property." International educational cooperation and exchange are the major education services that CCIEE provides. One of the main departments in CCIEE is called the Join Program Department, while IAP is the major program of this department. CCIEE entrusted China Bridge to develop and run the IAP program. There are some interesting ties between China Bridge and CCIEE. For example, the main leaders of China Bridge are also the employees of CCIEE.

CCIEE's relation to MOE is based on its affiliation with CEAIE, which was established in 1981 and administrated by MOE. In 1991, CEAIE was sanctified as a non-governmental organization by the Ministry of Civil Affairs (MCA) of the People's Republic of China. Both MOE and MCA are the departments of the State Council. If we trace the line from the State Council to China Bridge demonstrated in the graph (see Figure 5.1), we can find that the affiliations embody the privatization process of Chinese public institutions from the dot gov institution, dot edu organizations such as MOE and CEAIE, to dot com firm CCIEE and dot cn corporation China Bridge.[7] This is a typical example of the endogenous form of privatization that Ball (2007) underscores. This type of privatization is also one manifestation of social policy reform with Chinese characteristics. It signals the trend of the privatization of Chinese public institution.

When looking at the power relations between the social organizations bearing on China Bridge (see Figure 5.1), this study has found that the Central Government has strong control over MOE, as it does for MCA. The strength of the relationship between CEAIE and MOE is not as strong as that between the Central Government and MOE. However, although CEAIE is designated as a non-governmental organization, it still receives "guidance and supervision" from both MOE and MCA. The unique relations between CEAIE and MOE can be found in the evidence that the current president of CEAIE is the former Vice Minister of MOE. As a non-profit organization, CEAIE represents the Chinese education sector to conduct non-governmental, educational exchange and collaboration. Nevertheless, CCIEE deriving from CEAIE is a for-profit education company despite its position as "collective property." Affiliated with CCIEE, China Bridge is obviously a private for-profit firm. In this line, the further educational institutions are from the Central Government and MOE, the more likely they are to be businesses, and the less control the State has over them.

It is starting from CCIEE that education institutions become private. However, CEAIE as a non-governmental and non-profit organization is also problematic given its relation to CCIEE, a for-profit institution. Such similar problematic issues can be also found in the establishment of ACT Education Solutions, a for-profit subsidiary of ACT that is a non-profit organization. Although located in different contexts, the same strategies were used for the endogenous privatization of education. As corporate brands, both the IAP curricular program and GAC curricular program were developed for profit making by their respective corporations. Chinese educational reforms, in particular, the CFCRS policy, create opportunities for the private sector to participate in public sector education. As the graph shows, social organizations on the right side are from US and Australia and most of them are private educational institutions. Chinese organizational actors and curricular programs on the far left are public, while those in the middle are mixed. But it is very clear that China Bridge is at the center of the network and it is a private institution. As a central actor, the company has more connections with both Chinese and foreign private institutions. Given its multiple roles in the network, China Bridge brings "the 'informal authority' of diverse and flexible networks" into a changing Chinese educational landscape (Ball and Junemann, 2012, p. 3). This implies a new form of education governance in China, a network-based governance that goes beyond the nation-state.

Private-Public Partnership: Contractual Relations

As demonstrated above, China Bridge is a result of the endogenous privatization of Chinese public education institutions. When introducing itself, the education company always puts its background institutions, such as CCIEE and MOE, at the forefront. This company utilizes its unique relations to MOE as social and political capital when seeking partnerships with Chinese elite public schools and marketing its educational services to schools and parents. Besides initiating partnership and building networking with other private firms, the public-private partnership between Sunny High and China Bridge is even more crucial among the relationships in the network because this relation is the precondition for foreign private sectors to be involved in the Chinese state education system. Furthermore, this public-private partnership marks the exogenous form of privatization in education. As Ball (2012) reminds us, the public-private partnership is more likely to blur the public-private divide. This is best represented in the quasi-public and quasi-private identity of the Sunny High IAP program. As mentioned in the

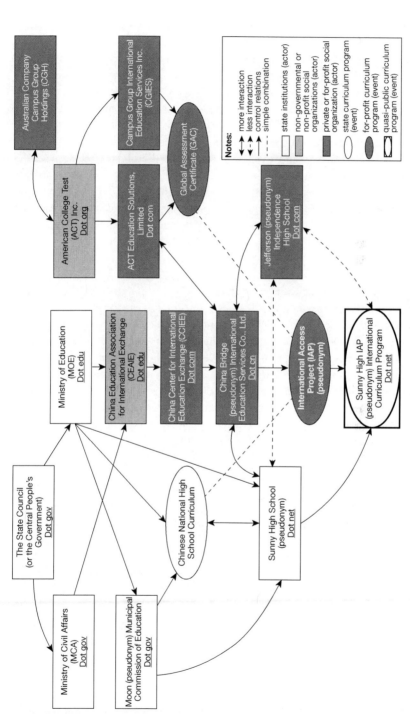

FIGURE 5.1 The network of Sunny High IAP international curriculum program

introduction and confirmed in Principal Wang's statement, such a program is ostensibly public but requires families to pay high tuition fees.

Finally, the contractual relations between these two institutions deserve further discussion. According to the agreements in their contracts, Sunny High is responsible for providing school infrastructure, recruiting students, teaching Chinese high school curriculum, administrating IAP students, and issuing Chinese high school diplomas. China Bridge is primarily in charge of running the GAC curriculum system and consultancy services for students' overseas studies, including hiring foreign teachers and managing them, monitoring the GAC teaching quality, and providing students with career counseling. As school administrators from Sunny High all expressed, the contractual relations are filled with tensions and conflicts, which require continuing negotiations surrounding the distribution of profits and responsibilities between the two institutions.

Implications and Conclusion

This chapter has located the emergence of Chinese international high school curriculum programs in both the Chinese and international contexts. The introduction of the CFCRS policy context highlights the marketization of Chinese education and international education. It emphasizes that emerging international high school programs marked the new development of Chinese educational reforms towards modernizing and internationalizing the Chinese basic education system. Based on my network analysis of the Sunny High IAP international program, this study argues that the CFCRS policy is the unique institutional structure of the new program, which brings both domestic and foreign private sectors into Chinese education reforms. Through identifying and examining the participation of organizational actors in the development of the international program, this study demonstrates that various Chinese and foreign private organizations were involved in the network of the international program for profit-making purposes. Their participation in Chinese and international education markets denotes the exogenous form of privatization in education (Ball, 2007). This exogenous privatization intertwined with the endogenous privatization of Chinese public education institutions points out the neoliberal character of education reforms in China—the privatization of education, which also reflects the reform characteristics in other social domains in contemporary China. The growth of forms of privatization in education was interwoven with the marketization of education and existing hierarchical power of the State, which implies changes in the modalities of the State.

As facilitated by the CFCRS policy, "collaboration" and "partnership" are the effective managerial tactics in developing emerging international high school programs, which points to a network-based education governance. The use of both private-private and public-private partnerships make these new programs transform education into a business (Ball, 2012). The participation of foreign education institutions in the program demonstrates that the program has also become a global education business, which informs that education governance in the era of neoliberal globalization is not limited to the activities of the state. This observation resonates with what Ball (2012) calls "global education policy," a concept that could apply broadly to countries beyond the Chinese context.

My analysis of the IAP program points out that a so-called international program is in nature a university preparation program that offers a "seamless pathway" for wealthy Chinese high school students to access elite global universities. This finding has rendered the problematics of the newly established international curriculum programs because they serve to transform public services to private individual interests. By tracing the flow of the GAC program, this research argues that curriculum has been seen as a commodity, being sold, bought, exported, and imported. The selling process of the curriculum program is concomitant with the selling of international education services to international students, who are becoming the subjects of neoliberal education reforms in both the local and global contexts. This study suggests that further studies should explore the quality of the newly established international curriculum programs and in-depth studies are needed to examine students' educational experiences with these curriculum programs.

In addition, this study questions the effects of the introduction of foreign curricula into the Chinese education system. It raises a serious question about what counts as high-quality foreign education resources when the State expects public schools to import such resources from foreign countries. The presence of the U.S.-based assessment firm ACT and its for-profit subsidiary in the network has some interesting implications that merit further studies. In particular, attention needs to be paid to the influence of the importation of the GAC–ACT bundle. As far as policy borrowing and policy learning is concerned, the involvement of the American private school in the new international program in China may imply the expansion of traditional education services for homeschooling in the US into a global education market. Its presence in the networking shows the potential impact of the private schooling in the US on Chinese education reforms. This issue also deserves further attention. The research agenda described here will help further develop a critical understanding of the impacts of "advocacy and dissemination of 'private' and social enterprise solutions to the 'problems' of state education" in changing local and global contexts (Ball, 2012, p. 1). The work of challenging the dominant way to modernize and internationalize state education will contribute to collective efforts to improve public education for a more equitable and just society.

Acknowledgements

I would like to thank Michael W. Apple, Wayne Au, and Joseph J. Ferrare for their helpful comments on earlier drafts of this paper.

Notes

1   The reform of decentralization and financial diversification was initially issued by the *Decision of the Central Committee of the Chinese Communist Party of China on the Reform of the Educational System* in 1985. It was also enhanced by the *Outline for Reform and Development of Education in China* in 1993 (Mok et al., 2009; Ngok, 2007).
2   Basic education in China covers grades 1–12 education, including six-year elementary education, three-year middle school education, and three-year high school education.
3   State-run schools have dominated the Chinese education system since the founding of the People's Republic of China in 1949. Historically, the Chinese government has invested more educational resources in urban areas, particularly, small numbers of urban "key" state schools. Key government schools that mostly concentrate in urban areas represent quality education, due to their enjoyment of more educational resources from the government, better teaching facilities, and more quality teachers than non-key schools. However, key schools, particularly those in the stage of compulsory education (grade 1–9), have been criticized due to its negative impacts on educational equality. Although the Chinese government has cancelled the name of key schools, it introduced demonstration senior high schools in the mid-1990s (State Education Commission, 1995). This has been viewed as the continuation of the key school policy, which can be confirmed by the fact that the new demonstration schools are more likely to be those former key schools. What I call elite public high schools here refers to demonstration high schools. One useful book that can provide more details on the evolution of the key school system is Wu's (2014) School Choice in China: A Different Tale?
4   According to the 1986 Compulsory Educational Law, compulsory education in China includes six-year elementary education and three-year middle school education. Three-year high school education and post-secondary education belong to non-compulsory formal education (MOE, 1986).
5   In the 2003 CFCRS policy, Article 6 states that "Chinese and foreign cooperators in running schools may cooperate to establish educational institutions of various types at various levels. However, they shall not establish institutions offering compulsory education service or special education services such as military, police and political education services." High school education is non-compulsory education, which not only allows the implementation of the CFCRS policy at high school level, but also makes high school education services in China open to the global education market.
6   Pseudonyms are used for all interviewees in this study. Interviews with these research participants were conducted in Chinese. I translated the transcripts quoted in this chapter into English.
7   See Howard, 2002.

References

Apple, M. W. (2006). *Educating the 'right' way: Market, standards, god, and inequality* (second ed.). New York: Routledge.
Au, W. and Ferrare, J. J. (2014). Sponsors of policy: A network analysis of wealthy elites, their affiliated philanthropies, and charter school reform in Washington State. *Teachers College Record, 116*(11), 1–24.
Ball, S. J. (2007). *Education Plc: Understanding private sector participation in public sector education*. New York: Routledge.
Ball, S. J. (2012). *Global education Inc.: New policy networks and the neo-liberal imaginary*. New York: Routledge.

Ball, S. J. (2013). *Education debate* (second ed.). Bristol: The Policy Press.

Ball, S. J. and Junemann, C. (2012). *Networks, new governance and education*. Bristol: The Policy Press.

Bourdieu, P. (1984). *Distinction: A social critique of the judgement of taste*. Cambridge, MA: Harvard University Press.

Chen, G. and Xie, L. (2010). *Approaching internationalization: Research on international exchange and cooperation of education in China* [in Chinese]. Guangzhou: Guangdong Education Publishing.

Cheng, B. (1997). Exploring the practice and theory of Chinese private schools. *Chinese Education & Society*, 30(1), 23–37.

Crabb, M. W. (2010). Governing the middle-class family in urban China: Educational reform and questions of choice. *Economy and Society*, 39(3), 385–402.

Ding, X., Yue, C., and Sun, Y. (2009). The influence of China's entry into the WTO on its education system. *European Journal of Education*, 44(1), 9–19.

Ferrare, J. J. and Apple, M. W. (2010). Spatializing critical education: Progress and cautions. *Critical Studies in Education*, 51(2), 209–221.

Guan, Q. and Meng, W. (2007). China's new national curriculum reform: Innovation, challenges and strategies. *Frontiers of Education in China*, 2(4), 579–604.

Gulson, K. N. and Symes, C. (Eds.). (2007). *Spatial theories of education: Policy and geography matters*. New York: Routledge.

Hannum, E. (1999). Political change and the urban-rural gap in basic education in China, 1949–1990. *Comparative Education Review*, 43, 193–211.

Hannum, E., An, X., and Cherng, H. Y. S. (2011). Examinations and educational opportunity in China: Mobility and bottlenecks for the rural poor. *Oxford Review of Education*, 37(2), 267–305.

Harvey, D. (2005). *A brief history of neoliberalism*. Oxford: Oxford University Press.

Huang. Z. (2012). The road to internationalization of education in Shanghai under the concept of plural symbiosis [in Chinese]. *Exploring Education Development*, 18, 7–12.

Howard, P. N. (2002). Network ethnography and the hypermedia organization: New media, new organizations, new methods. *New Media & Society*, 4(4), 550–574.

Lao, K. (2002). Chinese education facing the challenges of WTO [in Chinese]. *Journal of Beijing Normal University (Social Science Edition)*, 2, 86–96.

Law, W. W. (2014). Understanding China's curriculum reform for the 21st century. *Journal of Curriculum Studies*, 46(3), 332–360.

Li, P., Li, Q., and Sun, L. (2004). *Social stratification in China today* [in Chinese]. Beijing: Social Sciences Academic Press.

Liu, F. (2013). Re-discussion on Chinese high school "international curriculum class" [in Chinese]. *Sichuan Education*, 7–8, 45–46.

Liu, Y. (2013). Meritocracy and the Gaokao: A survey study of higher education selection and socio-economic participation in East China. *British Journal of Sociology of Education*, 34(5–6), 868–887.

Liu, Y. and Dunne, M. (2009). Educational reform in China: Tensions in national policy and local practice. *Comparative Education*, 45(4), 461–476.

Ministry of Education of the People's Republic of China (MOE). (1986). *The compulsory education law of the People's Republic of China*. Retrieved February 2, 2011 from www.npc.gov.cn/englishnpc/Law/2007–12/12/content_1383936.htm

Ministry of Education of the People's Republic of China (MOE). (2003). *Regulations of the People's Republic of China on Chinese-foreign cooperation in running schools* [in Chinese].

Retrieved March 18, 2014 from www.moe.edu.cn/publicfiles/business/htmlfiles/moe/moe_861/200506/8646.html

Ministry of Education of the People's Republic of China (MOE). (2004). Implementation measures for the regulations of the People's Republic of China on Chinese-foreign cooperation in running schools [in Chinese]. Retrieved March 18, 2014 from www.crs.jsj.edu.cn/index.php/default/news/index/6

Ministry of Education of the People's Republic of China (MOE). (2010). *National guidelines for medium- and long-term educational reform and development (2010–2020)* [in Chinese]. Retrieved May 6, 2012 from www.moe.gov.cn/publicfiles/business/htmlfiles/moe/moe_838/201008/93704.html

Mok, K. H. (2009). The growing importance of the privateness in education: Challenges for higher education governance in China. *Compare, 39*(1), 35–49.

Mok, K. H., Wong, Y. C., and Zhang, X. (2009). When marketisation and privatisation clash with socialist ideals: Educational inequality in Urban China. *International Journal of Educational Development, 29*(5), 505–512.

Ngok, K. (2007). Chinese education policy in the context of decentralization and marketization: Evolution and implications. *Asia Pacific Education Review, 8*(1), 142–157.

Rhodes, R. A. W. (1997). *Understanding governance: Policy networks, governance, reflexivity and accountability*. Buckingham: Open University Press.

Robertson, S. (2010). 'Spatializing' the sociology of education: Stand-points, entry-points, vantage-poits. In M. W. Apple, S. J. Ball, and L. A. Gandin (Eds.), *The Routledge international handbook of the sociology of education* (pp. 15–26). New York: Routledge.

Robertson, S. L., Bonal, X., and Dale, R. (2002). GATS and the education service industry: The politics of scale and global reterritorialization. *Comparative Education Review, 46*(4), 472–495.

Shao, Z. and Zhang, L. (2013). Why is it so difficult to solve the problem of school choice [in Chinese]. *Educational Research, 4*, 38–45.

Shi, Q. (2013). Education modernization is the inevitable choice to realize national modernization: Commemorating Deng Xiaoping's "Three Orientations" Inscription for 30th Anniversary. *Educational Research, 9*, 4–11.

State Education Commission (SEC). (1995). *Notice about the appraisal and designation of 1000 demonstration senior middle schools* [in Chinese]. Retrieved March 21, 2011 from http://law.chinalawinfo.com/newlaw2002/SLC/SLC.asp?Db=chl&Gid=85901

The Observatory on Borderless Higher Education. (2005). US assessment giant expands international presence through acquisition of Australian university preparation company. Retrieved January 7, 2013 from www.obhe.ac.uk/documents/view_details?id=403

Tsang, M. C. (1996). Financial reform of basic education in China. *Economics of Education Review, 15*(4), 423–444.

Wang, H. (2011). Access to higher education in China: Differences in opportunity. *Frontiers of Education in China, 6*(2), 227–247.

Wang, X. (2012). Using the concept of qualification competence in exploring the cultural construction of Sino-foreign Cooperation in Running Schools [in Chinese]. *Journal of Sichuang Normal University (Social Science Edition), 1*, 72–80.

Williams, P. (2002). The competent boundary spanner. *Public Administration, 80*(1), 103–124.

Wittel, A. (2000). Ethnography on the move: From field to net to internet. *Forum Qualitative Sozialforschung/Forum: Qualitative Social Research, 1*(1), Art. 21. Retrieved November 25, 2012 from http://nbn-resolving.de/urn:nbn:de:0114-fqs0001213

Wu, X. (2014). School choice in China: A different tale? New York: Routledge.

Yan, G. and Chang, Y. (2009). The circumstances and the possibilities of critical educational studies in China. In M. W. Apple, W. Au, and L. A. Gandin (Eds.), *The Routledge international handbook of critical education* (pp. 368–386). New York: Routledge.

You, Y. (2007). A deep reflection on the "key school system" in basic education in China. *Frontiers of Education in China, 2*(2), 229–239.

Zhang, X. (2003). Implementing the Regulations on Chinese-Foreign Cooperation in Running Schools [in Chinese]. *The China Higher Education, 11*, 4–5.

Zhong, Q. (2006). Curriculum reform in China: Challenges and reflections. *Frontiers of Education in China, 1*(3), 370–382.

Zhou, M. (2013). Consideration on the internationalization of basic education [in Chinese]. *Educational Research, 1*, 65–68.

Zhu, Z. (2013). Chinese high school international curriculum class: An analysis of current situation and policy expectations [in Chinese]. *Elementary and Secondary School Administration, 8*, 18–20.

6

MAPPING NEOLIBERAL REFORM IN CHILE

Following the Development and Legitimation of the Chilean System of School Quality Measurement (SIMCE)

Javier Campos-Martínez, Francisca Corbalán Pössel, and Jorge Inzunza

Introduction

One of the strategies used by neoliberal reformers in Chile and elsewhere is to disguise their interests in privatization and marketization of public goods, services, and institutions as common sense. They understand that for neoliberal governance there is no need to be formally part of the State. Moreover, if they are able to offer a convincing and almost self-evident economic, political, and social imaginary, they can easily govern from the side (Corbalán, 2012). In order to govern without formally being part of the State, these actors organize themselves in different ways. For example, they work as service providers, they also create extra-institutional groups that ally with the State to accomplish mutual benefit agendas, and they might even form part of the State but with independent, autonomous, and flexible positions. With these strategies and others, these actors create networks that permeate the governmental structures establishing an interwoven government into the State. Some authors have described this mode of ruling as "new governance" (Ball, 2008a, 2010; Jessop, 2002).

Globalization has expanded neoliberal reforms to a global scale, thus facilitating the emergence of new configurations of networks and actors across the world and scaling their governance agendas to a global reach. It is vital to render visible the networks purposely created to build legitimacy and support to neoliberal reforms. In this chapter we aim to apply "cartography" techniques to the public-private networks that have been and are being created as a result of the early neoliberalization of the Chilean educational system. Using the Chilean System of School Quality Measurement (Sistema de Medición de la Calidad de la Educación, a.k.a. SIMCE) as a case study, we explore the possibilities emerging from mapping and describing the shape of the public-private networks using the SIMCE to advocate for an educational system centered on competition, school choice, and the free market. These networks work as advocacy coalitions, influencing education leaders, administrators, and governments to support reforms in the direction of "standardization, charter schools, vouchers, and high-stakes testing" (Robertson and Verger, 2012, p.34). The exercise of inquiring into these networks and their changes allows for an analysis of both the continual adapting capacity of the neoliberal project and the public-private geography of the education system as an effect of neoliberal globalization.

Neoliberalism, the State, and New Educational Governance in the Times of Testing

Since the 1980s neoliberalism has arisen around the globe as the hegemonic system for cultural, economic, and political organization. Chile is widely known as the laboratory where the first attempts of global neoliberalism took place (Harvey, 2005), with the support of one of the longest Latin American dictatorships of the twentieth century (1973–1990). The neoliberal plan to strengthen the Chilean private sector worked by reducing taxes and prompting the transference of important public industries to the private sector, which generated conditions for the emergence of new large investors. These investors have the capacity that only the State could afford before financial venturing in the provision of services, including hospitals, road infrastructure, and universities. Although the weight and tasks of the State were reduced, it maintained a central role as funding source and coordination entity serving the needs of the new owners of public services. The Chilean experience, with its own nuances and particularities, resembles the way in which neoliberalism has spread across different territories (Harvey, 2005).

Holding a global perspective, it would not be an exaggeration to affirm that the denoted neoliberal reinvention of the State has had as its main target the education apparatuses (Ball, 2008b; Lauder et al., 2006; Popkewitz and Brennan, 1998). In fact, the spreading of neoliberalism as a new political-cultural-economic system has been propelled by similar waves of education reforms promoted by nation states and transnational entities committed to the neoliberal ideology (Ball, 2008b). The means to conduct these processes have mainly been consecutive deployments of multiple education policies (Lingard and Ozga, 2007).

Standardized tests have become an important resource used by neoliberal reformers in Chile and elsewhere to shape education systems. Marginson (1997) and Connell (2013) describe the role that high-stakes tests have in transforming education into a marketable commodity. They explain that in order to "create a market you have to restrict the service in some way. In this case you have to re-allocate education. What you sell, then, is a privilege—something that other people cannot get" (Connell, 2013, p. 105). To justify the existence of winners and losers, high-stake testing comes in handy. These categories are then linked to individual choices of families (or the failure of teachers) rather than broader inequalities generated by the neoliberal frame. Under this logic, "losing has to be legitimized, and not appear a matter of unfair discrimination or pure bad luck" (Connell, 2013, p. 106), i.e., to encourage people to pay to become winners, neoliberals need to legitimize the existence of known losers (Connell, 2013).

In Chile, SIMCE was created to support the implementation of neoliberal policies seeking to reform the education system. SIMCE plays an important role in creating a culture legitimizing education as a market commodity. Using standard neoliberal concepts such as freedom of choice and perfect information, SIMCE has been used to promote competition between families for limited educational resources, as well as competition among teachers and schools for achievement on standardized tests and student enrollment. SIMCE operates by ranking schools according to the results of their students in the tests, without consideration of the context in which these schools operate. Public schools that do not select students and serve the largest number of low-income students usually are located at the bottom of these rankings. This has damaged the status of public schools and decreased students' enrollment. Over the years, the SIMCE has worked as a pillar of the neoliberal reforms in education, thus supporting the construction of a common sense that transforms cultural capital into merit and makes the poor responsible for their "own failure" (Inzunza et al., 2013)

Additionally, SIMCE has had perverse effects on educational practices. Under its influence the curriculum has narrowed to the content and skills measured by the test, diminishing attention to the multiple ways students learn. The government also provides financial "incentives" and sanctions to schools and teachers based on students' achievement, assuming people feel motivated to change through external rewards. The pressure for performing well on the tests is felt by principals, teachers, and students, and distracts them from creating and enjoying rich opportunities for learning (Au, 2009; Inzunza et al., 2013). Moreover, as has occurred with similar measurements elsewhere (Au, 2009; Lipman, 2004), the test has been demonstrated to contribute to an increase in school segregation and inequality (Campos-Martinez, 2010; Cornejo et al., 2011). With the help of SIMCE, the Chilean education system has greatly increased segregation among people from different social classes, thus creating what has being described as a factual "educational apartheid" (Kremerman, 2007).

Despite these antecedents, since its creation SIMCE has operated with few—if any—obstacles. This measurement system has never been evaluated with respect to its crucial role in defining the Chilean educational neoliberal reforms. Because of its role sustaining the cultural framework, which transforms the privileges into merits, SIMCE emerged as one of the main tools of neoliberalism to impose its influence on education. The following section will explain in more detail the process and actors involved in the institutionalization of SIMCE during the transition from dictatorship to democracy.

The Beginning of SIMCE: Actors, Articulations and Policy Dissemination

The idea of introducing standardized educational measurements, understood as a tool to guide decisions in the emerging education market, was a notion logically discerned from the neoliberal principles imposed during the dictatorship; although, its final creation and legitimation occurred in the complex time of post-dictatorship governments. The initial developments of SIMCE during the dictatorship involved the largest private university in the country, the Pontific Catholic University of Santiago (PUC). A highlight to this fact is the institutional relationship between PUC and the dictatorship, founded within the domain of neoliberal economists, many of whom were educated between 1957 and 1963 under the agreement between the PUC and the School of Economics at the University of Chicago (a.k.a. the Chicago Boys). During the dictatorship, the "Chicago Boys" occupied several positions at the School of Economics and at the neoconservative Law School of the PUC. They also were appointed in various government positions (Gazmuri, 2001; Salazar and Pinto, 1999; Siqueira, 2009).

In 1978, commissioned by the Ministry of Education, PUC started the development of a test known as the Performance Assessment Test (PER). PER was used between 1982 and 1984 as one of the first attempts to develop a national test to compare schools (Benveniste, 2002). The role assigned to PUC led to the exclusion of the state-owned Center for Training, Experimentation and Pedagogical Research (CPEIP) from the direction and developments of educational measurement systems. This center was founded in 1965 in response to the state developmental momentum in educational research, planning and curriculum. It quickly became one of the most reputed centers of education research and development in the world (Leyton, 2010). Even though in 1986 CPEIP participated in an initiative to analyze the PER results, by 1988 the CPEIP was permanently displaced and PUC began to play an essential role in the development of educational policies, and still does to this day.

In 1988, PUC signed a three-year agreement with the Ministry of Education to develop the battery of tests known as SIMCE (1988–1991). At that time, PUC's commitment was to facilitate a process of institutionalization of know-how into the ministry that would enable it to later take control of the test (Briones, 2014). However, PUC retained a high degree of independence that allowed it to build a sphere of influence in public policy, training new technicians, standardizing, and extending the network to other educational domains. The hegemony of PUC and its functionaries remained after the transfer of SIMCE to the Ministry of Education in 1992 through the leadership of Erika Himmel—a professor and researcher from PUC.

With the origin of the SIMCE it is possible to identify not just the involvement of Chilean institutions, but international organizations, as well. With the return of elections in 1990, the Chilean authorities needed to seek legitimacy in their policies. The World Bank was one of the agencies that provided legitimacy to the new government while it sought to take advantage of the wealth of experience accumulated during the decade-long Chilean neoliberal experiment. Although the World Bank had accumulated a number of experiences from the 1960s in vocational technical education and school infrastructure, it lacked the experience that big scale education reforms, like those in Chile, may provide. Since the beginning of the 1980s, the World Bank aligned with the neoliberal policies found in the Chilean experience, providing an opportunity to rely on specific policies to examine and disseminate. This position of the World Bank was consistent with the assessment of the political right wing in Chile, which was looking for the continuity of the neoliberal model in education.

In the context of negotiations between Chile and the World Bank, this entity strongly promoted the continuity of policies initiated during the dictatorship. For example, consider the following communication between bank officials Ping-Cheung (Director of Country Department IV, Latin America and the Caribbean) and Shahid Husain (Vice President for Latin America and the Caribbean) from October 17, 1991:

> *You might wish to indicate* that the Bank applauds this and other pioneering measures in the social sectors, including targeting of fiscal social spending on the poorest subgroups, reducing university expenditures and instituting a voucher system that gives parents freedom to select schools. *The Bank encourages continuation and strengthening of decentralization of education, and looks forward to working with the Ministry of Education* via the institutional strengthening component of the proposed primary education project, to support the decentralization process. The Bank also encourages the Government to sustain a viable private-subsidized school system, thus providing parents with a wide range of choices for educating their children.
>
> *(Holsinger, 1991, p. 3, original emphasis)*

The second international player of relevance was the United Nations Educational, Scientific and Cultural Organization (UNESCO), whose Regional Office for Education in Latin America and the Caribbean Office (OREALC) was located in Santiago, Chile. OREALC was a protection space for dissidence to the dictatorship, where scholars, researchers and politicians expelled from public universities found a meeting place. Figures such as Juan Carlos Tedesco (Argentine researcher), José Rivero (Peruvian researcher), and Juan Casassus, Antonio Rojas and Ernesto Schiefelbein (Chilean researchers) were responsible for putting new energy into educational policy analysis during the 1980s.

At that time, the use of standardized information to support broad educational reforms was a subject of interest for UNESCO. This organization was promoting an international agenda to improve the collection and use of information for decision-making (Hallack, 1990). From this perspective, OREALC developed a plan to build learning assessment tests from 1988–1991. This plan included the participation of the Center for Educational Research and Development (CIDE), the Chilean Ministry of Education, UNICEF, and PUC. Part of this network was involved at the same time with the teams developing SIMCE in Chile. Thus, a critical mass was formed for the construction of standardized tests for Latin America, and they were based in Chile.

The use of SIMCE as a tool to focalize public resources placed Chile at the vanguard of Latin America in regard to policy evaluation. Chile quickly became one of the first countries to use standardized tests at a national level, which led to the creation of a network of people as well as national and international institutions for its development and improvement. Soon, two more government programs would be added in partnership with SIMCE: the Education Improvement Program (EMP), a competitive fund for development projects in schools; and the National Performance Assessment System (SNED), which awarded cash bonuses to teachers and schools on the basis of their SIMCE scores.

The World Bank was interested in developing the local capacity for testing student achievement in Latin America. The participation of the bank in the Principal Educational Project for Latin America and the Caribbean of UNESCO (PROMEDLAC, Quito, Ecuador, May 1991) aimed at promoting the installation of these systems of evaluation. Donald Holsinger of the World Bank fostered the necessity to enhance SIMCE and carried out a training seminar for Latin American measurement technicians in Santiago. In Ecuador, the meetings between Holsinger, Wadi Haddad (Senior adviser, Population and Human Resource Department of the World Bank) and Ernesto Schiefelbein (UNESCO-OREALC) seemed to close the deal to intervene in SIMCE:

> Despite its abundant superlative qualities, the SIMCE program is in need of considerable assistance in order to continue its good start and to overcome a range of serious impediments to efficient operation . . . the cost of this procedure is high relative to the cost of testing samples of students from the same grades . . . Consequently the government is not in a position to fully exploit the potential of its achievement data for planning purposes. It can send more money to low performing schools but it can't encourage "best practice" because it lacks the necessary information to form efficiency judgments.
>
> *(Holsinger, 1991, p. 3)*

One week later, there was a key meeting in Santiago to escalate SIMCE. In this meeting, the test was evaluated and as a result an agreement was reached to finance a consultancy to improve the test. This meeting was attended by:

- Donald Holsinger, an Education Specialist from the Word Bank who graduated from the University of Wisconsin and obtained a PhD from Stanford University;
- Cristián Cox, sociology graduate of PUC with a PhD in Sociology from the University of London, who served the role of interlocutor from MINEDUC for the project on Improving the Quality and Equity of Education while also doing work with CIDE and FLACSO;
- Josefina Olivares, director of SIMCE;
- Ernesto Schiefelbein, who was in charge at that time of the Regional Information System of Education for UNESCO-OREALC before becoming director of planning at MINEDUC in the 1960s, and founder of the Inter-disciplinary Education Research Program (PIIE) in PUC in 1971, as well as a visiting professor at Harvard Univeristy, World Bank official, coordinator of the Latin American Network of Educational Documentation (REDUC), and CIDE researcher; and
- Juan Carlos Tedesco, an Argentinean, graduate of Philosophy and Letters of the University of Buenos Aires. In 1976, he began working at UNESCO and led the Regional Office of Higher Education (Caracas, 1982–1986) and OREALC (Santiago, 1986–1992).

The World Bank hired UNESCO as an advisory body for improving the test. UNESCO invited Anthony Somerset, who was part of the Kenya Examination Council during the late 1970s, to assess SIMCE and participate in a regional seminar to work in the dissemination of student achievement systems. The mistrust that the World Bank might have created was remedied by involving the "progressive" networks of UNESCO in Chile and Latin America. In addition, the World Bank worked as a promoting agent of the International Association for Educational Assessment, an organization that was trying to sell their testing instruments and advise on testing.

The initial triad of the World Bank, UNESCO-OREALC, and the Chilean SIMCE team was removed later due to the conflicting interests of the two international organizations. The World Bank supported adherence to the PISA and TIMSS international tests. At the same time, UNESCO-OREALC was forming its own project, which culminated in 1994 with the foundation of the Latin American Laboratory for the Assessment of Quality of Education (LLECE), supported by the Inter-American Development Bank (IDB). Despite this difference, the two entities used Chile as a reference to promote the installation of standardized assessment systems in various countries of Latin America.

A network of researchers was formed around LLECE. Three Chileans excelled in advocacy actions to promote standardized tests in Latin America:

- Juan Casassus, PhD in economics of education from PUC, and coordinator of LLECE from UNESCO;

- Erika Himmel, trained in evaluation at the University of Chile. Himmel and her teacher, Erika Grassau, created the Scholastic Aptitude Test (PAA) used as a selection tool for admission to universities in the 1960s. Years later, she was one of the developers of SIMCE; and
- Viola Espínola, PUC Educational Psychologist, PhD in Sociology of Education at the University of Wales, former official CIDE and IDB.

Inzunza (2014) highlights the role played by the figure of Erika Himmel, who supported the creation of the Unit for Measuring Educational Quality in Peru (1994), the National Assessment of Quality in Argentina (1994), and Educational Measurement Unit Results in Uruguay (1994). Another strategy to spread the SIMCE experience was the organization of research trips. For example, during 1995 there were several immersion trips to Chile and Mexico as part of the Project Honduras Morazámica School (1995), which ended with the creation of the Mexican Unit for Measuring the Quality of Education (1995).

These international coalitions gave external legitimacy to SIMCE, transforming it into the model for standardized assessment in Latin America (Wolff, 1997). The networks developed around SIMCE continued expanding the scope of standardized evaluation. After 1990 SIMCE continued to be refined and the Chileans who originally worked at designing the instrument were invited to lead international teams in organizations such as OREALC-UNESCO, the International Association for the Evaluation of Educational Achievement (IEA), and the Organization for Economic Cooperation and Development (OECD) (Valdés, 2013).

The spread of SIMCE, as the Latin American model for education policy assessment, was possible with the support of a myriad of actors. Many of them were linked to educational agencies that fulfilled the role of the State during the military dictatorship. Two of these agencies were linked to the work of the Catholic Church: PUC, "Alma Mater" of the "Chicago Boys"; and CIDE, an NGO that hosted many progressive education intellectuals banned from working in the Chilean public sector by the dictatorship. While PUC positioned itself as a technical agency with the capacity to coordinate the developments of the assessment tools, CIDE provided many of the progressive human resources that were able to link this assessment tool with the goals of the post-dictatorial State policies. International agencies, such as UNESCO and the World Bank, reinforced the utility of SIMCE and provided both international expertise and material resources to escalate the model to other Latin American countries. Chile became a regional example and both of these international agencies used the experience of SIMCE, and the people trained in this network, to develop their own educational international assessment tools. Figure 6.1 helps us visualize how during the first stages of SIMCE the limits between the State, the private sector, and the international agencies were blurred or almost nonexistent.

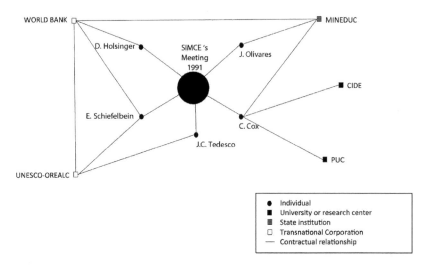

FIGURE 6.1 Key actors involved in the initial linkages of SIMCE

New Conditions of Possibility, Multiple Adjustments, and New Actors

The legitimation of SIMCE, as provider of useful information for the development of neoliberal educational policies, was used to support its transformation into a high-stakes assessment system. Broadly speaking, these transformations involved legal, institutional, and technical reforms that increased the SIMCE's relevance, as well as its capacity to impact different levels and actors of the education system. All of these transformations were tied to the progressive privatization of the measurement process and to the increasing presence of new private actors not completely aligned with the aims of the State. The increased complexity promoted by these new conditions shaped a grid of public-private alliances and interests supporting SIMCE policy, which were far more complex than those presented during its initial stage. Before explaining the construction of the new grid of actors, we will briefly describe the different waves of particular changes that had shaped the current form of the Chilean high stakes measurement system (SIMCE).

SIMCE's Adjustments: From Policy Feedback to High Stakes Accountability

According to reports released by official organizations, the changes to SIMCE did not all happen at one time. Instead, they occurred in a gradual and fragmented way through experimentation with specific measures driven by the Ministry of Education (Bravo, 2011; Briones, 2014; ACE 2013). The first measure driven by the Ministry happened in 1995 when it sought to expand the use of the information that the test provided. This expansion occurred through the individualization of school performance, which was done by the individualized publication—using a ranking format—of school test scores. In 1996, these scores started being directly linked to teachers' incomes when the teachers from the top 25 percent of schools received a financial incentive. Finally, in 1998, the Ministry created an official unit to oversee the logistics of SIMCE. This unit was composed of mostly PUC technicians who directed the efforts of the State to: increase the technical sophistication of the SIMCE by aligning the tests to recent curricular reform; make the annual results comparable from one year to another and between schools; create standards for students' achievements, teachers' perform-ance and head teachers' work; and develop models for the efficient management of the schools (Bravo, 2011).

Over the years, the subjects and grades being measured by SIMCE increased. While during the 1990s only two subjects (Reading Comprehension and Math) were tested every four years in 4th and 8th grade, by the year 2014 both subjects were annually assessed in 2nd, 4th, 6th, 8th, and 10th grade. New subjects were incorporated to SIMCE, although they were less frequent and tested in fewer grades (i.e., Geography, History and Social Sciences, Natural Sciences, Writing, Physical Education, English, and Use of Information Technologies).

The Organic Constitutional Law of Education (Act N° 18.962, March 1990, a.k.a. The LOCE) became the legal structure sustaining SIMCE. This legislation was passed just one day before the end of the dictatorship and officially secured the existence of SIMCE for almost two decades. This legal framework also allowed the linkage of schools' performance to their budget and to broad national resource allocation policies. In 2006 massive student demonstrations threatened the legal support of SIMCE when they pushed towards the abolition of the LOCE. However, the lobby of the Chilean conservatives trumped the students' efforts by substituting the LOCE with a General Education Law (LGE) (Act No. 20.370, September 2009), which ultimately reconfirmed many of the principles of the LOCE and strengthened even more the role of SIMCE in the allocation of resources for schools. With the LGE, school choice policies were legally preserved and the existence of a national and periodical measure of the students' performance was finally legitimized by the parliament. Further, the LGE also created the Education Quality Agency (EQA), a semi-independent institution that acquired the prior responsibilities of the Ministry of Education regarding assessment of schools. The EQA is currently in charge of promoting education improvement by constructing and applying standardized tests, analyzing its data, and informing citizens about the quality of each school based on that data (Act No. 20.529, September 2011).

Concurrent to these legislative and institutional adjustments, a gradual privatization process of the evaluation system itself took place. This privatiza-tion at different stages included distinctive areas of SIMCE apparatus. First, the development of the test as well as the data collection process were outsourced. By the mid-1990s, the only task regarding the logistics of the test not directly done by State functionaries was the optical scanning of the answer sheets (Olivares, 1997). Later, when the goals, frequency, and areas of testing grew and more work was needed, the Ministry opted to hire external agencies, hence creating the financial and political conditions required to develop a measurement industry.

Second, due to two strong incentives related to SIMCE that generated economic circuits and specific costs for schools administrators, a whole market related to the improvement of the schools' testing performance was promoted. On the one hand, SIMCE's relevance within the system managed to become a high measure of pressure for schools. On the other, the State gave money to schools with the only goal of improving SIMCE results. This money might be used to hire private consultant agencies, defined by the law as ATE (Education Technical Assistance) (SEP Law, No. 20.458). Thanks to this budget, created to improve SIMCE, an entire market niche grew. This market included the creation of multiple services such as: those offered by ATEs towards improving SIMCE results; specialized teachers promoting their expertise in raising outputs; and multiple materials such as software training tests and exercise books.

A third trend of privatization relates to the development of recommendations to adjust the SIMCE. The privatization of the adjustments of the SIMCE has been attained by two mechanisms. One of them is tendering the responsibility of evaluating the system to international companies. A second mechanism, which may be complementary to the first one, is the creation of advisory boards mostly composed of technicians from private agencies, representatives of think tanks, representatives of guilds, and a small number of state technicians.

In the following section we will deepen our study, particularly into the dimension of the development of policy recommendations, further describing the "Comisión SIMCE" created in the year 2003 with the purpose of reviewing the system and making recommendations regarding the direction of its future development. However, before introducing the logistical aspects of this advisory board, we will present some of the discursive conditions that made this instance possible.

Private-Public Discourses and Actors Supporting SIMCE's Renewal and Expansion

The adjustments to SIMCE presented earlier were framed as the response to the concern for improving the quality of education. Since the second half of the 1990s, quality was depicted as the natural challenge of a second stage of liberalization after having expanded school access by means of privatization (Himmel, 1997). However, the struggle for quality was strategized only in narrowed terms, by making individuals and schools accountable for the test scores and strengthening efforts to enhance school competition by improving the information for parental school choice.

Although conservative leaders prompted this narrative (Libertad y Desarrollo, 2000), it quickly permeated the language of the official government through the relations between these leaders and members of the Christian Democrat Party (PDC). After the dictatorship, the Christian-Democrats occupied strong positions in the government, which placed them in a strategic position to introduce the need of accountability practices as a way to face and solve this issue. This discourse became the dominant framework shaping the way in which resources aimed at education improvement were allocated (Contreras and Corbalán, 2010).

The shift towards accountability also might be considered a new example of the Chilean state's allegiance to transnational agencies, such as the World Bank. In 1998 a group of experts from the World Bank created a report called *Beyond the Washington Consensus* (Burki and Perry, 1998). This report described some possible paths to implement a "second generation of reforms" (1998, p. 99), which curiously fits with the stages undergone by the Chilean measurement system:

> While the first phase of reforms often established a basic database, the second phase of reforms needs to ensure that this database is used by the actors to facilitate and ensure accountability. Two particular actions will be required for this to occur: First, the management information systems that have been designed and piloted need to be made accessible as tools for the public and parents to obtain usable information, and for education researchers to have access to the raw data. Second, the student assessment systems that have been piloted in most countries need to be made universal; they need to provide student-specific information that helps teachers diagnose learning problems, and they need to provide school-specific information that permits ministries to identify schools that need additional support. Such assessment systems also provide parents with the information they need to carry out their role in ensuring accountability.
>
> *(Burki and Perry, 1998, pp. 101–102)*

Despite the influence international agencies had on the development of SIMCE, it is also fundamental to consider how an important political sector, and a broad range of academics, constructed a consensus regarding the equivalence between educational quality and standardized tests scores. Moreover, when the history of SIMCE is described (ACE, 2013; Bravo, 2011; UCE, 2012), it is repeatedly argued that the definitive shift of SIMCE towards reinforcing accountability was decided in 2003, when the Minister of Education Sergio Bitar appointed a special commission to analyze and improve the system (Comisión para el Desarrollo y Uso del SIMCE, 2003).

Figure 6.2 depicts the "SIMCE Commission" portraying the links of its members to agencies and institutional actors. The commission included fifteen "experts" from a range of academic institutions, philanthropic foundations, think tanks, and trade organizations. In addition to these experts, two foreign consultants were part of the commission representing the interest of international agencies and testing corporations. Compared to the previous map (in Figure 6.1) this one allows us to grasp how the network of interest around SIMCE grew over a short period of time, thus gaining complexity and including new types of actors. The private-public network that the SIMCE Commission formed illustrates the type of actors with whom the neoliberal state sought to share the processes of policy making. It shows one of the problems of public-private partnership in which only specific groups are given power to negotiate political decisions.

To start breaking down Figure 6.2, it is important to explain that the task of organizing and systematizing all the work was conducted by an executive team appointed by the Ministry of Education and led by Cristián Cox. He was the same person who in the 1990s mediated between PUC, CIDE and the Ministry to institutionalize SIMCE (Comisión para el Desarrollo y Uso del SIMCE, 2003).

The Commission members' academic backgrounds were an interesting combination, which included scholars with a more critical perspective regarding SIMCE. However, as a group they still allowed the dominance of an uncritical point of view. Three of these academics worked at PUC and were involved in the birth of the SIMCE. One of these, Erika Himmel, assumed the role of president of the commission.

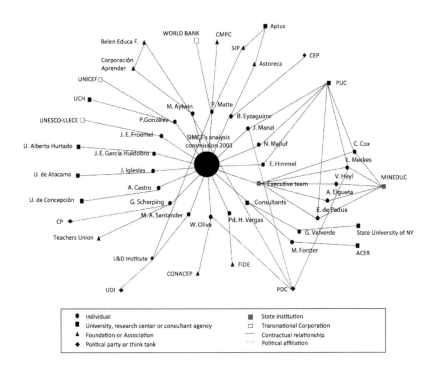

FIGURE 6.2 Key actors involved in SIMCE's renewal

The importance of PUC in relation to SIMCE has varied across the years. While PUC has lost some of its influence in the decisions around the development of SIMCE, it has also gained from SIMCE's reform diversifying the range of services offered to the State and schools around this measurement. This strategy generated significant resources for the university, which in 2006 allowed the creation of an agency highly specialized in psychometric measurements, MIDE-UC. Since its creation MIDE-UC had worked in the creation of SIMCE's question banks and had developed their own battery of tests to measure the added value that schools provide to their students. The story of MIDE-UC is especially interesting within the SIMCE trajectory, given that its founder and current CEO, Jorge Manzi, was one of the members of the 2003 SIMCE Commission. PUC also administrates schools and sells services via its ATE and is the owner of an editorial, "Editorial UC," which produces SIMCE training books for teachers.

The 2003 commission tried to balance the presence of scholars directly related to PUC. To attain this, five more scholars coming from different public and private universities were invited. One of them was Juan Eduardo García-Huidobro, who was part of the University Alberto Hurtado, a Jesuit university founded by the CIDE. García-Huidobro also had an important role in the early 1990s at the Ministry of Education. He was one of the main promoters and director of the "P-900 project," a governmental program that used the SIMCE results to develop compensatory policies directed to the 900 State-founded schools holding the lowest scores in this test. Another important scholar was Juan Enrique Froemel, who participated as an expert from LLECE-UNESCO and after its service in the commission moved to the OECD.

While some of the scholars previously mentioned were invited because they have technical expertise in educational measurement, others were invited because they represented private stakeholders of different school services. One of them was the former Christian-Democrat Minister of Education, Mariana Aylwin. Among other memberships, Aylwin participated on the board of an important Catholic foundation that owns a significant number of privately subsidized schools and also sells programs to other schools to enhance their SIMCE performance. One of these foundations was the "Educating Together Foundation," which reunites bankers such as Angelico Lucksic, retail and university owners, such as the Larrain Family, representatives of conservative factions of the Church, former Ministers of Education, such as Mariana Aylwin and Monica Jimenez, and others members of the traditional Chilean elite.

Other participants who were invited to the commission based on their political kinship included Bárbara Eyzaguirre and María de los Ángeles Santander. Both of them were prolific members of two of the most influential conservatives think tanks in Chile, i.e., the Centro de Estudios Públicos (CEP) and Libertad y Desarrollo (LyD). In addition, like Aylwin, Eyzaguirre was part of a foundation that used public subsidies to run private schools (Fundacion Astoreca). When the right wing occupied the government in 2010, Eyzaguirre was invited to the

Ministry of Education and became one of the intellectuals behind the intensification of the use of high-stakes tests.

One of the most powerful conservative leaders invited to this commission was Patricia Matte, who was a member of one of the wealthiest families in Chile (second according to the world millionaire's rank in Forbes, March, 2012). Patricia Matte also sat on the board of two organizations mentioned before, the Educating Together Foundation and the conservative think tank "Libertad y Desarrollo" (Corbalán, 2012). Figure 6.2 helps us identify the relation of Bárbara Eyzaguirre and Patricia Matte with another organization named Aptus. Aptus offers different sorts of materials such as SIMCE practice tests and strategies seeking to improve students' test scores.

Two members of the commission were also invited to represent associations of private schools owners. These members were Walter Oliva who, like Aylwin, was an important Christian-Democrat militant, and the priest Héctor Varas. While Oliva represented the interest of the association of subsidized for-profit schools (CONACEP), Varas did the same with the association of non-subsidized private Catholic schools (FIDE). Whereas the government had previously invited right-wing think tanks to policy-making instances, neither FIDE nor CONACEP had ever been considered until this commission. Maybe a factor that contributed to its inclusion is the fact that private schools were steadily increasing as a result of the neoliberal reforms imposed during the previous years (Campos-Martinez, 2010; OECD, 2004). It is also important to state that both organizations have historically benefited from the use of rankings based on SIMCE scores, using them as a marketing tool.

Guillermo Scherping, a member of the Communist Party, was the only participant of the commission who represented the teachers' perspective. He was invited because of his work at the national Teachers' Union, but his inclusion seemed more like an attempt to gain legitimacy than a genuine interest for including a different point of view. His isolation on the commission also highlighted the other voices that were excluded from the process. The commission did not have any other representative advocating for parent associations, students' unions, public schools, schools leaders, or people who might have been interested in other types of assessments. The Commission placed Scherping as a token, hence legitimizing with his presence the strategic exclusion of other social actors.

Finally, it is worth mentioning that two foreign experts were allocated to the 2003 commission, not as proper members, but as consultants. One of them was Gilbert Valverde from the State University of New York. The other one was Margaret Forster, who was hired as a professional of the Australian Council for Educational Research (ACER). ACER is similar to MIDE UC in Chile, which sells expertise and also tools of standardized assessment to schools, universities or countries (www.acer.edu.au). After 2003, Forster continued working with the Chilean Ministry of Education, strongly influencing the type of information that was produced to give pedagogical feedback to schools (Bravo, 2011). In 2012

ACER won a contract over Educational Testing Service (a.k.a. ETS) to assess the validity of SIMCE. ETS was previously hired by the Ministry to solve technical issues. ACER concluded in their report that SIMCE is a highly sophisticated tool, which adheres to all the international standards (ACER, 2013).

Conclusion

In the last 40 years, Chile has been affected by several educational policy modes, which have ultimately changed the role of the State established during the twentieth century. Mapping the complex path of SIMCE allows us to visualize the progression of this enormous transformation and the effects of the neoliberal experiment of the 1980s. The role of the State has been dislocated from its central position leading the development of educational policies, being now just another stakeholder within a network that disproportionally represents the corporative, market, and conservative interest of the traditional global elite. The absence of parent organizations, local government representatives, school teachers, school principals, community leaders, and students from the decision-making spaces gives a fair impression of the agendas behind the development of national education policies. These absences also raise questions regarding the health of the Chilean democracy and the legitimacy of evaluation policies targeting the broad population, but tailored to the needs of a cluster of neoliberal entrepreneurs.

The maps help us understand the important role that the Catholic Church has played regarding the design of school measurements policies in Chile. Both maps show the enormous influences that institutions directly linked to the Church had during the first stages of SIMCE. During the 1990s PUC and CIDE, both linked to different factions of the Church, were the main providers of technicians supporting the implementation of SIMCE. By 2003, many of these technicians migrated to international agencies to spread SIMCE's legacy. Others became part of the State using SIMCE for the development of policies focalized in disenfranchized populations. A third group maintained their institutional locations and became contractors of the State; hence, profiting from collaborations with the shrinking State and enabling the advance of neoliberalism. Because of this mobility, these technicians became key actors in the development of SIMCE-related policies and most of them were invited again in 2003.

The 2003 commission also included a new type of actor who did not clearly fulfill a technical profile. Coincidently, many of them were members of the Christian Democratic Party and represented private interests profiting from SIMCE's role as a market organizing tool. Other "non technical" members of the commission were representatives of conservative think tanks and the traditional elite. They were no representatives of progressive think tanks invited to this commission. Other non-traditional actors were the international testing agencies and the Teachers' Union. Both of them were invited because they were instrumental for the commission, although the expected contribution for each one was different. While the representative of the Teachers' Union was there with legitimation purposes, the representative of the international testing agency was there to align the instrument with the international trends, such as the neoliberal agenda promoting high-stakes testing, accountability policies, and markets as the silver bullet for all the educations system. The Chilean State partnerships with ACER, ETS, the World Bank, and other transnational organizations brings up questions about the decision-making process behind national policies in education and who stands to benefit from this process plays.

We started this chapter claiming the emergence of new education governance. We also claim that the laboratory characteristic of Chile is an opportunity to understand how neoliberalism looks during its advanced stages. The changes and regularities between both maps present the new and old players of the neoliberal governance. They also present the sporadic and permanent alliances created around SIMCE, and some of the resources they use to influence the direction of the education policy. These maps help us understand the power that concrete people have to direct the policy agenda, and the role that history plays in facilitating the consolidation of networks connecting similar interests through multiple institutions.

Since 2013, the authors of this chapter have been participating in a national campaign against SIMCE. The connection of this campaign with the actors excluded from the neoliberal technocratic frame has been essential. This is one of the reasons for the campaign's relative success. Our activism has generated great corporate reactions defending the core of SIMCE actions that allow us to better identify the actors, roles and alliances on the map. The activity of this network behind SIMCE pushed the government to insist on a technocratic answer to the important criticisms raised. A new commission of experts has been appointed, though many of these members are part of the same networks portrayed in this chapter. Lorena Mekes, the president of this new commission and right hand of Christian Cox back in 2003, defended SIMCE explaining that "it is a great tool, but its use has been distorted and exaggerated by us" (Urquieta and Carmona, 2014). We are looking forward to the results of this new commission, and while we wait for them, we are starting the initial drafts mapping its participants.

References

Agencia de la Calidad de la Educación (ACE) (2013). *Informe Técnico Simce 2012*. Retrieved July, 2013 from www.agenciaeducacion.cl

Au, W. (2009). *Unequal by design: High-stakes testing and the standardization of inequality*. New York: Routledge.

Australian Council for Education Research (ACER) (2013). *Evaluación de los procesos y los productos asociados a la elaboración de instrumentos, las operaciones de campo y a gestión de datos de las pruebas nacionales de SIMCE*. Santiago, CL: ACER and ACE.

Ball, S. J. (2008a). New Philanthropy, New Networks and New Governance in Education. *Political Studies, 56*(4), 747–765. doi:10.1111/j.1467–9248.2008.00722.x

Ball, S. (2008b). *The Education Debate*. Bristol, UK: The Policy Press.

Ball, S. (2010). New states, new governance and new education policy. In M. Apple, S. Ball, and A. Gandin (Eds.), *The Routledge International Handbook of the Sociology of Education* (pp. 155–167). London, UK: Routledge.

Benveniste, L. (2002). The political structuration of assessment: Negotiating state power and legitimacy. *Comparative Education Review, 46*(1), 89–118.

Bravo, J. (2011) SIMCE: Pasado, presente y futuro del sistema nacional de evaluación. *Estudios Públicos, 123*, 189–212.

Briones, J. (2014). La huella del neoliberalismo en el sistema evaluativo de la educación nacional. Aproximación a las directrices implícitas en el Sistema de Medición de la Calidad de la Educación (SIMCE). 1988–2012. Bachelor Thesis, Pontificia Universidad Católica de Valparaíso, Facultad de Filosofía y Educación. Valparaíso, Chile.

Burki, J. and Perry, G. (1998). *Beyond the Washington Consensus. Institutions matter.* Washington, DC: World Bank.

Campos-Martinez, J. (2010). *Las desigualdades educativas en Chile.* Buenos Aires: Foro Latinoamericano de Politicas Educativas.

Comisión para el Desarrollo y Uso del SIMCE (2003). *Evaluación de aprendizajes para una educación de calidad.* Santiago, CL: Ministerio de Educación.

Connell, R. (2013). The neoliberal cascade and education: an essay on the market agenda and its consequences. *Critical Studies in Education, 54*(2), 99–112.

Contreras, P. and Corbalán, F. (2010). ¿Qué podemos esperar de la Ley SEP? *Revista Docencia, 41*, 4–16.

Corbalán, F. (2012). *Governing education from the side: Case study of a neoliberal think tank in Chile.* Unpublished master's thesis. Institute of Education, University of London, London.

Cornejo, R., Gonzalez, J., Sanchez, R., Sobarzo, M., and the OPECH Collective. (2011). The struggle for education and the neoliberal reaction. In X. de la Barra (Ed.), *Neoliberalism's Fractured Showcase: Another Chile is Possible* (pp. 153–177). Leiden, The Netherlands: Brill.

Gazmuri, C. (2001). *Notas sobre las elites chilenas, 1930–1999.* Documento de Trabajo No. 3, Santiago: Instituto de Historia, Pontificia Universidad Católica de Chile.

Hallak, J. (1990). Preface. In K. Ross and L. Mahlck (Eds.) *Planning the Quality of Education. The Collection and Use of Data for Informed Decision-Making. Instituto Internacional de Planejamento Educacional* (pp. vii–viii). UNESCO. Oxford: Pergamon Press.

Harvey. D. (2005). *A brief history of neoliberalism.* Oxford, UK: Oxford University Press

Himmel, E. (1997) Impacto social de los sistemas de evaluación: El caso chileno. In B. Álvarez and M. Ruiz-Casares (Eds.), *Evaluación y reforma educativa. Opciones de política.* Santiago, CL: PREAL.

Holsinger, D. (1991). Office memorandum "Ecuador and Chile: Conference and technical assistance mission back-to-office report", May 16, 1991.

Inzunza, J. (2014). *A reforma educacional chilena na América Latina (1990–2000): circulação e regulação de políticas através do conhecimento. Campinas.* Doctoral dissertation, Universidade Estadual de Campinas, Faculdade de Educação.

Inzunza, J., Santa Cruz, E., Contreras, P., Corbalán, F., Campos-Martinez, J., and Salina, I. (2013, August 29). Manifiesto para superar la estandarización educativa en Chile. *Ciper Chile.* Retrieved August, 2014 from http://ciperchile.cl/2013/08/29/manifiesto-para-superar-la-estandarizacion-educativa-en-chile/

Jessop, B. (2002). *The Future of the capitalist state.* Cambridge, UK: Polity Press

Kremerman, M. (2007). *Radiografía del financiamiento de la educación Chilena: Diagnóstico, análisis y propuestas* [Radiography of the financing of Chilean education: Diagnosis, analysis and proposals]. Santiago, CL: OPECH. Retrieved August, 2014 from www.opech.cl/inv/investigaciones/Kremerman_Radiografia_Financiamiento_Educacion.pdf

Lauder, H., Brown, P., Dillabough, J., and Halsey, A. (2006). Introduction: The prospects for education: Individualization, globalization, and social change'. In H. Lauder, P. Brown, J.-A. Dillabough and A. Halsey (Eds.), *Education, globalization, and social change* (pp. 1–70). Oxford, UK: University Press.

Leyton, M. (2010). Los inicios del Centro de Perfeccionamiento, Experimentación e Investigaciones Pedagógicas (CPEIP). *Revista Docencia, 40*, 85–91.

Libertad y Desarrollo (2000) Un análisis de las nuevas propuestas en educación, *Temas Públicos, 499, 1–3*. Retrieved June, 2011 from www.lyd.cl.

Lingard, B. and Ozga, J. (2007). Globalization, education policy and politics. In B. Lingard and L. Ozga (Eds.), *The Routledge Falmer Reader in Education Policy and Politics* (pp. 65–82). London: Routledge.

Lipman, P. (2004). *High stakes education: Inequality, globalization, and urban school reform.* New York: RoutledgeFalmer.

Marginson, S. (1997). *Markets in education.* Sydney: Allen & Unwin.

Olivares, J. (1997) Sistema de medición de la calidad de la educación de Chile: SIMCE, algunos problemas de la medición, *Revista Iberoamericana de Educación, 10*, 177–196.

Organization for Economic Co-operation and Development (OECD) (2004). *Evaluación de políticas nacionales de educación: Chile.* Paris: OECD Publishing.

Popkewitz, Th. and Brennan, M. (1998). Restructuring of social and political theory in education: Foucault and a social epistemology of school practices. In Popkewitz and Brennan (Eds.), *Foucault's Challenge. Discourse, knowledge, and power in education.* New York and London: Teachers College Press.

Robertson, S. L., and Verger, A. (2012). Governing education through public private partnerships. In S. L. Robertson, K. Mundy, A. Verger, and F. Menashy (Eds.), *Public private partnerships in education. New actors and modes of governance in a globalizing world* (pp. 21–42). Northampton, MA: Edward Elgar Publishing.

Salazar, G. and Pinto, J. (1999). *Historia contemporánea de Chile I. Estado, legitimidad y ciudadanía.* Santiago: Lom Ediciones.

Siqueira, A. (2009). As reformas da educação superior no Chile no período 1970–2000. In Adriao, T. and Gil, J. (Eds.), *A educação no Chile: olhares do Brasil* (pp. 34–59). São Paulo: Xama.

The World's Billionaires. (2012, March). Eliodoro, Bernardo and Patricia Matte. *Forbes Magazine.* Retrieved August, 2014 from: www.forbes.com/profile/eliodoro-bernardo-patricia-matte/

Unidad de Evaluación y Curriculum (UCE). (2012). *Plan de evaluaciones nacionales e internacionales.* Santiago, CL: Ministerio de Educación.

Urquieta, C., and Carmona, A. (July 14, 2014). El jugoso negocio vinculado al Simce. *El Mostrador.* Retrieved August, 2014 from www.elmostrador.cl/pais/2014/07/30/el-jugoso-negocio-vinculado-al-simce/

Valdés, M. (2013). ¿Leen en forma voluntaria y recreativa los niños que logran un buen nivel de comprensión lectora? *Ocnos, 10*, 71–89. Retrieved August, 2014 from www.revista.uclm.es/index.php/ocnos/article/view/330

Wolff, L. (1997). Avaliações educacionais: uma atualização a partir de 1991 e implicações para a América Latina. In Bomeny, H. (Ed.) *Avaliação e determinação de padrões na educação latino-americana: realidades & desafios* (pp. 1–8). Rio de Janeiro, Brasil: Editora Fundação Getúlio Vargas.

Laws

LOCE-Constitutional Organic Law of Education, Act No. 18.962 (1990). Retrieved May, 2014 from www.bcn.cl

SEP-Preferential Education Subvention Law, Act No. 20.458 (2008). Retrieved August, 2014 from www.bcn.cl

LGE-General Education Law, Act No. 20.370 (2009). Retrieved August, 2014 from www.bcn.cl

SAG-System of Education Quality Insurance Law, Act No. 20.529 (2011). Retrieved August, 2014 from www.bcn.cl

7

MAPPING THE DISCOURSE OF NEOLIBERAL EDUCATION REFORM

Space, Power, and Access in Chicago's Renaissance 2010 Debate

Sarah Bell

Introduction

During the years 2004–2010 Chicago Public Schools (CPS) underwent a massive restructuring through its *Renaissance 2010* (Ren2010) initiative, around which much of Chicago's school choice debate is still centered. Ren2010 was billed to the public as a CPS game changer that would fix failing schools by providing parents across the city with the freedom to choose the right education path for their children through the introduction of 100 new "school choice" schools called "Renaissance schools." These new schools were to be comprised of one-third charter schools, one-third contract schools, and one-third CPS-run performance schools (Lipman and Haines 2007, p. 474), making two-thirds of the Renaissance schools privately-run schools within CPS. These new schools were not the only measure of the Ren2010 plan; the controversial school choice initiative also included shuttering 60–70 traditional public schools that city officials deemed to be under-enrolled, underperforming, or failing. However, these officials provided no list of schools on Ren2010's chopping block at the time the initiative was announced.

The power granted through Ren2010 to shutter schools and shuffle students frustrated many parents and teachers. The students of closed schools were oftentimes expected to attend CPS schools far outside their own neighborhood while waiting for new Renaissance schools—schools not bound to hiring any union-represented teachers—to be established near their home. Clear lines emerged in this new public debate on Ren2010. On one side there were school choice advocates such as corporate sponsors of charter schools and mayor-appointed city officials, while on the other side there were teachers' unions, and many parents and students of shuttered schools. As the debate unfolded in prominent news media, powerful voices of the Ren2010 debate squelched the voices of students and parents who were most impacted by Ren2010's intentionally destructive path.

This chapter analyzes the discourses of the Ren2010 debate as it played out in Chicago's two largest newspapers, the *Chicago Sun-Times* and *Chicago Tribune*. I do this by exploring the media access and content differential between elite voices and parents. The theoretical concepts of social space and linguistic markets are crucial to this analysis. As will be presented in this chapter, those who have the most power to opine their side of social debates in linguistic markets—news media in this case—have a privileged power in the creation, maintenance, and alteration of social spaces. After laying out social space and its connection to linguistic markets within the context of the Ren2010 news media debate, I will describe the thematic coding process I used to analyze the Ren2010 debate within Chicago's two major newspapers. Next, I show how these themes have differentially constructed the physical space of the city by using GIS and correspondence analysis. Finally, I conclude by discussing the implications of highly restricted access to media engagement in general and in the context of contemporary educational reform movements.

It is important to situate Ren2010 in relation to its roots within the corporate movement. Ren2010 policy was authored by Chicago city officials and corporate elites from the Civic Committee of the Commercial Club of Chicago (Commercial Club). Since Ren2010's inception, city officials have been open about the policy's corporate co-sponsorship, insofar as the partnership is utilized as a marketing tool to tout the validity of Ren2010. In fact, the public announcement of Ren2010 in June 2004 was delivered at a Commercial Club meeting by Mayor Richard M. Daley. Established in 1877, the Commercial Club's membership today is comprised of Chicago's most powerful business elites. Prior to becoming key players in the school choice movement, the Commercial Club's mission consisted of strengthening Chicago as a global city. Following the implementation of Ren2010, the Commercial Club now employs a full-time staff dedicated to establishing charter schools throughout Chicago via its New Schools for Chicago (NSC) organization (formerly the Renaissance School Fund). NSC has raised over $70 million in charter school start-up funds since 2004.[1]

In the weeks following Mayor Daley's Ren2010 announcement, Chicago's major news media reported that the initiative would "hand over day-to-day control of a significant number of the city's schools to independent operators" thus "freeing them [schools] from traditional methods" (Cholo and Dell'Angela, 2014). As time went on, however, and after CPS began shuttering traditional public schools to make way for privately operated charter and contract schools, the media's tone on Ren2010 shifted from a liberating education policy to a contentious battle between city officials and teachers and parents. The most powerful voices from both sides of the school choice reform debate ramped up their utilization of news media to publicly opine the ills or benefits of Ren2010 (Bell, 2014).

This chapter builds upon the well-established literature (e.g., Lipman, 2004, 2007; Lipman and Haines, 2007) by contributing new socio-geographic knowledge to the story of corporate education reform in Chicago by centering on the manner through which dominant discourse surrounding the school choice policy debate in Chicago manifests itself spatially—both in physical space and theoretically constructed "discursive" space. By first understanding neoliberal policies as space-contingent and space-changing, this chapter presents geo-visual aspects of school choice advocates' spatial rhetoric campaign in Chicago as a part of the greater neoliberal project.[2] Within the framework that considers school choice policies as part of a larger neoliberal spatial agenda that restructures urban spaces in order to reflect or support free market values, the project presented in this chapter maps—geographically and theoretically—the discourses of the school choice debate over time as deliberated in Chicago's two largest newspapers.

Ren2010's Shake-up of the Seemingly Natural Order of Chicago's Social Space

Just as we exist in physical spaces, we are also positioned in social spaces that are constituted by "the subset of physical space that is colonized, reproduced, and transformed by human societies" (Sayer 2000, p. 110). Thus, as a social construct, social space serves as text for *where* people and their actions can occur. Social space's hegemonic imposition causes such space to seem natural, yet the naturalization of human-occupied space is a constant production maintained by all members of a society. It is important to understand socio-spatial production and reproduction in the context of Ren2010 because the initiative was a very spatial agenda hyper-focused on changing schools that served a specific socio-demographic in order to reflect or support a global capitalist economy. This section shows that the architects of Ren2010 swiftly moved forward with their school choice agenda while ignoring obvious implications and frustrations that CPS students and parents would experience due to the sudden disruption of educative space.

Since socio-spatial production is often directly related to state and market powers, the layout of human-occupied space that contextualizes our sense of spatial belonging—while in constant flux—is an artifact that reflects and usually serves the state and the predominant mode of production (Soja, 1989, p. 87). Chicago's thousands of students and families who were shuffled, displaced, and disrupted by Ren2010 experienced rather abruptly the reality that space exists as a commodity that is controlled by those who control production. Many Chicagoans who were directly impacted by the Ren2010 shake-ups protested the unexpectedly abrupt changes imposed by the policy:

"We need a traditional high school like Austin was. That's the bottom line," said Betty Robinson, a mother of four sons, only one of whom attends public school. "You have to have a home (school) to go to, or you are just left out in the cold. We've got to find them a space. We don't want them to drop out."

(Dell'Angela, 2007)

While the Austin neighborhood that Betty Robinson speaks of did not physically move, the neighborhood's sudden lack of a traditional public high school positioned Austin into a now-present category due to Ren2010's effect on the city's landscape: neighborhoods with no successful schools. The emergence of these new categories of "failure" that many Chicago public schools and neighborhoods were now placed into following the implementation of Ren2010, in turn, created a counterpart category of neighborhoods that were *not* subject to school closures. Voicing her dissatisfaction that her neighborhood underwent dozens of school closures, Kenwood resident Juti Brown recognized these newly created spaces of exemption:

"These actions have destabilized education in a community that desperately needs performing schools," says Juti Brown, of the Kenwood Oakland Community Organization. "Transferring students from school to school— that's a violation of these students' rights. CPS would never have subjected students in Lincoln Park or the Gold Coast to this sort of treatment."

(Ahmed-Ullah, 2012)

Kenwood-Oakland is a neighborhood in Chicago's Mid-South area with an 80 percent African American population, while the Lincoln Park and Gold Coast neighborhoods are 86 and 90 percent white, respectively (U.S. Census Bureau, 2013). Neither Lincoln Park nor Gold Coast experienced the massive school closures that the Mid-South and other predominantly African American neighborhoods underwent.

Fields and Discourses

The evolution of relational positions in Chicago characterized by schools of success and failure is aptly understood through Bourdieu's field theory (Bourdieu, 1986), which states that a person's or organization's position in social space is determined by the volume and composition of capital (cultural, economic, social, etc.) relative to all others in that space (Bourdieu, 1998, p. 9–12). The differentiating characteristics of positions in social space contribute to an individual's habitus, which is the embodied dispositions or "feel for the game" that is learned over a lifetime of experiencing various socializing circumstances (Bourdieu, 1998, p. 8), which "literally mold the body and become second nature . . . provid[ing] individuals with a sense of how to act and respond in the course of their daily lives" (Thompson, 1991, p. 12).

The way we conduct ourselves through certain circumstances depends on the access to the various markets that our habitus and capital provide and a market's rules of engagement (sanctions) (Bourdieu, 1991; 1998; Foucault, 1972, p. 25–26; Gee, 2005, p. 35). *Markets* in this sense means any arena where a person can utilize the capital that they earn based, in part, on their habitus (set of cultural dispositions) in order to earn more capital. The level of formality for each market determines the discourse necessary to engage that market (Gee, 2005, p. 35–40). As the formality of the market increases, so does the required level of specialization necessary to gain capital in that market. The term *formality* here simply refers to the exclusive norms that a person knows to follow; street gangs, symphony concerts, and job interviews each have their specific sets of norms that a person follows in order to be recognized by others as one who belongs. While these three domains may all require the same level of formality, the specializations required to engage within them do not carry the same level of legitimacy by dominant members of society. The more legitimate the specialization, the more authority it tends to carry, especially as the domain becomes more restricted to only the dominant discourses.

Linguistic Markets of the School Choice Debate

People leverage their own discourses in various kinds of markets. This chapter analyzes discourses within the *linguistic* market of news media, where dominant voices were able to shape the rhetoric of the Ren2010 debate. Discourses are "rhetorical devices" that demonstrate "how social goods are thought about, argued over, and distributed in society" (Gee, 2005, p. 2). Discourses are often part of a greater social discussion, or "Conversation" defined by James Gee as:

> [D]ebates in a society or within specific social groups (over focused issues such as smoking, abortion, or school reform) that large numbers of people recognize, in terms of both what "sides" there are to take in such debates and what sorts of people tend to be on each side.
>
> *(2005, p. 35)*[3]

Conversations are intertextualized with added-value discourses; people who participate in Conversations add value to their own argument by citing others' various discourses that support their own desired outcome. An example of intertextualization in the Ren2010 Conversation is provided from a news article reporting on a September 2004 study conducted by the Fordham Institute.[4] Just months after Ren2010 was announced, Fordham reported that 38.7 percent of

CPS teachers send their own children to private schools—a much higher rate than the 22 percent of non-teacher families in Chicago who choose private schools. Supporters and critics alike used this report to tout their estimation of the benefits or drawbacks of school choice reform. Chester Finn, president of the Fordham Institute, used his organization's report to both criticize Chicago school teachers and promote school choice for all.

> "It's a damn shame that more of their [teachers'] own schools aren't good enough for their own kids, but everyone should be able to choose his or her children's school, teachers included."
>
> *(Ihejirika, 2004)*

Arne Duncan, who was the Daley-appointed CEO of CPS at the time, used Fordham's report to justify Ren2010's shuttering of some schools in order to make room for charter and contract schools:

> "I think obviously it shows, particularly in those low-performing schools, that the board is doing the right thing," said Schools CEO Arne Duncan. "We need to create schools that both the community and teachers can be proud to send their children to, because if a school is just good enough for someone else's children, then it's not good enough."
>
> *(Ihejirika, 2004)*

While Finn and Duncan used the report to add value to their support of Ren2010, CTU President, Marylin Stewart connected that same report to critique the study's funders, and to defend Chicago teachers:

> "This is a conservative group that supports contract schools. You have to question the objectivity," said Stewart, who maintains there are many reasons teachers choose private schools—reasons that have nothing to do with the quality of public schools. Those range from religious choices to parents who are alumni, to seeking after-school programs, she said.
>
> *(Ihejirika, 2004)*

These three contributors to the Ren2010 debate, Finn, Duncan, and Stewart, each have a well-attuned *linguistic habitus* in the sphere of the school choice Conversation, and thus are able to anticipate the rules and sanctions of the linguistic market (Bourdieu, 1991). This is evident in each of their executive positions held at their respective organizations: the Fordham Institute, Chicago Public Schools, and the Chicago Teachers Union. The combination of executive status and their well-attuned linguistic habitus gives each of their discourses influential weight shaping the Ren2010 debate.

Methods of Representing Space and Discourse in the Ren2010 Debate

Phase I: The Chicago Tribune and Sun-Times News Articles

The data for this project's discourse sample comes from the *Chicago Tribune* and the *Chicago Sun-Times* newspapers, which are the city's most widely read and the ninth (*Tribune*) and tenth (*Sun-Times*) most widely read newspapers in the United States with a regular daily readership of 414,590 and 422,335 and Sunday readerships of 779,440 and 434,861, respectively (Audit Bureau of Circulations, 2012). By using both of these papers' online archive subscriptions, the reading sample consisted of 100 percent of the news and opinion articles that were returned upon searching for the letter strings *renaissance 2010, renaissance2010, ren2010* or *ren 2010*, providing 173 and 216 pieces written in the *Chicago Tribune* and *Sun-Times* respectively, for a total of 389 articles. Of these, 298 were traditional news reports (articles), 24 were editorials, 56 were letters to the editor, eight were announcements, two were special columns, and one was a newspaper political endorsement. For the purpose of this study, the collective term for all of these written pieces will be *articles*. Their specific type will be referenced whenever their distinction is necessary.

This project has benefitted greatly from the journalism represented in the news article sample; there is a wealth of information found in news articles reporting on Ren2010 that simply cannot be provided by a literature review on school choice. Yet the act of engaging media to report on Ren2010—a policy that proves to be very spatial in nature—is treated and analyzed in the same way as critical cartography treats the act of mapping. Critical cartography examines the rhetorical power embodied by maps, suggesting mapped data is dependent on the cultural perspective of the cartographer and map's sponsors (Harley, 1989). Likewise, within this paper's news article sample, that which is able to reach the media is brought forward by those who have an interest in conveying the story of Ren2010, whether it is to oppose or support the initiative. The media sample analyzed for this project contains various types of reports ranging from broadcasting the contextualization of space that benefits the elite population of Chicago's residents and outside corporate and global interests, to motives that challenge the hegemony imposed by such interests. The methodologies in this project were conducted with this fuzzy boundary between reported facts and knowledge production in mind.

Phase II: Coding Themes as they Emerged from the Discourse

The second phase involved thoroughly reading and coding each of the 389 articles according to the themes that emerged from the discourse contained within them. A theme is a "researcher-generated construct that symbolizes and thus attributes interpreted meaning to each individual datum for later purposes of pattern detection, categorization, theory building, and other analytic processes" (Saldaña, 2013, p. 4). The articles were read in random order to avoid any temporally linear bias in the coding process. The themes by which these articles were coded were either/or: a) informed by literature regarding neoliberalism, school choice policy, and how these two areas relate to the spatialization of society, and b) through the constant-comparative method, which requires re-reading previously coded articles as new themes emerge (Corbin and Strauss, 2008).

Since this project focuses specifically on the manner through which schools are spatialized through neoliberal discourse, schools were coded by their appropriate themes whenever a particular school was discussed in terms of Ren2010. The following excerpt contains an example of eight schools that were coded for this project:

> When the Renaissance 2010 plan was announced in June, its success was contingent on the support of the business and civic community, which promised to raise $50 million to create innovative public schools across the city . . .
>
> Each of the eight schools will be eligible to receive $500,000 in start-up funds over three years . . .
>
> The schools that will receive funds are Galapagos Charter, DuSable Leadership Academy, Aspira Haugen Middle School, Chicago International Charter School-South Shore campus, Erie Elementary Charter, University of Chicago Charter-Donoghue campus and Legacy Charter School. Pershing West, also included in the list, is a performance school.
>
> *(Cholo, 2010)*

The above excerpt is an example where, in this case, each of the eight mentioned schools was coded by the theme *private funding*. Since Ren2010 is a major restructuring of Chicago Public Schools, schools were the most commonly referenced geographic features within the reading.

Phase III: Mapping

Median Income and Schools of the Ren2010 Conversation

After coding the 389 articles into their themes, the distribution of schools mentioned within the articles was mapped in geographic space, followed by mapping the distribution of the schools' themes in theoretical space with the goal of understanding how the articles' characterizations of schools are distributed across the social geography of Chicago. The map in Figure 7.1 below focuses on the schools included within the articles reporting on Ren2010, highlighting the schools' juxtaposition within Chicago's income distribution. This was performed by superimposing the CPS schools onto Chicago ZIP codes. The ZIP codes were symbolized by a sequential color scheme representing median income, while CPS schools are symbolized by dots differentiated by whether or not they were referenced within the entire 389 articles that reported on Ren2010. This method generated visualization of median income's spatial bias on CPS schools' inclusion in Chicago's highly-politicized school choice debate.

Race and Schools of the Ren2010 Conversation

Table 7.2 below was created by aggregating the majority racial ethnicity for each 2010 U.S. Census tract in Chicago. Following this step, the expected value of schools mentioned per aggregated racial category within the article sample was determined by the overall contribution of schools from each category to the total population of schools. For example, if Census tracts with a white majority contained 40 percent of the total CPS schools, the expected percentage of schools mentioned from these tracts would also be 40 percent. This allows for a simple calculation to determine the distance above or below the expected value.

Correspondence Analysis of Themes

The goal of this correspondence analysis is to explore the relationship between CPS' nine different school types and their themes from the articles. Correspondence analysis (CA) is a powerful tool that helps interpret the underlying structure of this type of thematic relationship. CA is a data reduction technique used to represent similarities between objects (e.g., themes, neighborhoods, school types, etc.) in a contingency table as distances in a low dimensional space (Greenacre and Blasius, 2006). In CA, distances are typically interpreted as a weighted form of Euclidean distance:

$$d_{x,y} = \sqrt{\sum_{j=1}^{p} w_j \left(x_j - y_j \right)^2} \quad ,$$

where w_j refers to the specific weight of the jth dimension.

Correspondence analysis allows for the comparison of each school type to the average or expected value, or expected amount of times that each school type would be coded by a particular theme. The primary output of CA is a map representing the dissimilarity between the column and row objects (in this case, school types and themes) in a contingency matrix. Thus the CA for this project (see Figure 7.2 below) will reveal the dissimilarity between the school themes and the nine school types, as schools of these types were coded by the themes.

Which Schools and Where? Income and Schools of the Ren2010 Conversation

It is apparent in Figure 7.1 that ZIP codes with a higher median income level were less likely to have their schools injected into the ideological school choice policy debate than ZIP codes with a lower median income. In addition to mapping the

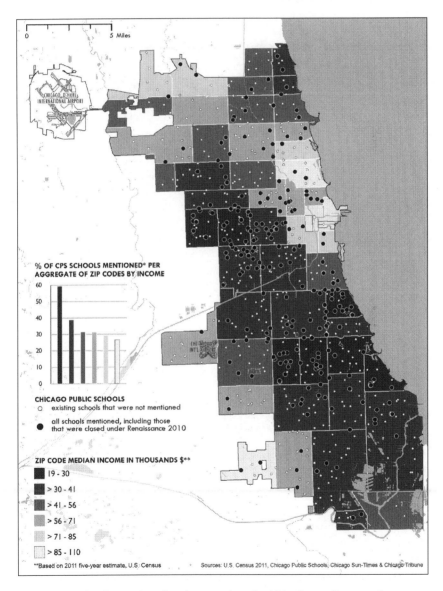

FIGURE 7.1 Schools mentioned and unmentioned within the reading sample per Chicago's aggregated ZIP codes based on median income

mentioned schools in the Ren2010 media debate, the map in Figure 7.1 also shows each unmentioned[5] public school that was still functioning as of the 2012–2013 school year, symbolized by a smaller white dot. By having all schools on this map, it allows readers to see the entire geographic spread of CPS schools, and compare the whole with the news-media-mentioned schools. This geo-visual distribution of mentioned and unmentioned schools presents the income-based spatial bias in the rate of schools mentioned per ZIP code. Further comparison of the percentage of all CPS schools mentioned per income category (see Table 7.1) reveals that nearly 60 percent of schools in ZIP codes for the lowest-income category (households earning $19,000–$30,000 annually) were included in the 389-article sample. Only 27 percent of schools in the aggregate of highest earning ZIP codes ($85,000–$110,000 annually) were mentioned in the entire news article sample.

Table 7.2 supports the argument that school choice, as a neoliberal policy, is a spatial strategy as much as it is an educational strategy. As Chicago news

TABLE 7.1 CPS schools mentioned in the 389-article sample reporting on Ren2010 and Chicago ZIP codes symbolized by median income

Median income in thousands	Number of ZIPs	Number of schools mentioned	Number of schools not mentioned	Percentage of schools mentioned
19–30	7	79	54	59
>30–41	13	125	196	39
>41–56	12	34	74	31
>56–71	11	36	79	31
>71–85	5	7	17	29
>85–110	11	4	11	27
Totals	59	285	431	40%

TABLE 7.2 Expectancy of CPS schools' mentioned status per aggregated U.S. Census tract categories based on racial ethnicity majority

Aggregated census tract categories based on racial ethnic majority (>50%)	Number of mentioned schools (NMS)	Number of unmentioned schools (NUS)	Total schools per category (TSC)	Expected value (EV): (TSC/726)	Actual value (AV): (NMS/292)	Distance from expected value (AV-EV)
African American	188	194	382	.526	.644	+11.8
Latino/a	48	108	156	.215	.164	−5
Asian	0	4	4	.006	0.0	−0.06
Caucasian	46	119	165	.227	.158	−7
No majority	10	9	19	.026	.034	−0.8
Total	292	434	726	1 or 100%	1 or 100%	

consumers read the debate presented to them by their city's two most popular newspapers, they read about the schools portrayed in Figure 7.1—connected to themes of failure and to themes of privatized rescue *of* such failure (see Table 7.3 below)—juxtaposed onto the racial layout of their city.

The news article sample reported on 292 CPS schools. Many of these schools have been shuttered or replaced since the 2004 introduction of Ren2010. Of total CPS schools that existed during the 2012–2013 school year, 494 schools were not mentioned within the articles, providing a total of 726 schools from which to analyze the expected percentage of schools that would be mentioned from Table 7.2's aggregated census tracts based on racial ethnicity.[6] Table 7.2 shows that expected value for the percentage of schools per category was determined to be the total schools per category divided by the total schools analyzed. The expected value of schools that are mentioned within Caucasian-majority census tracts is 0.227, since schools in this category make up 22.7 percent of the total schools. The distance from the expected value was determined by subtracting the expected value from the actual value per each category. The negative values for Latino/a, Asian, and Caucasian indicate that, for these categories the percentage of schools that were included in the Ren2010 news media debate is lower than the expected value. For African American majority census tracts, the value was 11.8 percent higher than the expected value.

School Themes

Table 7.3 contains the themes for schools that emerged throughout the coding process. These themes contribute and/or reflect and perpetuate the labels of "success" or "failure" that stem from high stakes testing results (Klaf, 2013) and other school choice policy actions carried out in Chicago. The themes are grouped into two columns that, after an exhaustive literature review and investigation of Ren2010, can confidently be connected to schools as a space of success or failure. The third column contains themes that are neutral or ambiguous in their contribution to the schools as a space of success or failure.

It was clear in some instances that schools were consciously described in terms of failure. For example, when schools were coded by *suffered budget cuts* or *high mobility rate* the sentiment was that these schools were experiencing circumstances that made it difficult to be a space of success, and thus much easier for readers to view these schools as spaces of failure. Yet, when schools were tied to gentrification in their reporting, it was not always in a positive or negative light. However, the full investigation of Ren2010 combined with the literature review on neoliberalism and school choice strongly indicates that if a school is being discussed alongside the theme of gentrification it is likely that the school is subject to the changing mechanisms of neoliberalism, i.e., the school is likely considered to be standing in the way of a politically spatial agenda that supports neoliberal policy. Ultimately, if the residents who attend a particular school were displaced as part

TABLE 7.3 School themes as they emerged through the coding process

Themes of success	Themes of failure	Neutral or ambiguous themes
1. cronyism	19. closing	41. demographics
2. good model	20. compliance to save	42. free market
3. growing	21. consolidating	43. school type
4. improving	22. displaced students	44. segregation as part of
5. new facilities	23. divided up	reform
6. new program	24. failing	
7. new school(s)	25. gentrification	
8. NIMBY protest	26. high mobility rate	
9. outgrowing space	27. labor cuts	
10. prestigious	28. labor replacement	
11. private funding	29. needs transformation	
12. private mode of governance	30. new ways to oppress	
13. public funding	31. overcrowded	
14. rescued by school choice reform	32. poor facility conditions	
15. succeeding	33. inadequate funding	
16. survived Budget Cuts	34. program cuts	
17. good staff/teachers	35. protest	
18. waitlist	36. received displaced students	
	37. Ren2010 failure	
	38. replaced	
	39. suffered budget cuts	
	40. violence	

of gentrification, it was a strong indication that the school itself would likely soon be closed. Gentrification is part of the Chicago-style spatial pattern of school choice reform. The following news article excerpt reporting on McCorkle Elementary School in the Mid-South neighborhood of Bronzeville provides an excellent example of this pattern where seemingly unrelated development projects can predict the likely extinction of Chicago's neighborhood schools:

> Principal Janet House said she thinks REAL (Recognizing Excellence in Academic Leadership) drew quality candidates to her school [McCorkle Elementary], located across the street from the now-toppled Robert Taylor Homes, and hopes the program will encourage them, and others, to stay.
> REAL requires that all teachers be observed at least four times a year by the principal or teacher leaders, using an eight-page scorecard.
> *(Rossi, 2007)*

The above excerpt comes from a news article that was boasting the changes that McCorkle Elementary was undergoing in order to retain teachers and be attractive to real estate developers. The phrase "located across the street from the now-toppled Robert Taylor Homes" is the reason that McCorkle Elementary was coded by the theme *gentrification* in this instance. Robert Taylor Homes was a Chicago Housing Authority subsidized housing project that was torn down in 2005, resulting in the displacement of thousands of residents, most of whom are African American. Gentrification is not the article's topic, but by mentioning that the now-toppled public housing is located directly across the street from a school that is taking measures to appease city officials and private developers, gentrification is discursively tied to McCorkle Elementary. Incidentally, McCorkle Elementary was permanently closed in 2010.

A simple question to ask when deciding whether the theme should be considered one that contributes to a school's success or failure is "Does this theme *cost* or *benefit* the school?" It is important to note that these themes do not reflect an opinion. Rather, the themes are considered as labels of "success" or "failure" almost in an evolutionary sense of the words. These themes help predict an answer to the question "Will this school survive *Renaissance 2010*?" So the themes *Cronyism* and *NIMBY Protest* can be considered as themes that help a school's survival in a district that is focused on school choice even if we may or may not think of these as positive terms to be attached to public schools.

The Discursive Space of the Ren2010 Debate

Figure 7.2 depicts the discursive space of Chicago's public school types and the themes that those school types were coded by during the coding process. This figure was generated by using correspondence analysis (CA) from a contingency table containing the school types as rows and their themes as columns. Each object (school type or theme) in Figure 7.2 is marked by a corresponding point. Within this map, a small square and their labels indicate theme positions and larger circles and their labels indicate the school type positions. A general way to read CA maps is to consider that the closer each object is to another object, the more similar they are, and conversely the further they are apart, the greater the dissimilarity. The CA map gives us a two-dimensional output that orients these objects (school types and themes) along the two axes (i.e., factors) with the highest variance in the CA analysis. Along the horizontal factor, traditional neighborhood schools fall on the far left and charter and contract schools fall on the far right. The polarization of these two school types within this space is due to the themes that these schools took on within the Ren2010 news articles and opinion pieces. Along the vertical factor, small schools are at the far top while special education schools fall at the far bottom. The first two dimensions (factors) explain 28.0 percent and 19.9 percent, respectively, of the variance among the entire population of objects when schools are coded by the themes from Table 7.3.

Each theme in Figure 7.2 is grayscale shaded to correspond with the columns in Table 7.3; themes of success are marked by a light grey label, and themes of failure are marked by a black label. The medium grey themes represent the neutral or ambiguous themes. Figure 7.2 reveals an actual space of CPS school types

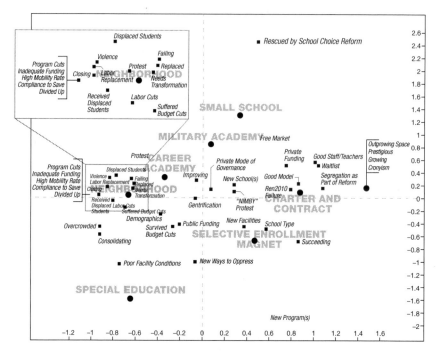

FIGURE 7.2 Correspondence analysis map of mentioned schools by their coded themes

positioned in their relation to one another based on the themes by which they were coded. In this space, the themes that foster spaces of failure cluster around the neighborhood schools on the far left of the first factor. In fact, the only one of these failure themes that falls near the opposite side of the factor is *Ren2010 Failure* as this theme was used to code Renaissance schools that were opened and then reported as closed or criticized as failures within the news article sample. The light grey themes that foster spaces of success are more dispersed than the themes of failure, and tend to cluster near the *Charter and Contract* school type.

Figure 7.2 reveals that school type can predict whether a school will be discursively presented as a space of success or failure within the Ren2010 debate as it played out in the linguistic market of news media. Privately-run school choice schools were almost always reported as spaces of success and models to repeat. Likewise, neighborhood schools were most commonly connected to the "failure" labels that Suzanna Klaf and others have written about:

> They [labels of "failure"] are a mechanism intended to identify failure and name and shame schools publicly (Stoll and Myers 1998; Nicolaidou and Ainscow 2005) . . . Labels are a means of maintaining power, and

hegemonize social values and practices (Armstrong 2003). Government and nongovernment stakeholders use the labelling of schools and districts as a mechanism to regulate behaviour. Labels are used to manage the Other by aligning school behaviour to government-established norms (Foucault 1980; Armstrong 2003).

(Klaf, 2013, p. 299)

The space depicted in Figure 7.2 indicates that the "other" in Chicago's school choice policy debate is neighborhood schools. These are the school types that require regulated behavior and penalizing mandates within school choice policies, making the students of these school types the human manifestations of Chicago's "other" in the Ren2010 debate. This continual production of Chicago's social spaces was increasingly conducted by those who have what is considered legitimate linguistic habitus, since, over the lifetime of Ren2010, the journalistic production of education space grew more restricted to elite voices, even as parents and students protested the school choice initiative. This is evident in that nearly 70 percent of the editorial letters from these news articles were authored by a person holding a political and/or private executive position.

Discussion and Conclusion

Mass news media journalism, as a spatial-identity-forming process, is accessible to only a few (Howe, 2009). Due to the differential access to the journalistic process, those who are able to express their discourses in news media control this particular branch of place creation. The business of journalism implicitly maps places through *semantic geographies*, which are "the actual process[es] of situating people and places in space and in relation to one another" (Howe, 2009, p. 44–45). News media outlets represent the cultures on which they report, but also assist in maintaining the infrastructure for how people map out their own sense of place (Buchanan, 2009, p. 63; Howe, 2009, p. 44).

Much like socio-spatial order, the differential access to certain linguistic markets, news media included, is taken for granted so often that it, too, is almost accepted as "natural" (Gee, 2005, p. 71–72). The hegemony of the seemingly natural order of who may participate within certain linguistic markets is extended to the power that each market grants, i.e., the power differential is also taken for granted as "natural." A group of parents who meet in a coffee shop to discuss their opinions about Ren2010 is part of the Conversation about this piece of education policy. However, the chances of any one of these parents' opinions achieving mass media distribution is far smaller than that of a charter school operator's CEO. This imbalanced access to the political debate represents one of the many boundaries that a society constructs in order to uphold the commonsense view of what is politically doable (Bourdieu, 1991, p. 172–181) and who may do or say it. One of the reasons these boundaries perpetuate is that the dominant voices in political debates stand to gain from restricting access to the Conversation. The profit in a greater political debate about school choice reform can manifest as a political victory, real estate development and investment opportunities, or other forms of social, cultural, and even monetary capital.

By using empirical GIS and cartography, this investigatory mapping project has illustrated that school choice policies are part of a spatial strategy carried out by a neoliberal rhetorical campaign, where it has become strikingly evident that space must be considered a significant factor as critical education studies moves forward (Ferrare and Apple, 2010). As Figure 7.1 and Table 7.1 indicate, the gravity of the Ren2010 Conversation is weighted toward lower-income neighborhoods with a high percentage of African American residents. Figure 7.1 and Table 7.1 show that socio-spatial configuration is a principal predictor of whether or not Chicago's sub-regions will be inserted into the school choice policy debate. Figure 7.2 and Table 7.3 demonstrate that, within the dominant linguistic market of news media production, these exploited sub-regions' traditional neighborhood schools will be discursively contextualized as blights on the city. Figure 7.2 also indicates that, in the Ren2010 debate, private charter and contract schools are promoted by and large as the only remedy for these reported-as-suffering regions. The exhaustive news article analysis performed for this project has shown that it is the dominant corporate and political supporters in Chicago's school choice policy debate who advertise these privatized schools as the free market solution that will rescue Chicago's residents from the "plagued" public system.

The intersection of the data presented in this paper—the geographic and CA maps, and supporting tables and figures—exposes a neoliberal school choice campaign that not only pathologizes schools, but also pathologizes the social geography of those schools. The lower-income African American residents who are subject to the school closures and revitalization (gentrification) projects carried out via a powerful civic–corporate partnership become the personification of the themes within the place-shaping process of news media production, bearing the brunt of the neoliberal doctrine's shock from corporate spatial commodification. That is to say, the residents in these spaces are those whom news media readers will consider as in need of new schools and violent; they are also the residents who are expected to accept labor replacement and school closures as part of their schools' contribution to school reform. The residents of these ailing spaces are also the same people who are expected to allow their children to become the displaced students for the "greater good" of long-term revitalization through education reform founded on free market values. The residents who live in Chicago's spaces where the gravity of the Ren2010 debate is concentrated are expected to transform the most—to become more like the whiter, affluent spaces of the city—in order to retain and improve the city's global status, while whiter and more affluent spaces are largely exempt from being inserted into the school choice debate.

Chicago Today

In 2004, Mayor Richard M. Daley's Renaissance 2010 set out to close 60–70 neighborhood schools and replace them with 100 Renaissance schools by the year 2010. School closures in Chicago have not halted, however. Mayor Rahm Emanuel took Chicago's highest office in May 2011 and has continued Daley's legacy of shuttering neighborhood schools to make way for privately-run charter schools (Ahmed-Ullah, 2013). In fact, Mayor Emanuel's school closure initiatives included the second-largest mass school closure in Chicago's history; in spring 2013 Mayor Emanuel announced that CPS would be closing 50 public schools prior to the start of the 2013–2014 school year (Ahmed-Ullah, Chase, and Secter, 2013). The mass school closure announcement marked the 2012–2013 school year as one bookended with extreme controversy for CPS; the school year started off with a week-and-a-half-long CTU strike as teachers battled with city officials to negotiate more union-friendly re-hiring practices as neighborhood schools were continually shuttered and replaced by charter schools (Rado, 2012). Chicago's new charter schools are still not bound to hiring any union-represented teachers (Lutton, 2013), thus the neoliberal theme of anti-organized labor continues in Chicago's education reform to this day.

Future Approaches

A decade after an alliance between corporate and civic elites began shuffling and displacing Chicago's lower-income minority public school students, and replacing open-enrollment neighborhood schools with competitive enrollment privatized schools, the story of school reform in Chicago seems to only be repeating itself: Measures that are propelled by the discourses of Chicago's most dominant voices use public schools as an arena to vend free market values of competition and individual choice (Apple 2000), displacing Chicago's under-represented residents. On the surface, school choice policies are sold as a path toward egalitarianism through a market from which all may equally choose and participate (Lipman, 2004; Ravitch, 2010), but as this project has clarified, neoliberal education reform is concerned not with equality, but rather with reframing urban space so that it may fit the dominant capitalist economy centered on private competition.

The presence of dominant voices in news media combined with the lack of voices from the Ren2010-shuffled families supports Pierre Bourdieu's *linguistic markets* and *linguistic habitus* theories (Bourdieu, 1991). The evidence described above illustrating that these dominant voices concentrate on a particular social geography in Chicago indicates that the spatial layout of the city is indeed not detached from policies, but rather arranged by them (Lefebvre, 1976). Moving forward, in terms of school choice reform, geographers, sociologists, and education researchers more broadly can now understand space itself as a subject of education reform, understanding that changing only very particular space is at the heart of neoliberal reformists' agenda. Mapping the spatial objects of this agenda, and how those objects are discursively fashioned into spaces of failure is only the beginning to counter-cartographic ventures confronting hegemonic discourses that re-contextualize and exploit urban space. Counter-discourses in education reform (see Ferrare and Apple, 2010; Lipman, 2004) must move forward by including a local-democratic discursive contextualization of educative space. Cartographies of these counter-discourses are also necessary to amplify the voices that have been shut out of the school choice policy debate.

Notes

1   New Schools for Chicago website (2014). http://newschoolsnow.org
2   See Apple 2000 (60–62), Harvey 2005 (38–41), and Peck and Tickell 2002 (383) for more on the *neoliberal project*.
3   James Gee's term *Conversation* is, therefore, used interchangeably with *debate* throughout this paper.
4   The Fordham Institute is an Ohio-based conservative think tank that focuses on school choice reform. The institute runs several charter schools in the state of Ohio (www.edexcellence.net/ohio-charters/fordham-sponsored-schools.html).
5   "Unmentioned" refers to all CPS schools that were not included in any of the 389 news articles analyzed and coded for this project.
6   This analysis does not include schools that were not mentioned in the news articles that were shuttered or replaced.

References

Ahmed-Ullah, N. S. (2012, January 9). CPS has shut 15 in 12 years and plans 2 more, but area decries 'destabilized education' for kids. *Chicago Tribune*.

Ahmed-Ullah, N. S. (2013, August 25). CPS' first day awaits amid budget cuts, school closings. *Chicago Tribune*.

Ahmed-Ullah, N. S., Chase, J. and Secter, B. (2013, May 23). CPS approves largest school closure in Chicago's history. *Chicago Tribune*.

Apple M. W. (2000). Between neoliberalism and neoconservatism: Education and conservatism in a global context. In N. C. Burbules and C. A. Torres (Eds.), *Globalization and education: Critical perspectives* (pp. 57–78). New York: Routledge.

Armstrong, F. (2003). *Spaced out: Policy, difference and the challenge of inclusive education*. London, UK: Kluwer Academic Publishers.

Audit Bureau of Circulations (2012). *Standard certificates of circulation: US newspapers*.

Bell, S. (2014). The spatial manifestation of neoliberal discourse: Mapping Chicago's education reform debate. Master's thesis, Huxley College of the Environment, Western Washington University, Bellingham, WA.

Bourdieu, P. (1986). The forms of capital. In J. Richardson (Ed.), *Handbook of theory and research for the sociology of education* (pp. 241–248). New York: Greenwood Press.

Bourdieu, P. (1998). *Practical reason*. Stanford: Stanford University Press.

Bourdieu, P. (1991). *Language and symbolic power* (trans. by G. Raymond and M. Adamson). Cambridge: Polity Press.

Buchanan, C. (2009). Sense of place in the daily newspaper. *Aether: The Journal of Media Geography*, 4, 62–84.

Cholo A. B. (2010, February 23). Businesses help new schools; $37 million in grants for Renaissance 2010. *Chicago Tribune.*

Cholo, A. and Dell'Angela, T. (2014, June 23). 100 new schools to be created; Charter, small sites envisioned. Chicago Tribune.

Corbin, J. M. and Strauss, A. L. (2008). *Basics of qualitative research: techniques and procedures for developing grounded theory* (third ed.). Los Angeles, CA: Sage Publications.

Dell'Angela, T. (2007, May 31). Students in area feeling displaced; new sites assailed as lacking spots for many local teens. *Chicago Tribune.*

Ferrare, J. J. and Apple, M. W. (2010). Spatializing critical education: Progress and cautions. *Critical Studies in Education, 51*(2), 209–221.

Foucault, M. (1972). *The Archaeology of knowledge and the discourse on language* (trans. by A. M. Sheridan Smith). New York: Pantheon Books.

Foucault, M. (1980). *Power/knowledge: Selected interviews and other writings, 1972–1977* (edited by C. Gordon). Brighton, UK: Harvester.

Gee, J. P. (2005). *An introduction to discourse analysis: Theory and method* (second ed.). New York: Routledge.

Greenacre, M. and Blasius, J. (Eds.). (2006). *Multiple correspondence analysis and related methods.* Boca Raton, FL: Chapman & Hall/CRC.

Harley, J. B. (1989). Deconstructing the map. *Cartographica, 26*(2), 1–20.

Harvey, D. (2005). *A brief history of neoliberalism.* New York: Oxford University Press.

Howe, P. D. (2009). Newsworthy spaces: The semantic geographies of local news. *Aether: The Journal of Media Geography,* 4, 43–61.

Ihejirika, M. (2004, September 26). 38% of public teachers pick private school for their kids. *Chicago Sun-Times.*

Klaf, S. (2013). School labelling as technology of governance: Problematizing ascribed labels to school spaces. *The Canadian Geographer, 57*(3), 296–302.

Lefebvre, H. (1976). *Reflections on the politics of space* (trans. by M. Enders). *Antipode, 8*(2), 30–37.

Lipman, P. (2004). *High stakes education: Inequality, globalization, and urban school reform.* New York: Routledge.

Lipman, P. (2007). Education and the spatialization of urban inequality: A case study of Chicago's Renaissance 2010. In K. Gulson and C. Symes (Eds.), *Spatial theories of education: Policy and geography matters* (pp. 155–174). New York: Routledge.

Lipman, P. and Haines N. (2007). From accountability to privatization and African American exclusion: Chicago's "Renaissance 2010." *Educational Policy, 21*(3), 471–502.

Lutton, L. (2013, August 13). Just months after closing 50 schools, Chicago issues RFP for more charter schools. Retrieved September 6, 2013 from www.wbez.org/news/education/just-months-after-closing-50-schools-chicago-issues-rfp-more-charter-schools-108398

Nicolaidou, M. and Ainscow, M. (2005). Understanding failing schools: Perspectives from the inside. *School Effectiveness and School Improvement, 16*(3), 229–248.

Peck, J. and Tickell, A. (2002). Neoliberalizing space. *Antipode, 34*(3), 380–404.

Rado, D. (2012, September 17). Chicago teacher strike: Issues at the center of contract negotiations. *Chicago Tribune.*

Ravitch, D. (2010). *The death and life of the great American school system: How testing and choice undermine education.* New York: Basic Books.

Rossi, R. (2007, September 4). New incentive for teachers: Bonuses also would go to principals, and even janitors and clerks. *Chicago Sun-Times.*

Saldaña, J. (2013). *The coding manual for qualitative researchers*. Los Angeles, CA: SAGE.

Sayer, A. (2000). *Realism and social science*. London: SAGE.

Soja, E. W. (1989). *Postmodern geographies: The reassertion of space in critical social theory*. New York: Verso.

Stoll, L. and Myers, K. (Eds.). (1998). *No quick fixes: Perspectives on schools in difficulty*. London, UK: Falmer Press.

Thompson, J. B. (1991). Editor's introduction. In P. Bourdieu, *Language and symbolic power* (pp. 1–31). Cambridge: Polity Press.

United States Census Bureau TIGER Geo-database and demographic profiles. (2013). Retrieved September 25, 2013 from www.censusgov/geo/maps-data/data/tiger-datahtml

8

OTHER PEOPLE'S POLICY

Wealthy Elites and Charter School Reform in Washington State[1]

Wayne Au and Joseph J. Ferrare

Introduction

Charter schools have become a prominent education reform in the United States. Once upon a time charter schools were part of a progressive education reform agenda, where teachers and their unions took the lead in building innovative schools and practices in partnership with families and communities, all in the interest of improving public education for all children, but especially those low-income black and brown kids currently underserved by the public school system (Fabricant and Fine, 2012; Karp, 2013). However, the charter school movement shifted, and those politicians and business leaders invested in free market, capitalist, corporate-styled reforms for the public sector saw charter schools as an opportunity to deregulate public education, weaken teachers' unions, and access the vast market offered by state-run school systems (Fabricant and Fine, 2012; Ravitch, 2010).

The corporate education reformers seized the opportunity presented by charter schools and worked to build a strong coalition of both major political parties, billionaire philanthropists, venture capitalists, business leaders, and a growing network of non-profit organizations and research centers to help shift the national commonsense surrounding charter schools and concepts of school choice (Barkan, 2012; Scott, 2009) as part of a larger packet of reforms (e.g., high-stakes testing, school closings, and value-added measures of teacher performance, among others). Buoyed by rhetorics of "choice," the charter school movement has thus evolved from being a much more public, grassroots, and school- and community-based education reform to one being driven by corporate and political elites interested in shrinking the public sector (Fabricant and Fine, 2012; Karp, 2013). These elites combine financial largesse with networks of non-profit and for-profit organizations, and strategically seize upon discontent with public schools originating in marginalized communities (see, e.g., the Black Alliance for Educational Opportunities, as discussed in, Apple and Pedroni, 2005; Apple, 2014; Pedroni, 2007) to establish a popular image of serving those who are underserved.

In this chapter we look at the campaign to pass charter schools into law in Washington State as an illustrative example of the elite interests invested in charter school reform. We begin here with a brief history of charter school reform in the state and campaign to get Initiative 1240 (I-1240) passed. Then, using social network analysis, we analyze publicly available data and "map" important relations of actors connected to the successful campaign to pass I-1240. We conclude with a discussion of the political implications of our findings, including how such elitism threatens the democratic impulses provided by the public sphere, and how the network of policy actors surrounding the Yes On 1240 WA Coalition for Public Charter Schools (hereafter, Yes On 1240) campaign functionally illustrates wealthy elites developing policy for other peoples' children—a concept that itself is both raced and classed.

Indeed, we'd like to take a moment to acknowledge that the main title of our chapter, "Other People's Policy" draws loosely from Delpit's (1995) work *Other People's Children*, where she explicitly and sharply addresses the racial dynamics of middle-class, professional, and white teachers working with low-income kids of color in urban public schools. As Delpit points out, too often our teachers are teaching "other peoples' children," and this relationship raises all sorts of serious and substantive issues with regards to race and class. Similar to Delpit's (1995) argument, we see wealthy, predominantly white elites pushing for free market education reforms, charter schools in this case, ostensibly for low income kids of color in public schools—schools to which these same wealthy elites would never send their own children. In this sense we are arguing that in Washington State and elsewhere, charter school policies are not the will of the communities that proponents claim they will be serving, but instead represent "other people's policy."

Initiative 1240 and The Path to Legalized Charter Schools in WA State

As of 2012, all but nine U.S. states allowed charter schools (National Alliance for Public Charter Schools, 2013), and in one of those nine, Washington State, charter school legislation was passed by popular vote in November of 2012 (Reed, 2012). November 2012 was not the first time that charter schools appeared on Washington ballots. Washington State has a substantive and unique history with regards to charter school reform. The state allows for popular votes on whether or not various initiatives, measures, or referenda (put on the ballot by petition) become law, and since 1996 there have been four opportunities for voters to decide if charter schools would be allowed in the state. Washington State voters have affirmed opposition to charter schools three times: In 1996 54 percent opposed charters; in 2000 51.8 percent opposed charters; and in 2004 58.3 percent opposed charters (Corcoran and Stoddard, 2011).

After a failed effort tó have charter school laws passed through the Washington State Legislature in the 2011–2012 legislative session, charter advocates drafted I-1240, which was filed with the state by the League of Education Voters (LEV) chief of staff, Tania de Sa Campos (League of Education Voters, 2012; Sa Campos, 2012). Initiative 1240 contained provisions to establish 40 charter schools over five years, establish two charter authorizers (local school boards or an appointed state-level charter school commission), set up appointed charter school boards for charter oversight, and to allow for a parent-teacher charter conversion trigger, among other details (Sa Campos, 2012). With $2.26 million in donations mostly from Bill Gates Jr., Amazon.com's Bezos family, venture capitalist Nick Hanauer (also a LEV board member), and Microsoft cofounder Paul Allen, enough signatures were collected by paid signature gatherers to successfully put I-1240 on the Fall 2012 Washington ballot (Callaghan, 2012).

With the initiative on the ballot, I-1240 supporters Stand for Children, LEV, Partnership for Learning, and Democrats For Education Reform (DFER) then co-founded the Washington Coalition for Public Charter Schools (Washington Coalition for Public Charter Schools, 2012a), the organization that publicly took responsibility for the Yes On 1240 campaign (Washington Coalition for Public Charter Schools, 2012b). Based on records of "in-kind" donations of services and staff time, these organizations provided leadership in coordinating every aspect of the campaign—financial management, field organizing, press releases, TV, web, and radio advertising, messaging, and public presentations, among others (Washington State Public Disclosure Commission, 2012b). As of election day, November 6, 2012, the Yes On 1240 campaign had received $10.9 million in donations (Washington State Public Disclosure Commission, 2012a). At the time the $10.9 million spent to support charter school reform via the Yes on 1240 campaign represented the third largest sum spent on an initiative campaign in Washington State history (Washington State Public Disclosure Commission, 2012d).

Leading up to election day Partnership for Learning (2012), working with researchers from the Center on Reinventing Public Education (CRPE), published a report, "Examining Charters: How Public Charter Schools Can Work in Washington State" (Lake, Gross, and Maas, 2012), which explicitly refers to I-1240 as a "good" charter school law. Further, CRPE founder and charter school proponent, Dr Paul Hill, was prominently featured in a Yes On 1240 television advertisement advocating for the passage of I-1240 (Yes on 1240, 2012b). In the November 2012 election voters in Washington approved Initiative 1240 (I-1240) 50.69 percent to 49.31 percent, or a 41,682 vote margin out of just over 3,020,000 total cast (Reed, 2012), legalizing charter schools in the state. After 18 years, advocates finally legalized charter schools in Washington State, and, as we shall see, the wealthy elites provided the tipping point.

Data Sources

We collected data for this chapter from multiple sources. Basic organizational information and relationships came from web pages formally associated with the Yes On 1240 campaign (Washington Coalition for Public Charter Schools, 2012a), those of affiliated non-profit organizations taking credit as founding leadership for the Washington Coalition for Public Charter Schools (Washington Coalition for Public Charter Schools, 2012b)—also evidenced by staff time and other organizational resources donated to the campaign (Washington State Public Disclosure Commission, 2012c)—and a local organization that through the research process we identified as explicitly connected to the Yes On 1240 campaign, the Center On Reinventing Public Education. Funding relationships were identified using foundation databases (e.g., Bill & Melinda Gates Foundation, 2013), tax returns for foundations (Foundation Center, 2013), and institutional reports (e.g., University of Washington Bothell Office of Research, 2013). Cash and in-kind contributions to the Yes On 1240 campaign were tracked using the Washington State Public Disclosure Commission database (Washington State Public Disclosure Commission, 2012a, 2012c). For the purposes of this study we only included what we deemed were significant contributors to the Yes On 1240 campaign (see Table 8.1) by setting a parameter of those donors that contributed $50,000 or more to the campaign in cash or in kind, which resulted in a list of 21 donors being responsible for 98 percent of the total campaign funds.

Corporate Elites and the Network of Influence behind Yes On 1240

In this section we present the findings of our analysis in two phases. First, in Tables 8.1 and 8.2 we present data on cash and in-kind contributions to the Yes On 1240 campaign and funding relationships between campaign donors, affiliated philanthropies, and organizational campaign supporters. Second, we visualize these relationships through a simple directed graph (see Figure 8.1 on p. 155) that traces the connections between policy actors associated with Yes On 1240 (see Chapter 1 for more on these methods).

Yes On 1240 Campaign Contributions

Several important findings arise when we analyze the contributions to the Yes On 1240 campaign.

Table 8.1 highlights that in total $10.65 million, or almost 98 percent of the $10.9 million raised for the Yes On 1240 campaign was funded by 21 individuals and organizations who each donated more than $50,000 to the campaign (Washington State Public Disclosure Commission, 2012a).

Notably, Bill Gates Jr. is the biggest contributor ($3M) to the campaign, nearly doubling the next biggest contributions coming from Walmart heiress Alice Walton

TABLE 8.1 Yes On 1240 campaign cash and in-kind contributions $50k and greater (Washington State Public Disclosure Commission, 2012a)

Yes On 1240 donor	Donation amount
1. Bill Gates Jr.—Microsoft co-founder and current chairman	$3,053,000.00
2. Alice Walton—heiress daughter of Walmart founder, Sam Walton	$1,700,000.00
3. Vulcan Inc.—founded by Paul Allen, Microsoft co-founder	$1,600,000.00
4. Nicolas Hanauer—venture capitalist	$1,000,000.00
5. Mike Bezos—father of Amazon.com founder Jeff Bezos	$500,000.00
6. Jackie Bezos—mother of Amazon.com founder Jeff Bezos	$500,000.00
7. Connie Ballmer—wife of Microsoft CEO Steve Ballmer	$500,000.00
8. Anne Dinning—managing director D.E. Shaw Investments	$250,000.00
9. Michael Wolf—Yahoo! Inc. Board of Directors	$250,000.00
10. Katherine Binder—EMFCO Holdings Chairwoman	$250,000.00
11. Eli Broad—real estate mogul	$200,000.00
12. Benjamin Slivka—formerly Microsoft, co-founder DreamBox Learning	$124,200.00
13. Reed Hastings—Netflix CEO	$100,000.00
14. Microsoft Corporation	$100,000.00
15. Gabe Newell—formerly Microsoft, co-founder Valve Corporation	$100,000.00
16. Doris Fisher—Gap co-founder	$100,000.00
17. Kemper Holdings LLC—local Puget Sound developer	$110,000.00
18. CSG Channels	$60,000.00
19. Education Reform Now	$50,000.00
20. Bruce McCaw—founder McCaw Cellular	$50,000.00
21. Jolene McCaw—spouse of Bruce McCaw	$50,000.00

Source: Washington State Public Disclosure Commission (2012a)

($1.7M) and Vulcan Inc. ($1.6M),[2] Microsoft cofounder Paul Allen's company. These amounts illustrate how a number of wealthy individuals with no direct connection to Washington State (e.g., Eli Broad and Alice Walton) demonstrated a vested interest in charter school policy in the state. Notably, 12 of the top 21 contributors to Yes On 1240 are strongly connected to the technology sector. As might be expected given the prominence of the technology sector donors, several of these individuals have historical and industry-related connections to Microsoft Inc. and Microsoft Inc. cofounder and Chairman, Bill Gates Jr.

The $50,000 donation to the Yes On 1240 campaign from Education Reform Now! Advocacy illustrates the pivotal interconnectedness of organizations and funding structures associated with corporate education reform policy. New York State tax records from 2006 explicitly indicate that Education Reform Now! Inc., Education Reform Now! Advocacy, and DFER all share officers, personnel, office space, and paymasters (Libby, 2012). Tax records from 2007 further indicate that Education Reform Now! Inc. and Education Reform Now! Advocacy share these same resources (New York State Office of the Attorney General, 2013). Thus it is difficult to determine where DFER, Education Reform Now! Inc., and Education Reform Now! Advocacy begin and end individually because in essence they are an interconnected cluster of three organizations with overlapping staff and resources. Consequently, even though tax records do not allow us to fully understand the exact relationship, the $50,000 donation to the Yes On 1240 campaign from Education Reform Now! Advocacy is functionally also a donation from Education Reform Now! Inc., and DFER.

Organizations Associated with Yes On 1240

In addition to the direct financial contributions from wealthy elites, a number of non-profit organizations played crucial roles in the network of influence shaping the outcome of I-1240. As discussed above, four organizations, LEV, DFER, Stand for Children, and Partnership for Learning, took credit for leading the Yes On 1240 WA Coalition for Public Charter Schools (Yes on 1240, 2012a). This leadership is confirmed if we look at the in-kind donations to the Yes On 1240 campaign (that is, donations of labor or other services that are given cash value and added to the campaign donation total). These four are the only organizations listing "staff time" as donated in kind to the Yes On 1240 campaign (Washington State Public Disclosure Commission, 2012c). Further, the CRPE played an important role by contributing their expertise vis-à-vis being highlighted prominently in a campaign video (Yes on 1240, 2012b) and authoring, in conjunction with Partnership for Learning, a research report explicitly in support of I-1240 (Lake et al., 2012).

Yes On 1240 Campaign Philanthropic Support

The fact that Bill Gates Jr., Eli Broad, and Alice Walton supported the Yes On 1240 campaign with their individual wealth is not coincidental. Each of their respective foundations, the Bill & Melinda Gates Foundation (Gates Foundation), the Eli and Edythe Broad Foundation (Broad Foundation), and the Walton Family Foundation (Walton Foundation) are often referred to as the "big three" philanthropies in education reform, and all of the big three have demonstrated consistent ideological and financial commitments to supporting charter schools and charter school policy nationally (Barkan, 2011, 2012; Ravitch, 2010; Reckhow, 2013; Saltman, 2010). The presence of Bill Gates Jr., Alice Walton, and Eli Broad as individual contributors to the Yes On 1240 campaign prompted us to examine whether or not their respective philanthropies funded the non-profit organizations coordinating and actively supporting the campaign. This exploration then led us to look at whether other major individual contributors to the Yes On 1240 campaign also had philanthropies funding campaign-related organizations.

By cross-referencing information gathered from the Google (2013) search engine, philanthropic foundation websites, and available tax records (Foundation Center, 2013) we found 11 foundations directly connected to major donors to the Yes On 1240 campaign (in alphabetical order): the Apex Foundation (formerly the Bruce & Jolene McCaw Foundation), the Bezos Family Foundation, the Gates Foundation, the Corabelle Lumps Foundation (formerly the Anne Dinning and Michael Wolf Foundation), the Donald and Doris Fisher Fund, the Broad Foundation, the Goldman Sachs Philanthropy Fund (connected through the Connie and Steve Ballmer advised Biel Fund),[3] the Lochland Foundation (Katherine Binder, cofounder, officer and contributor), the Walton Foundation, and the Wissner-Slivka Foundation. Using foundation databases, foundation reports, available tax records, organizational websites, and institutional reports, we then looked for whether or not these foundations provided funding to the Yes On 1240 campaign-related organizations.

Looking at Table 8.2 we see that the philanthropic foundations connected to major individual contributors to the Yes On 1240 campaign provide a range of financial support to three of the four campaign-coordinating organizations and the CRPE: the Apex Foundation's $1,000 contributions to each LEV and Stand for Children being the smallest, and the Gates Foundation total contribution of $9,000,000 to Stand for Children being the largest. Further, while DFER received no direct philanthropic support, its sister organization Education Reform Now! receives ample support from campaign-connected philanthropies, and, as detailed above, the overlap of resources between the cluster of Education Reform Now! Inc., Education Reform Now! Advocacy, and DFER, appears to be very fluid. The Gates Foundation is the most prominent funder here with $27 million given to Yes On 1240 campaign-connected organizations across multiple years, grants, and contracts. The Walton Foundation is second-most prominent with $6.48 million given to campaign-connected organizations, followed by the Broad Foundation at $2.99 million in support for Yes On 1240 campaign-connected organizations. While there is a precipitous drop in total support after these three, regardless of the amount, foundation support of the organizations directly involved in the Yes On 1240 campaign indicates either explicit or implicit ideological alignment with specific education reforms (in this case, charter schools).

The Yes On 1240 Campaign Network

In order to more clearly visualize and understand the relationships between individual and organizational supporters surrounding the Yes On 1240 campaign, we developed a simple directed graph that illustrates connections among and between significant campaign actors and the philanthropic organizations that support them. This graph essentially synthesizes the information contained in Tables 8.1 and 8.2, as well as the textual/narrative information relayed above.

TABLE 8.2 Philanthropic support for Yes On 1240 connected organizations (Bill & Melinda Gates Foundation, 2013; Foundation Center, 2013; Libby, 2012; New York State Office of the Attorney General, 2013; Stand for Children, 2013; University of Washington Bothell Office of Research, 2013; University of Washington Bothell Office of Sponsored Programs, 2013)

Organization	Amount	Foundation
Center on Reinventing Public Education	$8,578,000	Gates Foundation
	$701,000	Walton Foundation
	$512,813	Broad Foundation
Education Reform Now! (Democrats for Education Reform)	$2,925,000	Walton Foundation
	$2,481,716	Broad Foundation
	$600,000	Doris and Donald Fisher Fund
	$500,000	Corabelle Lumps Foundation
	$15,000	Bezos Family Foundation
League of Education Voters	$4,790,000	Gates Foundation
	$257,000	Lochland Foundation
	$160,139	Bezos Family Foundation
	$1,000	Apex
Partnership for Learning Stand for Children	$4,700,000	Gates Foundation
	$9,000,000	Gates Foundation
	$2,857,945	Walton Foundation
	$350,000	Goldman Sachs Philanthropy Fund
	$120,304	Bezos Family Foundation
	$55,000	Wissner-Slivka Foundation
	$25,000	Lochland Foundation
	$1,000	Apex Foundation

Source: Bill & Melinda Gates Foundation, 2013; Foundation Center, 2013; Libby, 2012; New York State Office of the Attorney General, 2013; Stand for Children, 2013; University of Washington Bothell Office of Research, 2013; University of Washington Bothell Office of Sponsored Programs, 2013

As the focus of our analysis, it isn't surprising that the Yes On 1240 campaign is the most connected or "prestigious" actor in this directed graph. All but one of the arcs represents financial donations, with the arc coming from CRPE representing symbolic support via a formal endorsement and a technical report written in in favor of the initiative. The Gates Foundation is the most central *transmitter*

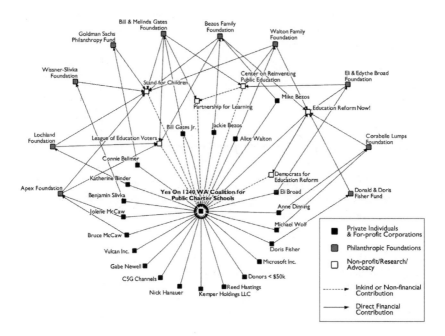

FIGURE 8.1 The Yes On 1240 campaign network

of resources in the graph, funding all of the coordinating organizations except for DFER. It is important for us to note here that the number of connections of an individual node is not necessarily a direct measure of power, nor is their relative centrality within the network. For instance, Bill Gates Jr. is not a central actor in the network and he transmits "only" two arcs. However, he is a powerful actor within this network because he was by far the largest direct donor to the campaign and his wealth is largely responsible for funding the most central acting foundation in the network, the Gates Foundation. In this sense, our representation of the campaign network fails to capture the relative weight of the relationships.

Next to the Gates Foundation, the Bezos Foundation and Walton Foundation are also relatively central to the network around the Yes On 1240 campaign. The Bezos Foundation funds LEV, CRPE, and Stand for Children, and the Walton Foundation, meanwhile, makes similar contributions to CRPE and Stand for Children, along with Education Reform Now!. The remaining foundations are more selective in their support. On the "west" side of the network, the Apex and Lochland foundations each fund LEV and Stand for Children, while the Wissner-Slivka Foundation and the Goldman Sachs Philanthropic Fund only fund Stand for Children. The "east" side of the network is populated by foundations without immediate regional connections. The Corabelle Lumps Foundation and the Donald and Doris Fisher Fund only support Education Reform Now!, whereas the Broad Foundation funds Education Reform Now! and the CRPE.

The "west" and "east" split in the network does show a pattern of support for different organizations relative to the Yes On 1240 campaign. Most of the foundations on the "west" side of the network (Gates, Bezos, Wissner-Slivka, Lochland, and Apex) are local to Washington State, and these foundations funded regionally based non-profit organizations coordinating the Yes On 1240 Campaign. The only apparent exception to this pattern is the Goldman Sachs Philanthropy Fund's donation to Stand for Children, since Goldman Sachs is located in New York. However, Goldman Sachs supports Stand for Children at the direction of Connie and Steve Ballmer (Stand for Children, 2011), both residents of Washington. The "east" side of the network, conversely, is populated by non-local foundations, and save for Stand for Children and CRPE, they mostly fund non-local organizations. The relative social positions of the foundations within the network, then, approximately align to a "local/non-local" geographic differentiation vis-à-vis proximity to the statewide initiative.

Corporate Policy Networks and Democratic Accountability

Elsewhere (Au and Ferrare, 2014) we have analyzed the network of the relationships surrounding the Yes On 1240 campaign in terms of "sponsorship," as an extension of Brandt's (1998) work on "Sponsors of Literacy." For Brandt, sponsors are, "any agents, local or distant, concrete or abstract, who enable, support, teach, model, as well as recruit, regulate, suppress or withhold" access to resources, "and gain advantage by it in some way" (p. 166). We found Brandt's conception of sponsorship particularly powerful for use in critical education policy studies because in Brandt's words, "Although the interests of the sponsor and sponsored do not have to converge (and, in fact, may conflict) sponsors nevertheless set the terms for access . . . and wield powerful incentives for compliance and loyalty"(pp. 166–167). In our previous work (Au and Ferrare, 2014) we identified two specific forms of policy sponsorship at play in the network surrounding the Yes On 1240 campaign: material sponsorship and symbolic sponsorship. Material sponsorship refers to the transmission and flow of material resources to campaigns or ancillary organizations (e.g., research centers and non-profit coalition groups). Material sponsorship also includes direct labor, which in this case includes the coordina-tion of the Yes On 1240 campaign. Symbolic sponsorship, on the other hand, represents the transmission or flow of nonmaterial resources. Such nonmaterial resources can include community representation, individual renown, intellectual prestige, or scientific support used to enhance the symbolic power of a given policy. As our network analysis of Yes On 1240 suggests, although policy sponsorship is the product of labor, the symbolic form does not carry the same weight as material sponsorship because financial resources are the strongest tool initiative campaigns can utilize. This strength of material sponsorship is also a key weakness. Simply put, material sponsors must stand naked and expose their influence and self-interest for the world to see. Symbolic sponsorship, on the other hand, is powerful precisely because of the appearance that it is driven by moral authority of doing the "right thing"—in this case under the guise of improving the outcomes of public education for underserved populations (Au and Ferrare, 2014).

As our network (Figure 8.1) illustrates, wealthy individuals leveraged significant influence on the adoption of charter school policy in Washington State, both directly through contributions to the Yes On 1240 campaign and indirectly through their affiliated philanthropic foundations. In this case the philanthropic foundations acted as a mediator for the material sponsorship of wealthy individuals to make its way to the organizations doing the local material and symbolic work to influence public discourse surrounding policy adoption. In this regard it is critical to point out that sponsorship is never neutral. As Brandt (1998) points out, "In whatever form, sponsors deliver the ideological freight that must be borne for access to what they have" (p. 168). In the case of the Yes On 1240 campaign policy actors, the "ideological freight" they must bear is a commitment to advancing charter school policy. Indeed, recent research suggests that philanthropists directly influence the work of these organizations and "see their investments . . . as a way to realize more promising and effective educational interventions whose 'profit' is understood to be a scaling up of reforms they favor" (Scott and Jabbar, 2014, p. 238).

Yet, whether or not these foundations directly "control" the non-profit and other organizations they fund is, in many ways, of peripheral importance. The fact remains that the non-profits and other organizations are funded by the philanthropies on the grounds that they align with and will follow through with the ideological and policy agendas set out by their funders. Indeed, this is a central tenet of venture philanthropic giving (Scott, 2009). In the end, directly controlled or not, these organizations do the bidding of their funders anyway. Hence, the non-profit organizations involved in the Yes On 1240 campaign are less "grassroots," and instead, as Barkan (2012) explains, are actually "astroturf" organizations funded to create the public image of local, community support:

> When an outside organization hires and pays for staff and vote solicitors and then "donates" their work to a candidate, the work looks like grassroots organizing but isn't. It is "astroturfing"—a term the late U.S. Senator Lloyd Bentsen is believed to have coined in 1985. Astroturfing is political activity designed to appear unsolicited, autonomous, and community-rooted without actually being so.
>
> *(p. 53)*

By furthering the education reform agendas of the philanthropies through their own work in support of I-1240, these pro-charter, non-profit and other organizations fundamentally help wealthy elites and their affiliated foundations legitimate charter schools within public discourse, and work to garner the support for charters from various constituencies within Washington State (Au and Ferrare, 2014).

Given that I-1240 passed and charter schools are now legalized in Washington State, our findings raise concerns about the disproportionate power of super-wealthy individuals and their related philanthropic organizations in shaping public education policy. In the case of the I-1240, it is clear to us that these wealthy individuals wielded tremendous amounts of power well beyond that of the average person in the state of Washington. This is particularly disturbing because the power of these elites extends purely from their wealth and is not based on any expertise in public education reform whatsoever (Bosworth, 2011). As such, the passage of I-1240 in Washington State raises concerns that billionaires and their philanthropies have become what Karier (1972) refers to as a virtual "fourth branch of government" that is able to carry its reform agenda and ideology forward into fully realized education policy through sheer force of material and symbolic sponsorship.

Initiative 1240 is thus, literally, "other people's policy" in that wealthy elites are shaping education policy for other people's children. Bill and Melinda Gates' children, for instance, did not attend public schools. Instead they attended a private, elite college prep school in the Seattle area that is known for its small class sizes, rich curriculum, well-resourced campus, and is free from the confinements of the Common Core Standards and high-stakes, standardized testing (Lakeside School, 2014). In the case of I-1240 we see the combination of vast wealth and strong influence over education policy creating a situation where, as Scott (2009) explains,

> Wealth that comes largely from favorable public policies is now directed into mostly tax-exempt foundations, where trustees and philanthropists directly shape public policy for the poor, without the public deliberative process that might have been invoked over school reform policies were that money in the public coffers.
>
> (p. 128)

Scott's (2009) final point here is of particular importance: Because these wealthy elites and their foundations are completely disconnected from any form of democratic process, they are also completely disconnected from any form of democratic accountability to the public. As Ravitch (2010) points out:

> These foundations, no matter how worthy and high-minded, are after all, not public agencies. They are not subject to public oversight or review, as a public agency would be. . . . If voters don't like the foundations' reform agenda, they can't vote them out of office. The foundations demand that public schools and teachers be held accountable for performance, but they

themselves are accountable to no one. If their plans fail, no sanctions are levied against them. They are bastions of unaccountable power.

(p. 200)

Or, as Bosworth (2011) so eloquently put it, "To paraphrase F. Scott Fitzgerald, today's plutocrats are not like you and I; nor do they resemble the politicians we elect. Even when they assume the authority to set public policies, they are, I fear, not sackable" (p. 386). Speaking about his own reform agenda in September of 2013, Bill Gates Jr. himself admitted that, "It would be great if our education stuff worked, but that we won't know for probably a decade" (Strauss, 2013, n.p.). Given the disproportionate power outlined in our analysis and network (Figure 8.1), we are concerned with the complete lack of a mechanism for public accountability for these wealthy individuals, their affiliated philanthropies, and their agenda for education reform. For instance, should the venture philanthropists' agenda for public education reform fail and even make public education worse, there is no viable way to hold these organizations accountable for that failure.

Conclusion

The clearly disproportionate power wealthy elites demonstrated in the case of the Yes On 1240 campaign in Washington State is just a single case, but this case points to larger power dynamics that are in play. Locally and nationally, charter schools and charter school policy have been offered by proponents as a cure for ameliorating educational inequalities around race and economic class. The problem is that charter proponents, and their well-connected funders, continually make these claims despite all available countervailing evidence. There is a substantial, if contested, research base focusing on charter school effectiveness specifically related to test score achievement. The two largest, most comprehensive national charter school achievement studies found substantial variability in charter performance across multiple states, and found overall that charter schools sometimes outperformed regular public schools, but mostly performed the same or worse than their public school counterparts (CREDO, 2009, 2013). These findings have been generally confirmed in studies across a variety of contexts (e.g., DiCarlo, 2011; Furgeson et al., 2012; Miron, Coryn, and Mackety, 2007). Further, studies of charter school enrollment have raised serious concerns about the high selectivity of which students charter schools allow to enroll ("creaming" higher achievers and/or not accepting students with disabilities and English Language Learners), the number of students expelled, counseled out, or disappeared from their rosters, and increased segregation in charter school populations (see, e.g., Frankenberg, Siegel-Hawley, and Wang, 2013; Miron, Urschel, Mathis, and Tornquist, 2010; Simon, 2013; Welner, 2013). The deregulation associated with charter schools has also brought with it numerous instances of corruption, embezzlement, and scarce financial oversight (Rawls, 2013).

Considered within this larger policy picture, the passing of I-1240 in Washington State is troubling. Not only is there a lack of evidence that charters work consistently to challenge educational inequality, charter school policy in the state of Washington was not created, supported, nor organized by the working class communities of color that proponents claim to be serving in the first place. Given the network of policy actors we have outlined in this chapter, we cannot help but see the irony surrounding the Yes On 1240 campaign. As a policy I-1240 was not passed for the children of the wealthy, predominantly white elites who have used their vast resources to help make charter schools legal in Washington State, but for the children of working-class communities of color in which there was little explicit community or grassroots organizational support for the law. Indeed, given the history of resistance to charter schools in Washington State, I-1240 may not have passed at all without the influence of these elites.

Notes

1   Portions of Chapter 8 appeared in: Au, W. & Ferrare, J. P. (2014). Sponsors of policy: A network analysis of wealthy elites, their affiliated philanthropies, and charter school reform in Washington State. *Teachers College Record, 116*(8). www.tcrecord.org ID Number: 17387.
2   As of the November 6, 2012 election, the Washington State Public Disclosure Commission database listed Paul Allen as a Yes On 1240 contributor of $1.6 million. However, in a May 15, 2013 search of the same database Paul Allen was no longer listed as a donor and his company, Vulcan Inc., was listed instead.
3   The "Stand for Children Annual Report 2010" (Stand for Children, 2011) indicates that Connie and Steve Ballmer donated an amount between $50,000 and $99,999 via the Biel Fund of the Goldman Sachs Philanthropy Fund. This is in agreement with tax records for the Goldman Sachs Philanthropy Fund, which indicate they granted $75,000 to Stand for Children in 2010 (Foundation Center, 2013). Stand for Children also lists Connie and Steve Ballmer as donors at the $100,000–$249,999 level in both 2008 and in 2009 (Stand for Children, 2009, 2010) and at the $50,000–$99,999 level in 2011 (Stand for Children, 2012). However Stand for Children does not list the Goldman Sachs Philanthropy Fund as donating in any of those years despite that the Goldman Sachs Philanthropy Fund tax records show donations to Stand for Children for $100,000 in 2008 and 2009 each, and $75,000 in 2011 (Foundation Center, 2013). Given the discrepancy between the Goldman Sachs Philanthropy Fund tax record and the Stand for Children annual reports, and given the explicit link established between the two via Connie and Steve Ballmer in the Stand for Children 2011 Annual Report, and given that Connie and Steve Ballmer are listed at levels of support that correspond with those donations indicated by Goldman Sachs Philanthropy Fund tax records in years 2008, 2009, and 2011, the evidence suggests that all financial support from the Goldman Sachs Philanthropy Fund given to Stand for Children in the years 2008–2011 was at the direction of Connie and Steve Ballmer.

References

Apple, M. W. (2014). Educating the "right" way: Markets, standards, god, and inequality (third ed.). New York: Routledge.

Apple, M. W., and Pedroni, T. C. (2005). Conservative alliance building and African American support of vouchers: the end of Brown's promise or a new beginning? *Teachers College Record, 107*(9), 2068–2105.

Au, W., and Ferrare, J. J. (2014). Sponsors of policy: A network analysis of wealthy elites, their affiliated philanthropies, and charter school reform in Washington State. *Teachers College Record, 116*(8). Retrieved September 12, 2014 from www.tcrecord.org/content. asp?contentid=17387

Barkan, J. (2011). Got dough?: How billionaires rule our schools. *Dissent, 58*(1), 49–57. doi:10.1353/dss.2011.0023

Barkan, J. (2012). Hired guns on astroturf: How to buy and sell school reform. *Dissent, 59*(2), 49–57.

Bill & Melinda Gates Foundation. (2013). *How we work: Awarded grants.* Retrieved December 9, 2013 from www.gatesfoundation.org/How-We-Work/Quick-Links/ Grants-Database

Bosworth, D. (2011). The cultural contradiction of philanthrocapitalism. *Society, 48*, 382–388. doi:10.1007/s12115–011–9466-z

Brandt, D. (1998). Sponsors of literacy. *College Composition and Communication, 49*(2), 165–185.

Callaghan, P. (2012, July 3). Might be a record: Sponsors of charter schools initiative say they have enough signatures. *Political buzz: Talking WA politics.* Retrieved February 10, 2013 from http://blog.thenewstribune.com/politics/2012/07/03/might-be-a-record-sponsors-of-charter-schools-initiative-say-they-have-enough-signatures/

Corcoran, S. P., and Stoddard, C. (2011). Local demand for a school choice policy: Evidence from the Washington charter school referenda. *Education Finance and Policy, 6*(3), 323–353.

CREDO. (2009). *Multiple choice: Charter school performance in 16 states.* Stanford, CA: Center for Research on Education Outcomes (CREDO). Retrieved December 15, 2009 from http://credo.stanford.edu/reports/MULTIPLE_CHOICE_CREDO.pdf

CREDO. (2013). *National charter school study 2013.* Stanford, CA: Center for Research on Education Outcomes (CREDO). Retrieved November 15, 2013 from http://credo. stanford.edu

Delpit, L. (1995). Other people's children: Cultural conflict in the classroom. New York: The New Press.

DiCarlo, M. (2011). *The evidence on charter schools and test scores.* Washington, D.C.: The Albert Shanker Institute. Retrieved October 10, 2011 from www.shankerblog.org/ wp-content/uploads/2011/12/CharterReview.pdf

Fabricant, M., and Fine, M. (2012). *Charter schools and the corporate makeover of public education.* New York: Teachers College Press.

Foundation Center. (2013). *990 finder.* Retrieved December 11, 2013 from http:// foundationcenter.org/findfunders/990finder/

Frankenberg, E., Siegel-Hawley, G., and Wang, J. (2013). Choice without equity: Charter school segregation. *Educational Policy Analysis Archives, 19*(1). Retrieved November 19, 2013 from http://epaa.asu.edu/ojs/article/view/779

Furgeson, J., Gill, B., Haimson, J., Killewald, A., McCullough, M., Nichols-Barrer, I., Lake, R. (2012). *Charter-school management organizations: Diverse strategies and diverse student impacts.* Mathematica Policy Research; Center for Reinventing Public Education. Retrieved December 3, 2012 from www.mathematica-mpr.com/publications/PDFs/ Education/CMO_Final_updated.pdf

Google. (2013). *Google*. Retrieved from www.google.com

Karier, C. J. (1972). Testing for order and control in the corporate liberal state. *Educational Theory, 22*(Spring), 159–180.

Karp, S. (2013). Charter schools and the future of public education: It's time to refocus public policy on providing excellent public schools for all. Trenton, NJ: New Jersey Education Association. Retrieved March 29, 2013 from www.njea.org/news-and-publications/njea-review/march-2013/charter-schools-and-the-future-of-public-education

Lake, R., Gross, B., and Maas, T. (2012). *Examining charters: How public charter schools can work in Washington state* (p. 23). Seattle, Washington: Partnership For Learning; Center for Reinventing Public Education. Retrieved October 30, 2012 from www.partnership4learning.org/files/ExaminingCharters.pdf

Lakeside School. (2014). *Lakeside School – About Lakeside*. Retrieved July 31, 2014, from www.lakesideschool.org/podium/default.aspx?t=120812

League of Education Voters. (2012). *Staff*. Retrieved November 20, 2012 from www.educationvoters.org/about-2/staff/

Libby, K. (2012). *DFER Watch: About*. Retrieved January 12, 2013 from dferwatch.wordpress.com/about-4/

Miron, G., Coryn, C., and Mackety, D. M. (2007). *Evaluating the impact of charter schools on student achievement: A longitudinal look at the Great Lakes states*. Boulder, CO: Education Policy Research Unit, Division of Educational Leadership and Policy Studies, Arizona State University; Education and the Public Interest Center, School of Education, University of Colorado. Retrieved March 10, 2008 from http://epsl.asu.edu/epru/documents/EPSL-0706–236-EPRU.pdf

Miron, G., Urschel, J. L., Mathis, W. J., and Tornquist, E. (2010). Schools without diversity: Education management organizations, charter schools, and the demographic stratification of the American school system. Boulder, CO and Tempe, AZ: Education and the Public Interest Center and Education Policy Research Unit. Retrieved February 8, 2011 from http://nepc.colorado.edu/files/EMO-Seg.pdf

National Alliance for Public Charter Schools (2013). *The public charter schools dashboard: Schools*. Retrieved Mar 12, 2015 from http://dashboard.publiccharters.org/dashboard/schools/year/2012

New York State Office of the Attorney General. (2013). *Charities nys.com*. Retrieved December 9, 2013 from www.charitiesnys.com/RegistrySearch/show_details.jsp?id={4D9E71F8-0188-4433-9D6C-4892837A401C}

Pedroni, T. C. (2007). *Market movements: African American involvement in school voucher reform*. New York: Routledge.

Ravitch, D. (2010). *The death and life of the great American school system: How testing and choice are undermining education* (e-book.). New York: Basic Books.

Rawls, K. (2013). *Who is profiting from charters?: The big bucks behind charter school secrecy, financial scandal and corruption*. AlterNet. Retrieved May 8, 2013 from www.alternet.org/education/who-profiting-charters-big-bucks-behind-charter-school-secrecy-financial-scandal-and?paging=off

Reckhow, S. (2013). *Follow the money: How foundationa dollars change public school politics*. New York: Oxford University Press.

Reed, S. (2012, November 27). *November 6, 2012 general election results: Initiative measure no. 1240 concerns creation of a public charter school system*. Retrieved November 27, 2012 from http://vote.wa.gov/results/current/Initiative-Measure-No-1240-Concerns-creation-of-a-public-charter-school-system.html

Sa Campos, T. de. (2012). *Initiative measure No. 1240 concerns creation of a public charter school system*. Olympia, Washington. Retrieved November 27, 2012 from http://sos.wa.gov/_assets/elections/initiatives/FinalText_274.pdf

Saltman, K. J. (2010). *The gift of education: Public education and venture philanthropy*. New York: Palgrave Macmillan.

Scott, J. T. (2009). The politics of venture philanthropy in charter school policy and advocacy. *Educational Policy*, *23*(1), 106–136. doi:10.1177/0895904808328531

Scott, J. T., and Jabbar, H. (2014). The hub and the spokes: Foundations, intermediary organizations, incentivist reforms, and the politics of research evidence. *Educational Policy*, *28*(2), 233–257.

Simon, S. (2013). *Special report: Class struggle—how charter schools get the students they want*. Reuters. Retrieved March 12, 2013 from www.reuters.com/article/2013/02/15/us-usa-charters-admissions-idUSBRE91E0HF20130215

Stand for Children. (2009). *Stand for children annual report 2008*. Stand for Children. Retrieved September 13, 2013 from http://stand.org/sites/default/files/National/Documents/STANDFORCHILDREN_ANNUALREPORT_2008.pdf

Stand for Children. (2010). *Stand for children annual report 2009*. Stand for Children. Retrieved September 13, 2013 from http://stand.org/sites/default/files/National/Documents/STANDFORCHILDREN_ANNUALREPORT_2009.pdf

Stand for Children. (2011). *Stand for children annual report 2010*. Stand for Children. Retrieved September 13, 2013 from http://stand.org/sites/default/files/National/Documents/STANDFORCHILDREN_ANNUALREPORT_2010.pdf

Stand for Children. (2012). *Stand for children 2011 annual report*. Stand for Children. Retrieved September 13, 2013 from http://stand.org/sites/default/files/National/Final%20Annual%20Report%20070612.pdf

Stand for Children. (2013). *Annual report and financial statement*. Retrieved September 13, 2013 from http://stand.org/national/about/annual-report-financial-statement

Strauss, V. (2013). Bill Gates: "It would be great if our education stuff worked but . . ." *Washington Post: The Answer Sheet*. Retrieved August 1, 2014, from www.washingtonpost.com/blogs/answer-sheet/wp/2013/09/27/bill-gates-it-would-be-great-if-our-education-stuff-worked-but/

University of Washington Bothell Office of Research. (2013). *Office of research: Current awards*. Retrieved September 13, 2013 from www.uwb.edu/research/reports/current-awards

University of Washington Bothell Office of Sponsored Programs. (2013). *Request for information*. Retrieved September 13, 2013 from www.uwb.edu/research/reports/current-awards

Washington Coalition for Public Charter Schools. (2012a). *Key facts about I-1240: The Washington public charter school initiative*. Retrieved September 8, 2012 from http://yeson1240.com/wp-content/uploads/2012/08/YESon1240_Facts_QA.pdf

Washington Coalition for Public Charter Schools. (2012b). *WA public charter schools initiative now state law*. Retrieved November 20, 2012 from www.wacharters.org/wa-public-charter-schools-initiative-now-state-law/

Washington State Public Disclosure Commission. (2012a). *Washington State Public Disclosure Commission: 40 years of shining light on Washington politics: Cash contributions for Yes On 1240 WA Coalition for Public Charter Schools*. Retrieved February 29, 2013 from www.pdc.wa.gov/MvcQuerySystem/CommitteeData/contributions?param=WUVTIFdDIDUwNw====&year=2012&type=initiative

Washington State Public Disclosure Commission. (2012b). *Washington State Public Disclosure Commission: 40 years of shining light on Washington politics: Expenditures for Yes On 1240 WA Coalition for Public Charter Schools.* Retrieved February 29, 2013 from www.pdc.wa.gov/MvcQuerySystem/CommitteeData/contributions?param=WUVTIFdDID UwNw====&year=2012&type=initiative

Washington State Public Disclosure Commission. (2012c). *Washington State Public Disclosure Commission: 40 years of shining light on Washington politics: Inkind contributions for Yes On 1240 WA Coalition for Public Charter Schools.* Retrieved February 29, 2013 from www.pdc.wa.gov/MvcQuerySystem/CommitteeData/contributions?param=WUVTIFdDID UwNw====&year=2012&type=initiative

Washington State Public Disclosure Commission. (2012d). *Washington State Public Disclosure Commission's "most money" journal.* Olympia, Washington: Washington State Public Disclosure Commission. Retrieved February 29, 2013 from www.pdc.wa.gov/archive/home/historical/pdf/MostMoneyJournal.pdf

Welner, K. G. (2013). The dirty dozen: How charter schools influence student enrollment. *Teachers College Record.* Retrieved February 29, 2013 from www.tcrecord.org/Content.asp?ContentID=17104

Yes on 1240. (2012a). *Voters approve I-1240 to allow the option of public charter schools in Washington.* Retrieved November 12, 2012 from http://yeson1240.com/wp-content/uploads/2012/11/1240_Release_Nov10.pdf

Yes on 1240. (2012b). *Yes On 1240: Prof. Hill.* Retrieved January 30, 2013 from www.youtube.com/watch?v=tGLNzlImRNY

9

GANGSTA RAPS, POWER GAPS, AND NETWORK MAPS

How the Charter School Market Came to New Orleans

Kristen L. Buras

> Listen, homie, it's Dollar Day in New Orleans
> It's water water everywhere and people dead in the streets
> And Mr. President he 'bout that cash
> He got a policy for handlin' the niggaz and trash . . .
>
> *Mos Def (2005) in his rap song "Dollar Day,"*
> *also known as "Katrina Clap"*

The *Washington Post* published an article entitled, "In New Orleans, traditional public schools close for good" (Layton, 2014). It opened with the following declaration:

> With the start of the next school year [in August 2014], the Recovery School District will be the first in the country made up completely of public charter schools, a milestone for New Orleans and a grand experiment in urban education for the nation.
>
> *(para. 3)*

There are at least two fundamental questions that the *Washington Post* failed to consider in any meaningful way. First, how did politics and power shape New Orleans' ascendancy as the nation's first all-charter school district? Second, how has mass charter school reform in New Orleans affected black students, teachers, and communities? This chapter responds to both questions from a critical perspective, accounting for the ways that inequitable racial and political-economic power has shaped education reform in New Orleans, the model city for corporate takeover and privatization of urban public schools. It also draws on a decade of education research in New Orleans that the *Washington Post* ignored (Buras, 2005, 2007, 2009, 2011b, 2012a, 2013, 2015; Buras et al., 2010, 2013).

Unlike the *Washington* Post, which hailed New Orleans as a "grand" experiment, Mos Def's rap was right on the money. August 29, 2005—the day that Hurricane Katrina struck New Orleans—was "Dollar Day" indeed. Education reforms implemented since this time have perpetuated existing power gaps and fostered racial and economic domination by a network of education entrepreneurs and wealthy, white philanthropists. Moreover, they could not have done the "Katrina Clap" without local, state, and federal policymakers as allies. As I reveal in this chapter, it is no small irony to characterize Mos Def's song as *gangsta rap* or black students in New Orleans as *gangstas* in need of discipline and redemption, especially when the actions of education entrepreneurs and policymakers have been nothing short of a hustle, if not a deadly assault on black schools and communities.

In this chapter, I map key facets of the elite network of policy actors that have made New Orleans the nation's first all-charter school district. Along the way, I provide background and analysis on strategic interventions and policies, the flow of resources, and the overall infrastructure required for whites to take over and privatize a black working-class school district in a single decade. Finally, I conclude by discussing some of the gross inequities and injustices that have resulted and join affected communities in warning other cities not to follow the New Orleans model of reform.

After Hurricane Katrina, President George W. Bush flew over New Orleans in a plane to "witness" the destruction. In point of fact, Bush and his coterie initiated a series of destructive reforms that have been expanded ever since. With speed and precision, the city's public schools were taken over by Louisiana's state-run Recovery School District (RSD) and then handed over for management by private charter school operators. Veteran teachers, mostly African American, were terminated *en masse* and replaced by largely white, transient, inexperienced recruits from beyond the city. How did this happen? How did the education market make its way to New Orleans? In what follows, I detail part of the untold story of how "Dollar Day" became a profitable decade and a model for corporate takeover of urban public schools nationwide. However, I first want to probe the history and staying power of images of black criminality and raise questions about *whose* interests are served by such images and whether or not such images mask the criminal nature of white supremacy and corresponding forms of economic domination. This short discussion will underscore that the elite, largely white network of local, state, and national actors charted in this chapter are not innocently engaged in education reform efforts, but rather have undertaken an aggressive campaign of racial and economic warfare. As Mos Def unabashedly notes, those in power are "[a]bout that cash" and they have a policy for handling those they deem to be racially subordinate "trash."

Gangsta Culture and the Politics of Racial Representation

Disparaging depictions of African Americans have a long history and are illustrated by the case of Robert Charles, a black man born in Mississippi who resided in New Orleans during the turn of the twentieth century (see also Buras, 2014). Charles was shot for resisting the aggression of a police officer who assumed he was guilty of criminal behavior by virtue of sitting on a street corner one evening. When the officer drew his gun, Charles drew his. Both were shot and Charles fled, setting in motion the largest manhunt in New Orleans history. White newspapers described Charles as "an unreasoning brute," "cocaine fiend," "worthless, crapshooting negro," and "ruthless black butcher" (Hair, 2008, p. 2). In a piece titled "The Making of a Monster," one reporter pondered: "It is only natural that the deepest interest should attach to the personality of Robert Charles. What manner of a man was this fiend incarnate?" (in Wells-Barnett, 1900/2005, p. 45). The question of Charles' innocence was never considered by whites. They presumed he was a "fiend" because he was black.

When police received word that Charles might be hiding at a house on Saratoga Street, a crowd of whites swelled to 20,000 within days. At least 5,000 bullet holes penetrated the house. Charles defended himself to the end, but the house was set on fire and he was shot upon fleeing. For the white mob, his death was not enough. Repulsively violent behavior ensued:

> Men ran up and dragged the body from the doorway into the muddy street. More shots were pumped into the corpse . . . Those who possessed no guns cursed at or kicked the corpse, which soon became indistinguishable from the trodden mud of Saratoga Street . . . Shouts of "burn him burn him!" began to grow louder . . . When Charles's body [was thrown] on the [police] wagon it fell in such a position that the mutilated head hung over the end. As soon as the wagon wheels began to turn, hundreds ran after the vehicle.
> *(Hair, 2008, pp. 174–175)*

An autopsy later revealed 34 bullet holes in the torso, numerous arm and leg wounds, a skull "almost beaten to a pulp," and the penis shot (p. 180). Was Charles the fiend incarnate? Or did white supremacists epitomize a violent culture that had the force of law? As I soon demonstrate, such questions are relevant to understanding the current dynamics of education reform in New Orleans.

In the 1960s, white commentators were concerned about what they called the *culture of poverty* (Buras, 2008). Edward Banfield, for example, published *The Unheavenly City: The Nature and Future of Our Urban Crisis* (1968). Banfield directed his concerns to class culture (which he used as a proxy for race). "A slum is not simply a district of low-quality housing," contended Banfield, but rather a place where "the style of life is squalid and vicious" (p. 45). Banfield (1968) described the lower-class individual in this way:

His bodily needs (especially for sex) and his taste for "action" take precedence over everything else—and certainly over any work routine. He works only as he must to stay alive, and drifts from one unskilled job to another . . .

He feels no attachment to community, neighbors, or friends, [and] resents all authority (for example, that of policemen, social workers, teachers, landlords, employers) . . .

In managing the children, the mother . . . is characteristically impulsive: once they have passed babyhood they are likely to be neglected or abused . . .

The stress on "action," risk-taking . . . [and] fighting . . . makes lower-class life extraordinarily violent.

(pp. 53–54)

The culture of poverty has remained a common point of reference in explaining race and class inequities. In *Sweating the Small Stuff: Inner-City Youth and the New Paternalism*, written by David Whitman (2008) for the conservative Thomas B. Fordham Institute, Chester Finn announces in his introduction that "a healthy, forceful, modern version of paternalism" is what African American and Latino/a students need. According to him, schools that exhibit such paternalism are "preoccupied with fighting disorder." More to the point, "students are shown exactly how they are expected to behave . . . Their behavior is monitored closely at all times" (p. x). This provides them with a "way out of socio-cultural cul-de-sacs" and helps to "change their lifestyles for the better" (p. xiii). Perhaps not surprisingly, Whitman (2008) applauds the Knowledge Is Power Program (KIPP), a national charter school network, for its rigid disciplinary structure and alleged benefits for children of color. This, too, is relevant to understanding the racial and cultural politics of reform in New Orleans.

Notably and pertinent to the upcoming discussion, little is said about the violence of white supremacy, the foundation for savage depictions of black people. During the period that Charles resided in New Orleans, for instance, living conditions for blacks were reprehensible:

The problem of most blacks in the city was simply survival. With few exceptions their work was the lowest paying, their housing the flimsiest, their mortality rate the highest, their treatment by police the harshest, their education the most neglected, and public services for their residential areas the most inadequate.

(Hair, 2008, p. 72)

This was not by chance. Whites created and sustained these conditions through slavery and subsequent legal segregation. Mob rule, rather than appearing gangsta, was considered to be a stabilizing force. Leonardo (2009) challenges the "innocence" of whiteness and exposes the history of terror by whites against communities of color. Charter school reform in New Orleans and the network of actors behind such reform are certainly a part of this history. Policymakers and reformers gathered in the wake of Katrina like a cabal ready to take back "their" city.

Federal, State, and Local Aggressions in New Orleans

Within days of the hurricane's strike on August 29, 2005, the conservative Heritage Foundation had begun issuing reports on "solutions for rebuilding lives and communities" on the Gulf Coast. In a report on September 12, it warned against Congress taking any steps that would "cause dollars to be used inefficiently" (Meese, Butler, and Holmes, 2005, p. 1). Infused with the language of entrepreneurialism and markets, the Heritage Foundation offered the following guidelines for education:

> New approaches to public policy issues such as enhanced choice in public school education should be the norm ... The critical need now is to encourage investors and entrepreneurs to seek new opportunities within these cities ... The key is to encourage private-sector creativity—for example, by declaring New Orleans and other severely damaged areas "Opportunity Zones."
>
> *(Meese et al., 2005, p. 1)*

Hence was the start of Dollar Day. Marketeers conceived of the Gulf Coast, particularly the city of New Orleans, as an experimental site for deregulation, so-called innovation, and private entrepreneurial investment. *As soon as the wheels began to turn, hundreds ran after the wagon*: this gravy train ultimately depended on the battering of black communities.

Three days after the Heritage Foundation report was issued, President Bush (2005) delivered a national address from Jackson Square and urged that rebuilding efforts address "deep, persistent poverty in the region," a condition that "has roots in a history of racial discrimination" (para. 17). His answer: Congress should create a Gulf Opportunity Zone in Louisiana, Mississippi, and Alabama where the government "will take the side of entrepreneurs as they lead the economic revival of the Gulf Region" (para. 20). The very next day, Heritage followed up with "how to turn the president's Gulf Coast pledge into reality," stressing that "Congress should use existing federal charter school funding to encourage the development of charter schools" (Butler et al., 2005, para. 24). Such political-economic reconstruction of southern space, or regional zoning, was a federal mandate for state leaders—one soon to be bolstered by political pressure and strategic funding (see also Buras, 2015). This would not remedy the history of racial inequity, but instead advance such wrongdoing (Buras, 2007; DeVore and Logsdon, 1991).

State leaders in Louisiana made certain of this. In November 2005, Louisiana governor Kathleen Blanco called a special legislative session in Baton Rouge. This legislative session was the occasion for passing Act 35, which redefined what constituted a "failing" school so that most of the New Orleans public schools could be deemed failing and placed in a state-run Recovery School District (RSD).[1] Act 35 enabled 107 of the 128 schools to be folded into the RSD, whereas only 13 schools could have been assumed before the legislation was passed (UTNO et al., 2006). More specifically, through Act 35, the denotation of failure was shifted upward, with the School Performance Score (SPS) cut point moved from 60 to 87.4, just below the state average. A representative from the Louisiana Federation of Teachers, who was present during the passage of Act 35, reflected:

> The definitions are as we define them and the process is not driven by any kind of real data. It's driven by the powers, and the powers now had a very clear charge. And the charge was these schools are going to be taken over and they're going to be reformed, and they're going to be sold out, they're going to be chartered.
>
> *(Buras interview, 2009)*

Around this same period in 2005, Blanco signed Executive Orders 58 and 79 suspending certain provisions of charter school law, such as the need to consult and obtain the votes of affected faculty, staff, and parents before converting an existing public school into a charter school (LFT, 2005; LFT and AFT, 2007). Such decrees were executed with speed, precision, and scope that are terrifying. And disenfranchisement was not a by-product—it was a goal. While poor and working-class African American communities remained displaced and their neighborhoods completely destroyed (with "water everywhere and people dead in the streets"), public schools were abruptly taken over by charter school operators. Unfortunately, this exercise of raw power has been a central dynamic in New Orleans. In fact, "laws" have been capriciously manipulated to foster such dispossession (Crenshaw et al., 1995; Harvey, 2006).

The circuit of power was not limited to Washington, DC and Baton Rouge. It is equally essential to understand the roles of local government and education entrepreneurs in advancing racial-economic dispossession and the ways that national policy actors supported so-called reform initiatives on the ground in New Orleans. In October 2005, Mayor Ray Nagin established the Bring New Orleans Back Commission (BNOB). BNOB's leaders largely consisted of white business elites (Buras, 2005). For example, among the appointees was James Reiss, a shipping and real estate mogul and chair of New Orleans Business Council, who declared, "Those who want to see this city rebuilt want to see it done in a completely different way: demographically, politically, and economically" (Cooper, 2005, p. A1). In essence, whites conceived the rebuilding of New Orleans as a form of turf warfare—they were going to take back "their" city, which allegedly had been overrun by poor, uneducated, criminally disposed blacks.

A range of subcommittees were constituted under BNOB, among them city planning, economic development, culture, and education, and each was tasked with formulating a component of the larger plan. Headed by Tulane University president Scott Cowen, BNOB's education committee issued its vision in January 2006: an all-charter school district. Using an educational network model, providers would operate groups of charter schools coordinated by managers, and principals would be given oversight on budgets, hiring, and firing (BNOB, 2006). Many on the education committee agreed that free-market schooling was the way forward and consulted "top education experts" such as Wendy Kopp, founder of Teach For America, a business that profitably replaces veteran teachers with new recruits; Mike Feinberg, founder of the well-endowed KIPP charter school network; and Sarah Usdin, founding partner of The New Teacher Project and soon-to-form New Schools for New Orleans, a charter school incubator. Moreover, the education committee consulted the Gates Foundation, Broad Foundation, and Annenberg Institute—groups that would later support the materialization of BNOB's vision politically or financially (BNOB, 2006).

During this same period, it was announced that more than 7,000 New Orleans teachers and school employees would be fired and lose health insurance, enabling the recruitment of new "human capital" to the city (UTNO, LFT, and AFT, 2007). Veteran teachers, most of them black, were terminated *en masse* without due process and without any regard for either their contributions as educators or their hard-won rights and entitlements. When the New Orleans Public School system was dissolved and reorganized as a mere shadow of itself, and the state-run RSD was installed, those who had worked for 20 to 30 years effectively lost all protections and entitlements guaranteed by United Teachers of New Orleans' collective bargaining agreement.

As BNOB's plans were being issued, the federal government had already begun providing millions of dollars for the establishment of charter schools in New Orleans (UTNO, LFT, and AFT, 2006). Indeed, the actions of federal, state, and local government created an opportunistic space into which education entrepreneurs quickly stepped. In fact, the role of nongovernmental policy actors and education entrepreneurs in pillaging the city's schools was fundamental, including an entrepreneurial university and an array of locally situated, but nationally funded, charter school and human capital recruitment businesses—all of which aimed to advance what was portrayed as an innovative experiment in reengineering public education for the betterment of black children. Nothing could be further from the truth.

Entrepreneurial Gangbanging

In its report, BNOB's education committee suggested the need to transform itself into an "Implementation Oversight Committee" (BNOB, 2006, p. 36). Enter the Cowen Institute for Public Education Initiatives at Tulane University—an elite white institution—which provides shelter for a host of charter school and human capital development organizations in New Orleans. The Cowen Institute opened its doors in March 2007, fashioning itself as an "action-oriented think tank that informs and advances solutions—through policies, programs, and partnerships—to eliminate the challenges impeding the success of K-12 education" (e.g., see Cowen Institute, 2010, p. i). As one Cowen representative explained, education reformers recognized that Tulane could "move something along," particularly since it is "the largest employer in the city—we have more political capital in the state and DC than any other entity." The need was all the more pressing as "new [education] non-profits were arising." It was envisaged that Tulane could be a "convener of all of these" (Buras interview, 2009). In short, Cowen and its entrepreneurial associates would organize themselves like a gang wielding substantive power over education reform. Significantly, they had little *street cred* [credibility] with the black community they sought to "help" (see also Buras, 2015; Buras et al., 2013).

The Cowen Institute provides free room and board to some of the most aggressive charter school and human capital "heavies" in the city, including: New Schools for New Orleans (NSNO), a charter school start-up operation; New Leaders for New Schools (NLNS), a recruitment project for principals and charter school board members who seize control of the schools; and teachNOLA, an alternative teacher recruitment initiative consisting of the RSD and edu-businesses such as The New Teacher Project (TNTP) and Teach For America (TFA) (Buras, 2011b).

The strategy of NSNO is fivefold: it seeks founders to *start* charter schools, principals to *lead* charter schools, teachers to *teach* in charter schools, members to *serve* on charter school boards, and investors and philanthropists to *contribute* to these efforts (see NSNO 2008a, 2008b, 2008c). For example, its Incubation Program provides "resources to new school founders in the year before opening" and announces, "If you are an experienced, dynamic, entrepreneurial educator . . . then this is your chance" (NSNO, n.d., p. 7). From 2007 to 2010, the organization launched ten charter schools, seeded three local charter management organizations, and provided twenty-one start-up grants that have supported over 90 percent of newly approved charter schools (NSNO, 2010b).

NSNO has partnered with the national organization New Leaders for New Schools (NLNS) to recruit, train, and place principals and other school leaders in the public schools of New Orleans. "In schools, just as with businesses, strong leadership breeds results," reads its literature (NSNO, 2008a, para 1). NSNO (2010b) boasts the training of 36 charter school boards for over 90 percent of charter schools in the city by 2010. To facilitate this effort, NLNS maintains a Board Bank that includes the names and résumés of parties wishing to serve on charter school boards. The qualifications that NLNS expects from Board Bank members reveal the raced and classed dimensions of charter school take-over, including expertise in law, real estate, financial management, governance, marketing, fundraising, community outreach, education, or strategic planning (NSNO, 2010a). In this way, forms of capital closely linked to class and race status enable unelected charter school board members, most of them white, to exercise disproportionate power over public schools attended by black students. That's gangsta, without a doubt.

An additional "human capital" operation is teachNOLA, a teacher recruitment project with the state-run RSD and businesses such as TNTP, which "works with clients on a fee-for-service basis" to place "alternate route teachers" in "high-need schools" (TNTP, 2010). TNTP won the Social Capitalist Award in 2008 from *Fast Company* magazine (TNTP, 2007). Building on this ethos, teachNOLA claims to have "eliminated the city's teaching shortage so that there can now be an increased focus on long-term quality" (NSNO, 2010b). Skirting the fact that the shortage was engineered through state policy and the mass firing of black veteran teachers, teachNOLA placed new teachers in 96 percent of the city's charter schools from 2007–2010 (NSNO, 2010b). Most of the alternatively recruited teachers are white, inexperienced, and replace more experienced and more expensive veteran educators who are indigenous to the community and unionized (Buras, 2015; UTNO et al., 2007; UTNO, 2010). As I will discuss, veteran teachers' mass firing was ruled unlawful by the court. These actions were gangsta as well.

In sum, the charter school movement in New Orleans is closely bound to the protection of white racial and economic power, as the clearest beneficiaries are upper-class white (and a few black) entrepreneurs who seek to capitalize on public schools for their own advancement while dispossessing the very communities the schools are supposed to serve. While charter school advocates frequently refer to "fraud" that predated current reforms, there is much less talk about the fraudulent manner in which the schools were taken over or the ways in which their charterization enables the channeling of public monies into private hands through "legal" means.

A Closer Look at Mob Rule in New Orleans

Although I cannot chart it comprehensively in this chapter, I want to provide a map of the elite policy network that has shaped human capital and charter school development in New Orleans, with NSNO playing a central role.[2] Analysis of network relationships is revealing and a visual map (Figure 9.1) is provided to assist in following the complex interactions discussed. In referencing the map alongside the text, the local, state, and national connections among seemingly disparate actors are rendered clear. This understanding is essential: too often, when takeover by charter school operators is experienced locally, communities are not fully cognizant of the wider infrastructure behind the assault. Different shapes on the map indicate whether or not an actor's scale of operation is primarily at the local, state, or national level. Arrows, in turn, represent relationships, patterns of

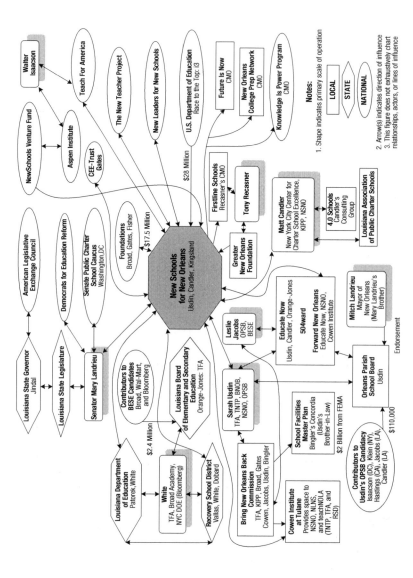

FIGURE 9.1 Policy ecology of New Schools for New Orleans

influence, the flow of human and financial resources, and the ways in which actors sometimes work and move among multiple nodes in the network. Although it is difficult, even impossible, to fully represent this evolving network, the map at least partly reveals the scope and mechanics of the exercise of power. It is a visual narrative of how the charter school market came to New Orleans.

NSNO's founder Sarah Usdin began her work in education in 1992 as a fifth-grade teacher in East Baton Rouge, Louisiana, where she taught for three years through TFA. From 1995–2000, she served as TFA's executive director in Louisiana, and from 2000–2005 she acted as founding partner for TNTP (Usdin, 2012). TFA and TNTP have played a crucial role in promoting alternative teacher recruitment, while demonizing veteran teachers and teachers unions for urban school failure.

Just six months after the storm, Usdin founded NSNO. NSNO initially received $500,000 in seed money from the Greater New Orleans Foundation, which connects philanthropic donors with local organizations (Childress, Bensen, and Tudryn, 2010, p. 386). Anthony Recasner, a member of the foundation's board, would receive support from NSNO for charter schools he cofounded and operated through the CMO Firstline Schools, illustrating a tight-knit circuit of power (Greater New Orleans Foundation, 2012; NSNO, 2012a). As Usdin's preexisting affiliations suggest, NSNO's founding and funding were not an accident, but were made possible by her and others' involvement in an elite policy network that stretches far beyond New Orleans.

Within weeks of the storm, Usdin rode in a National Guard helicopter alongside Walter Isaacson—native New Orleanian, president of the Aspen Institute (a think tank in Washington, DC), and chair of TFA's board at the time—to survey the city's destruction (Isaacson, 2007). Not only would the Aspen Institute become a hub for actors in a wider policy network supporting NSNO, but related philanthropies would provide financial resources. Isaacson (2007) explains:

> [Usdin's] work was supported by the NewSchools Venture Fund, a philanthropic investment fund started by two venture capitalists and Kim Smith, who launched it as her project when she had a fellowship at the Aspen Institute . . . For the past three summers, fund members have convened a meeting in Aspen of educational entrepreneurs, and at the July 2006 gathering, they decided to make New Orleans a focus of their involvement.
>
> *(para. 5)*

NSNO received funding from NewSchools Venture Fund as well as the attention, human resources, and capital of education entrepreneurs throughout this policy network. Isaacson continues: "The attendees decided that they needed a 'harbor master' in New Orleans, someone who could coordinate the various organizations, funders and school operators. So one of the group, Matt Candler, was recruited to become [Usdin's] chief executive officer at [NSNO]" (para. 6).

To understand the interpenetration of local, state, and national networks, consider Candler for a moment. Prior to becoming NSNO's CEO, Candler worked for the New York City Center for Charter School Excellence and acted even earlier as vice president of school development for KIPP, which would develop a network of schools in New Orleans—many of which received funding from NSNO (Childress et al., 2010). Within several years, Candler would develop his own consulting group in New Orleans called 4.0 Schools (2012), and also serve as chair of the Louisiana Association of Public Charter Schools, which NSNO says has been "instrumental in eliminating the charter cap, maintaining supportive finance laws, and generally protecting charter autonomy" (Brinson et al., 2012, p. 22).

By December 2007, Usdin and staff "fielded countless congratulatory phone calls from education reform leaders around the country" (Childress et al., 2010, p. 384). The Eli and Edythe Broad, Bill and Melinda Gates, and Doris and Donald Fisher Foundations had awarded $17.5 million jointly to NSNO, TFA, and NLNS to collaborate in recruiting new teachers and principals and opening new charter schools in New Orleans (Maxwell, 2007). These national foundations—all created and financed by wealthy venture capitalists—clearly grasped that New Orleans was a malleable and opportune place for implementing the market-based visions of education that have guided their investments.

Much of NSNO's early funding was based on its 2008 operational plan. This included building relationships with the Louisiana State Legislature, Louisiana Department of Education, Louisiana Board of Elementary and Secondary Education (BESE), and the state-run RSD (Childress et al., 2010). A few illustrations will demonstrate how state officials have embraced charter school reform to NSNO's benefit (see also Buras 2011b, 2012a).

Louisiana Senator Mary Landrieu and her colleagues have played a major role in providing the legislative infrastructure necessary for the proliferation of charter schools in New Orleans. In the wake of Katrina, Landrieu became a darling of Democrats for Education Reform (2010), a political action committee with a market-based agenda nearly indistinguishable from Republicans. She also organized a forum in Washington, DC around NSNO's *Guide for Cities* (Brinson et al., 2012), a report advocating the New Orleans model nationally. John White, former RSD superintendent and now state superintendent of education in Louisiana, has been a big supporter of charter school expansion. White is a former TFA teacher and a graduate of the Broad Superintendents Academy, and was deputy chancellor for the New York City Department of Education under Michael Bloomberg, who closed public schools and replaced them with charters (Cunningham-Cook, 2012; Simon, 2012). Much like NSNO's ascendancy in New Orleans, White's climb up Louisiana's political ladder was not by chance. A number of now familiar billionaires, such as Eli Broad, Wal-Mart heiress Carrie Walton Penner, and Michael Bloomberg, contributed $2.4 million to support the campaigns of market-oriented candidates to BESE. By comparison, teacher union-endorsed candidates had only $200,000. BESE must approve the governor's nominee for state superintendent of education and the state superintendent plays a role in deciding which charter schools can operate in Louisiana (Cunningham-Cook, 2012). Ensuring White's approval by a like-minded state education board was essential. Not surprisingly, Paul Pastorek, the state superintendent previous to White, was appointed to the board of the Broad Center for the Management of School Systems (Broad Foundation, 2012).

One of the above BESE candidates, Kira Orange Jones, is executive director of TFA for Louisiana—the position that Usdin once held—and was bankrolled during her campaign with $472,000 compared to a meager $14,000 by the teacher union-endorsed candidate (Cunningham-Cook, 2012). An ethics investigation surrounding Orange Jones' seat on BESE revolved around potential conflict of interest, since she simultaneously heads TFA in Louisiana and sits on a state board responsible for approving million-dollar contracts with TFA (Adelson, 2012).

Louisiana Governor Bobby Jindal is also a part of this policy network. Jindal advocated and signed anti-teacher union, pro-charter school legislation that is some of the most radical in the nation (Barrow, 2012a, 2012b), creating a hospitable operating environment for NSNO. Jindal received an award from the American Legislative Exchange Council (ALEC), a corporate front group that drafts model legislation for states. ALEC, which met in New Orleans in 2011, has had a startling influence on Louisiana's legislation (Center for Media and Democracy, 2012; Pocan, 2011; Underwood and Mead, 2012).

Perhaps most revealing was the membership of the BNOB education committee, which included not only Tulane's president Scott Cowen but also Leslie Jacobs, a wealthy New Orleans business woman whose role in charter school advocacy cannot be overstated (see below) (BNOB, 2006). While the Cowen Institute provides free room and board to NSNO, NLNS, and teachNOLA, Landrieu's former legislative aide worked for its public policy arm (Buras interview, 2009). Landrieu's brother, Mitch Landrieu, is mayor of New Orleans and endorsed Usdin during her school board campaign, to be discussed shortly (Vanacore, 2012a). Meanwhile, Usdin's brother-in-law, Steven Bingler, owner of Concordia architects, sat on BNOB's stakeholder advisory committee (BNOB, 2006). Concordia later emerged as one of only two consulting firms that helped develop New Orleans' School Facilities Master Plan (RSD, 2007; RSD & NOPS, 2008). It determined which schools would remain open, be closed, or be rebuilt. Ultimately, the plan was backed by $2 billion (billion, not million) from the Federal Emergency Management Agency (FEMA), a settlement partly negotiated by Landrieu (Chang, 2010a). The Usdin–Bingler connection is important because most charter schools in New Orleans are given free access to facilities, which Bingler had a hand in shuddering, renovating, or building and Usdin in filling with charter operators.

Jacobs is a case study of policy networking. While an insurance executive and member of the Orleans Parish School Board, she sold insurance to the school district. She also sat on BESE and had a hand in shaping legislation that created the RSD. Since 2005, Jacobs has used her political influence to push charter schools and alternative teacher recruitment (New Orleans Independent Media Center, 2009). She developed *Educate Now* (2012), an advocacy group focused on market-based education reform in New Orleans. Its advisory board includes Usdin, Candler, and Orange Jones as well as associates from the Cowen Institute. Jacobs likewise founded *504ward* (504 is New Orleans' area code). 504ward (2012) provides social networking opportunities for "new talent" in the city, with the goal of retaining young entrepreneurial newcomers. They are not the "gang" typically depicted—white, well educated, and upwardly mobile—but they have come in throngs, committing a host of offenses in the city's charter schools.

Usdin stepped down as NSNO's CEO in order to run for a seat on Orleans Parish School Board in November 2012 (Vanacore, 2012b). A group calling itself *Forward New Orleans for Public Schools*, which has Jacobs' imprint, asked candidates in the election to sign on to its guiding principles (Forward New Orleans, 2012). There is growing recognition by education entrepreneurs that the state-run RSD will need to return schools to governance by the locally elected Orleans Parish School Board, and thus a board guided by principles of charter school autonomy and development is priority one. Organizations affiliated with Forward New Orleans include NSNO, Educate Now, and Cowen Institute, among others (Forward New Orleans, 2012).

The financing of Usdin's race for school board in November 2012 reflected network relationships. Usdin raised $110,000, an amount unheard of in local school board campaigns (Vanacore, 2012b). Campaign finance reports from the state reveal noteworthy contributors, including Candler, Jacobs and her husband, and Jacobs' brother Stephen Rosenthal, who is chair of NSNO's board; Isaacson; former New York City schools chancellor Joel Klein; and Reed Hastings of Netflix, who co-founded Rocketship Education, a national CMO that relies heavily on computer-based instruction (Louisiana Ethics Administration Program, 2012). By comparison, Karran Harper Royal, a black public school parent and community-based education activist running for school board, registered $5,500 (Vanacore, 2012b). The local paper writes, "The list of contributors for Usdin stands as another testament to the national spotlight that has shined on New Orleans since the city began its controversial experiment with a system of autonomous charter schools" (Vanacore, 2012b, para. 6).

Aside from venture philanthropies, NSNO's other major funding stream is the federal Investing in Innovation program (i3), a component of the Obama Administration's Race to the Top. In 2010, NSNO received a $28 million grant to turn around schools in New Orleans and to extend its work to Memphis and Nashville; this was topped by $5.6 million in private funds, totaling $33.6 million (Brinson et al., 2012; Chang, 2010b). In part, the collaboration with Memphis and Nashville follows from Landrieu's affiliation with Senator Lamar Alexander from Tennessee, who co-chairs the Senate Public Charter School Caucus with her. In addition, NSNO has reached out to education entrepreneurs and policymakers in Denver, Detroit, Indianapolis, Seattle, and elsewhere, and participated on a panel in New Orleans for the Council of Chief State School Officers, which includes state and district superintendents from across the nation (NSNO, 2012b).

NSNO is a member of Cities for Education Entrepreneurship Trust (CEE-Trust), an undertaking to create the "ecosystem" necessary for charter school incubation and related reforms (Gray, Ableidinder, and Barrett, 2012). CEE-Trust is funded by the Gates Foundation, and policy partners include Mind Trust (CEE-Trust's founder), Center on Reinventing Public Education, and Fordham Institute—think tanks that have authored reports on New Orleans as a national model (e.g., see Hill and Hannaway, 2006; Hill et al., 2009; Meese et al., 2005; Mind Trust, 2011; Smith, 2012; for a response to Smith, see Buras, 2012b). The city's charter school enterprise is a vast scheme with a large and powerful network behind it.

Criminal Dispossession in New Orleans—One Decade Later

The results of network activity have been disastrous. I want to offer some illustrations of the effects as a way of countering the claim that New Orleans represents a model of urban school reform to be replicated nationally and to undercut the glowing depiction of education entrepreneurs and their allies as beneficent. Not only was the takeover anti-democratic, but would-be thugs continue to advance "reform" in the midst of legal and grassroots opposition.

Wrongful Termination of Veteran Teachers

On May 23, 2011, a class action lawsuit was initiated in the Civil District Court for Orleans Parish. In *Eddy Oliver et al. vs. Orleans Parish School Board et al.*, 7,000 tenured, certified teachers and school employees asserted they had been illegally fired, with teachers' due process and property rights violated by OPSB, Louisiana Department of Education (LDOE), BESE, and the RSD. Based on hundreds of documents and depositions, in fact, teachers claimed that local and state education officials "conspired to and committed wrongful conduct that included the wrongful termination of tenured employees and intentional interference with [their] employment contracts and/or property rights" (New Orleans Public School Employees Justice [NOPSE Justice], 2010). According to teachers, officials had not only enacted legislation to void property rights inhering in employment, but used the storm "as a once-in-a-lifetime opportunity to carry out an old political agenda to abolish the New Orleans Public School System . . . and replace it with quasi-private Charter Schools using public funds" (NOPSE Justice, 2007). A ruling in favor of teachers was issued by Judge Ethel Julien on June 20, 2012 (Civil District Court, 2012).[3]

Court findings in *Oliver* provide a disturbing account of the strategic racial-spatial reconstruction of the city's public schools by white leadership in Louisiana. For example, the court found the following:

- The LDOE and OPSB asserted that there was a shortage of teachers to hire. By October 2005, however, education officials had located nearly all OPSB employees, including thousands of certified teachers who had provided updated contact information and intent to return forms. Rather than hiring these teachers, the LDOE advertised nationwide for teacher positions with the RSD.
- Although there were thousands of certified, experienced OPSB teachers, the state approved a contract with TFA through BESE on April 20, 2006.
- Although the LDOE received over $500 million from the U.S. Department of Education based on the representation that it needed to pay the salaries and benefits of out-of-work school employees, it did not ensure that any of this money was used in such a manner. Rather, the money was diverted to the RSD and used in part to offer signing bonuses and housing allowances to teachers recruited from out-of-state.
  (Civil District Court, 2012, pp. 20–22)

Veteran teachers were fired illegally. It should be mentioned as well that these teachers constituted a substantial portion of New Orleans' black middle class. This fact cannot be considered apart from the rapacious campaign that ensued in 2006 through the efforts of policymakers and entrepreneurs, and that continues into the present.

Federal Civil Rights Violations Against Disabled Students

Charter schools in the RSD have had significantly fewer special education students than state-run public schools in the RSD, 8 and 13 percent, respectively (Cowen, 2011, p. 7). Cities adopting the New Orleans model are encouraged to do some of the following by NSNO:

- Allow charters to develop specialized programs for certain disabilities so that parents have choices that include programs tailored to their children's needs, and so that economies of scale can be captured in program delivery; and

- Create risk pools that individual schools can participate in to cover the potential costs of serving students with high needs.

(Brinson et al., 2012, p. 37)

The notion that each charter school should develop a specialized program for certain disabilities sounds like segregation. This defies the principal of main-streaming in the Individual with Disabilities Education Act (IDEA) and sets charter schools down a path of potentially violating federal law. Moreover, there is the distinct impression that such suggestions address charter schools' concerns about the financial costs of serving special education students, rather than concerns directly associated with students' right to learn. Special education appears as an afterthought or a matter of cost containment for charter schools.

In October 2010, a federal civil rights lawsuit (*P.B. et al. v. Pastorek*) documenting violations of IDEA in more than 30 schools in the RSD was filed by the Southern Poverty Law Center (2010a). This class action lawsuit represents some 4,500 students with disabilities who assert that they were denied appropriate services and/or access to public schools in New Orleans, the majority of them charters. In one case, for example, an eight-year-old student who is blind and developmentally delayed applied to eight different charter schools. Five said they would take the application but could not accommodate him; a sixth said it would accept him but was stretched thin; and a seventh said it had a solid program but access was not guaranteed due to a selective application process. The eighth school, which he attended, "had no services, materials, or support staff to help him" (Southern Poverty Law Center, 2010b). The lawsuit is ongoing, but the evidence appears compelling (Dreilinger, 2013; Southern Poverty Law Center, 2013).[4] This is concerning, especially when reformers legitimize their efforts by claiming to serve those students most in need, even as they are excluded.

Questionable Use of Federal Monies by Charter School Operators

The monies flowing through the policy network are substantial and the priorities set for using financial resources, some of which come from federal tax dollars, have been questioned.

In New Orleans, federal i3 monies have been allocated to pay six-figure salaries to CMO administrators (Harden, 2013; see also Thevenot, 2009). While NSNO and affiliated charter school operators fashion themselves as more efficient and accountable than former public school bureaucrats, their use of resources appears self-serving, if not worse. Harden (2013) reports on John McDonogh Senior High School, which was taken over by the CMO Future Is Now:

Despite being the recipient of an $800,000 federal grant, John McDonogh Senior High School [in New Orleans] is having serious money problems

... Future Is Now (FIN), the charter management organization (CMO) running the school, sent an email to board members expressing concern that without additional funding, they would not be able to make payroll ... FIN CEO Steve Barr announced a possible 20 percent salary cut across the board. And he said they may lose one of their principals. Principal Marvin Thompson makes an annual salary of $150,000. Angela Kinlaw was hired ... as the principal of the school's incoming freshman class with a salary of $115,000. Barr makes $250,000 ... The grant is part of the $28 million in federal funds awarded in 2010 to New Schools for New Orleans (NSNO), the Recovery School District, and the Achievement School District in Tennessee. John McDonogh was one of the recipients chosen by NSNO. Most of the grant money in New Orleans has been spent and is being spent on salaries and benefits—and not for teachers, but ... for upper management.

(p. 1)

In sum, around 55 percent of the grant monies from NSNO were designated for FIN salaries and benefits. In addition to the administrators already mentioned, grant monies paid 45 percent of the following FIN salaries: $130,000 for the director of community outreach; $150,000 for the president; $150,000 for the chief financial officer; and $135,000 for the director of policy development (Harden, 2013). Only $250,000 of the grant was allocated for a summer program attended by McDonogh students. In this case, 45 teachers were paid for five 40-hour weeks, three spent on preparation. The remaining two weeks included a morning program for 280 students and afternoon planning time for teachers (Harden, 2013). On the whole, monies were not used to support students. Not surprisingly, in 2012–2013, McDonogh's School Performance Score was 9 on a scale of 150.

Other CMOs in New Orleans have spent federal i3 grant monies from NSNO in a similar manner. Firstline divided $1 million during its first year among 20 different positions. Collegiate Academies spent 70 percent of $1.8 million on CMO salaries and benefits for employees working outside the schools in its network. Meanwhile, Firstline and Collegiate Academies are among the CMOs with the highest out-of-school suspension rates in New Orleans, alongside KIPP. Some NSNO board members also serve on CMO boards receiving i3 monies (Harden, 2013). Raynard Sanders, a past principal at John McDonogh and a longtime public education advocate in New Orleans, is concerned that the needs of students come last. Sanders concludes that NSNO and the CMOs it funds "act like private companies that don't have to answer to the public" and "are ripping off these communities" (Harden, 2013, p. 7).

Ongoing Allegations of Abuse and Violations of the Law

In 2014, a group of students, parents, and teachers filed a civil right complaint against Collegiate Academies in New Orleans, a CMO mentioned above that runs three charter schools. They called for local, state, and federal investigations of discipline policies and school culture. The complaint reads:

> Each of these three schools is based on harsh and punitive discipline culture . . . These policies and practices endanger the safety and welfare of students, violate students' rights under state and federal laws, push students out for minor infractions and ultimately deprive students of a right to education guaranteed by the Louisiana constitution.
>
> *(Calhoun, Lellelid, and Quigley, 2014, p. 2)*

The students attending these charter schools are African American and receive free and reduced lunch and, as mentioned, Collegiate Academies has one of the highest out-of-school suspension rates in New Orleans.

Community critiques of the culture in Collegiate Academies' charter schools are attempts to counter school practices and policies premised on the wrongful criminalization of black youth. The complaint continues:

> While most people would expect that suspension from school only happens when there is serious misbehavior or fighting or semi-criminal action, that is not the case at these schools. Rather suspensions at these schools can be triggered by violations of trivial and picky rules . . . These schools feature a culture of hyper-discipline that is punitive and demeaning to students.
>
> *(Calhoun, Lellelid, and Quigley, 2014, p. 4)*

Driven by the racially-inspired presumptions that led white journalists to depict Robert Charles as a "fiend," Banfield to critique lower-class "violence," and Whitman to advocate paternalism as a remedy for "disorder," Collegiate Academies imposes stringent codes of conduct upon students, such as requiring students to walk straight on a line; be silent "at level zero" in the hallways; sit in an upright position all day, hands folded on the desk, feet planted firmly on the floor, and looking straight ahead; and raise hands in lock-elbow position or else receive demerits (Calhoun, Lellelid, and Quigley, 2014, pp. 4–5).

Likewise, the complaint asserts that students are isolated in rooms by themselves for minor infractions without providing academic work (Calhoun, Lellelid, and Quigley, 2014, p. 5); sent home without notifying parents, a violation of Fourteenth Amendment Due Process rights to be informed of reasons for suspension (p. 6); and detained until after dark, undermining students' safety of return (p. 6). Children with special needs are reportedly bullied and harassed, such as a student with cerebral palsy who could not walk straight on the school line (p. 7). Students indicate that bathrooms are locked and that they are often refused permission to go. They also specify that food is withheld from those who refuse to serve lunch detention and that students are forbidden to bring food from home. Notably, parents say they were never given a copy of the student handbook (p. 9). Meanwhile, charter school board members have walked out of public hearings when parents sought to air concerns and students engaged in out-of-school protests have been penalized, violating their First Amendment rights of assembly (p. 10).

This kind of school culture raises serious questions about *who* has acted ruthlessly and underscores how those with authority have the capacity to violate the most basic humanitarian standards, if not civil rights law (see also Harden, 2014). Returning to Mos Def's words, these are policies for handling "niggaz" and "trash." It seems the charter school market in New Orleans has become the "monster" it sought to contain.

Conclusion: A Warning for Communities Nationally

From its early beginnings, the New Orleans model has been a means for dispossessing black teachers, students, and families of public education resources (Buras, 2005, 2007, 2009; Buras et al., 2010). This model has enabled charter school and human capital operations to proceed by undermining veteran educators and the teacher union, installing inexperienced staff from outside the community, and advancing the interests of charter school operators at the expense of the children they claim to serve (Buras, 2011b, 2012a, 2013). The voices of students and community members have been marginalized and ignored, even as they continue to be raised in opposition (Buras, 2011a, 2013; Buras et al., 2013). It is time to recognize that the New Orleans model is a guide for white education entrepreneurs (and select allies of color) to racially reconstruct the city, including its schools, for their profit (Buras, 2015).

Writing after Hurricane Katrina, one student reflected on the dire circumstances faced by her family, living in a homeless shelter without support to rebuild in New Orleans. Without bus tickets to get to school and school buses that "come when they want," this same student posed a telling question to policymakers and reformers: "New Orleans really is the murder capital, but now who's holding the gun?" (in Buras et al., 2010, p. 95). It is time for the real gangstas to take the rap for gutting the city's public schools and the children who attend them.

Notes

1   Act 35 targeted Orleans Parish by 1) analyzing School Performance Scores in Orleans Parish to provide a listing of the scores to be used in drafting the legislation so the highest number of OPSB schools could be taken over; 2) raising the SPS cut point immediately after the storm to 87.4; 3) specifying that the state's authority to takeover schools applied only to districts with more than 30 "failing" schools (Orleans Parish is one of the few districts in the state with more than 30 schools—50 of 64 districts have fewer than 30 schools); and 4) neglecting to takeover "failing" schools in three other districts, while

taking over the vast majority of "failing" schools in Orleans Parish (see UTNO et al., 2006; Civil District Court, 2012).

2   This section is adapted from "New Orleans education reform: A guide for cities or a warning for communities? (Grassroots lesson learned, 2005–2012)," Kristen L. Buras and Urban South Grassroots Research Collective, *Berkeley Review of Education*, 4(1), 2013.

3   If Judge Julien's decision is upheld, the case can be converted from seven plaintiffs, awarded $1.3 million, to a class action lawsuit that covers thousands of terminated employees, with damages estimated at $1.5 billion. These damages would be paid by either the LDOE or BESE (Dreilinger, 2013). After writing this chapter, the Louisiana Supreme Court reversed the judgments of the lower courts, which ruled in favor of the terminated school employees. Citing Louisiana's *res judicata* statute, the Louisiana Supreme Court asserted that an earlier settlement of cases answered the questions of the current suit; the court also said school employees' due process rights had not been violated, with two Chief Justices dissenting. The Louisiana Supreme Court decision will be appealed to the U.S. Supreme Court.

4   In 2013, Southern Poverty Law Center (2013) submitted a memorandum in support of seven discrete subclasses of disabled students that allege discrimination, and the court has been asked to certify them and extend the case beyond the initial plaintiffs. Among the subclasses are:

*   Students who have requested a special education evaluation that was *never completed* because the move to another school required the process to begin anew;
*   Students given a "Response to Intervention" (RTI) program rather than a special education evaluation, even though IDEA specified that RTI (interventions for students who fail to respond to traditional classroom instruction) cannot be used to delay or deny evaluations to students suspected of having a disability;
*   Students who have been given a less expensive 504 plan, meant to ensure that disabled students receive the same treatment as disabled ones, rather than a special education evaluation that qualifies the student for a level of services that may be costly;
*   Students removed for more than 10 days in a school year without the timely provision of the disciplinary safeguards or the educational services required by IDEA if they are removed from the classroom;
*   Students not provided services contained in their IEPs because autonomous schools cannot provide them cost effectively;
*   Students with disabilities who have been denied admission or instructed not to apply to a public school on the basis of their disabilities; and
*   Students with mobility impairments who have been denied access to programs and services of public schools as a result of structural or architectural barriers.

After writing this chapter, a class action settlement was reached in favor of disabled students and approved by a federal judge in the U.S. District Court for the Eastern District of Louisiana. Aside from defendants paying $800,000 in legal fees to Southern Poverty Law Center, this landmark settlement includes the appointment of an independent monitor to oversee charter school adherence to state and federal law, a review of school discipline policies, and other forms of oversight.

References

504ward. (2012). *Homepage*. Available at: www.504ward.com

Adelson, J. (2012, August 2012). Kira Orange Jones will keep seat on state board of education. *Times-Picayune*. Available: www.nola.com

Banfield, E. C. (1968). *The unheavenly city: The nature and future of our urban crisis*. Boston, MA: Little, Brown.

Barrow, B. (2012a, April 4). Louisiana Senate votes to expand vouchers, public charter schools. *Times-Picayune*. Available at: www.nola.com

Barrow, B. (2012b, April 4). Senate approves teacher tenure restrictions, pay changes. *Times-Picayune*. Available at: www.nola.com

Bring New Orleans Back Commission [BNOB]. (2006, January 17). *Rebuilding and transforming: A plan for world-class public education in New Orleans*. New Orleans: Author.

Brinson, D., Boast, L., Hassel, B. C., and Kingsland, N. (2012). *New Orleans-style education reform: A guide for cities (Lessons learned, 2004–2010)*. New Orleans, LA: New Schools for New Orleans. Retrieved from www.newschoolsforneworleans.org/guide.

Broad Foundation. (2012). *Broad Center for the Management of School Systems announces four new members of board of directors* [News release]. Los Angeles, CA: Author.

Buras, K. L. (2005). Katrina's early landfall: Exclusionary politics behind the restoration of New Orleans. *Z Magazine, 18*(12), 26–31.

Buras, K. L. (2007). Benign neglect? Drowning yellow buses, racism, and disinvestment in the city that Bush forgot. In K. Saltman (Ed.), *Schooling and the politics of disaster* (pp. 103–122). New York: Routledge.

Buras, K. L. (2008). *Rightist multiculturalism: Core lessons on neoconservative school reform*. New York: Routledge.

Buras, K. L. (2009). "We have to tell our story": Neo-griots, racial resistance, and schooling in the other South. *Race Ethnicity and Education, 12*(4), 427–453.

Buras, K. L. (2011a). Challenging the master's plan for the Lower Ninth Ward of New Orleans. *Z Magazine, 24*(5), 19–22.

Buras, K. L. (2011b). Race, charter schools, and conscious capitalism: On the spatial politics of whiteness as property (and the unconscionable assault on black New Orleans). *Harvard Educational Review, 81*(2), 296–330.

Buras, K. L. (2012a). "It's all about the dollars": Charter schools, educational policy, and the racial market in New Orleans. In W. H. Watkins (Ed.), *The assault on public education: Confronting the politics of corporate school reform* (pp. 160–188). New York: Teachers College Press.

Buras, K. L. (2012b, March). *Review of The Louisiana Recovery School District: Lessons for the Buckeye State*. Boulder, CO: National Education Policy Center.

Buras, K. L. (2013). "We're not going nowhere": Race, urban space, and the struggle for King Elementary School in New Orleans. *Critical Studies in Education, 54*(1), 19–32.

Buras, K. L. (2014). There *really is* a culture of poverty: On the history of black working-class struggles for education and equity. In P. C. Gorski and J. Landsman (Eds.), *The poverty and education reader: A call for equity in many voices* (pp. 60–74). Sterling, VA: Stylus Press.

Buras, K. L. (2015). *Charter schools, race, and urban space: Where the market meets grassroots resistance*. New York: Routledge.

Buras, K. L., Randels, J., Salaam, K. Y., and Students at the Center. (2010). *Pedagogy, policy, and the privatized city: Stories of dispossession and defiance from New Orleans*. New York: Teachers College Press.

Buras, K. L., and Urban South Grassroots Research Collective. (2013). New Orleans education reform: A guide for cities or a warning for communities? (Grassroots lessons learned, 2005–2012) [Postscript by A. D. Dixson, A. Bigard, and Walter Cohen High School students]. *Berkeley Review of Education, 4*(1), 123–160.

Bush, G. W. (2005, September 15). *Text of Bush speech*. Retrieved from www.cbsnews.com

Butler, S. M., Carafano, J. J., Fraser, A. A., Lips, D., Moffit, R. M., and Utt, R. D. (2005, September 16). *How to turn the president's Gulf Coast pledge into reality* (Webmemo 848). Heritage Foundation. Retrieved from www.heritage.org/research/reports/2005/09/how-to-turn-the-presidents-gulf-coast-pledge-into-reality

Calhoun, W., Lellelid, A., and Quigley, W. P. (2014). *Civil rights complaint* [document]. New Orleans, LA: Author.

Center for Media and Democracy. (2012). *ALEC Exposed* [Website]. Available at: www.alecexposed.org

Chang, C. (2010a, August 26). $1.8 billion from FEMA for Hurricane Katrina school rebuilding is "worth the wait," Sen. Mary Landrieu says. *Times-Picayune.* Retrieved from www.nola.com

Chang, C. (2010b, August 7). Charter incubator to get grant: It will help turn around more schools. *Times-Picayune.* Available from www.nola.com

Childress, S. M., Bensen, S., and Tudryn, S. (2010). New Schools for New Orleans 2008. In S. M. Childress (Ed.), *Transforming public education: Cases in education entrepreneurship* (pp. 384–410). Cambridge, MA: Harvard Education Press.

Civil District Court for the Parish of Orleans. (2012, June 20). *Eddy Oliver et al. v. Orleans Parish School Board et al.* [Reasons for judgment]. New Orleans, LA: Author.

Cooper, C. (2005, September 8). In Katrina's wake—Old-line families escape worst of floods and plot the future. *Wall Street Journal,* p. A1.

Cowen Institute. (2010). *The state of public education in New Orleans.* New Orleans: Author.

Cowen Institute. (2011). *NOLA by the numbers: School enrollment and demographics, October 2011.* New Orleans, LA: Author.

Crenshaw, K., Gotanda, N., Peller, G., and Thomas, K. (Eds.). (1995). *Critical race theory: The key writings that formed the movement.* New York: New Press.

Cunningham-Cook, M. (2012, October 17). Why do some of America's wealthiest individuals have fingers in Louisiana's education system? *The Nation.* Retrieved from www.thenation.com

Democrats for Education Reform. (2010, September 13). *Bursting the dam: Why the next 24 months are critical for education reform politics* [Brief]. Washington, DC: Author.

DeVore, D. E., and Logsdon, J. (1991). *Crescent City schools: Public education in New Orleans, 1841–1991.* Lafayette: Center for Louisiana Studies, University of Southwestern Louisiana.

Dreilinger, D. (2013, August 3). Unrelenting New Orleans special education problems alleged in new court filings. *Times-Picayune.* Available at: www.nola.com

Educate Now! (2012). Homepage. Available at: http://educatenow.net/

Forward New Orleans for Public Schools. (2012). Forward New Orleans for Public Schools [Pamphlet]. Available at: www.Schools.ForwardNewOrleans.com

Gray, E., Ableidinder, J., and Barrett, S. K. (2012, August). *Kick-starting reform: Three city-based organizations showing how to transform public education.* Indianapolis, IN: Cities for Education Entrepreneurship Trust.

Greater New Orleans Foundation. (2012). *Board of trustees.* Available at: www.gnof.org/about/who-we-are/board

Hair, W. I. (2008). *Carnival of fury: Robert Charles and the New Orleans race riot of 1900* (updated ed.). Baton Rouge, LA: Louisiana State University Press.

Harden, K. (2013, October 28). Implementation of i3 education grant being questioned. *Louisiana Weekly.* Available at: www.louisianaweekly.com/inplementation-of-i3-education-grants-being-questioned

Harden, K. (2014, April 22). Civil rights complaints are filed against three N.O. schools. *Louisiana Weekly.* Available at: www.louisianaweekly.com/civil-rights-complaints-are-filed-against-three-n-o-schools

Harvey, D. (2006). *Spaces of global capitalism: Towards a theory of uneven geographical development.* New York: Verso.

Hill, P. and Hannaway, J. (2006, January). The future of public education in New Orleans. In M. A. Turner and S. R. Zedlewski (Eds.), *After Katrina: Rebuilding opportunity and equity into the new New Orleans* (pp. 27–35). Washington, DC: Urban Institute.

Hill, P., Campbell, C., Menefee-Libery, D., Dusseault, B., DeArmond, M., and Gross, B. (2009, October). *Portfolio school districts for big cities: An interim report.* Seattle: Center on Reinventing Public Education.

Isaacson, W. (2007, September 6). The greatest education lab. *Time Magazine.* Retrieved from www.time.com/time/magazine/0,9171,1659767,00.html

Layton, L. (2014, May 28). In New Orleans, traditional public schools close for good. *Washington Post.* Available at: www.washingtonpost.com/local/education/in-new-orleans-traditional-public-schools-close-for-good/2014/05/28/ae4f5724-e5de-11e3-8f90-73e071f3d637_story.html

Leonardo, Z. (2009). *Race, whiteness, and education.* New York: Routledge.

Louisiana Ethics Administration Program. (2012, October 9). *Sarah Newell Usdin* [Candidate's report]. Available at: www.ethics.state.la.us/CampaignFinanceSearch/ShowEForm.aspx?ReportID=32542#TopOfFrom

Louisiana Federation of Teachers [LFT]. (2005, November 2). *Letter to Blanco regarding Executive Orders 58 and 79.* Baton Rouge: Author.

Louisiana Federation of Teachers [LFT] and American Federation of Teachers [AFT]. (2007, January). *The chronology: Scenario of a nightmare.* Baton Rouge: Author.

Maxwell, L. A. (2007, December 13). Foundations donate millions to help New Orleans schools' recovery. *Education Week.* Retrieved from www.edweek.org

Meese, E., Butler, S. M., and Holmes, K. R. (2005, September 12). *From tragedy to triumph: Principled solutions for rebuilding lives and communities.* Washington, DC: Heritage Foundation.

Mind Trust. (2011). *Creating opportunity schools: A bold plan to transform Indianapolis public schools* [report prepared by Public Impact]. Indianapolis, IN: Mind Trust. Retrieved from www.themindtrust.org/files/file/opp-schools-full-report.pdf.

Mos Def. (2005). *Dollar Day* [video]. Available: www.youtube.com/watch?v=Qo8NF9vv6TA

New Orleans Independent Media Center. (2009, July 20). *Behind the curtain of the Louisiana charter school experiment* [Article]. Available: http://neworleans.indymedia.org/print.php?id=14120

New Orleans Public School Employees Justice [NOPSE]. (2010, June 9). *Frequently asked questions.* Retrieved on April 21, 2012 from www.nopsejustice.com/faq.htm

New Orleans Public School Employees Justice [NOPSE]. (2007). *About NOPSE Justice* [Pre Katrina political agenda]. Retrieved on April 21, 2012 from www.nopsejustice.com/about.htm

New Schools for New Orleans [NSNO]. (n.d.). *Transformations* [Informational folder]. New Orleans: Author.

New Schools for New Orleans [NSNO]. (2008a). *Lead.* Retrieved from http://newschoolsforneworleans.org/

New Schools for New Orleans [NSNO]. (2008b). *Serve.* Retrieved from http://newschoolsforneworleans.org/

New Schools for New Orleans [NSNO]. (2008c). *Start.* Retrieved from http://newschoolsforneworleans.org/

New Schools for New Orleans [NSNO]. (2010a). *Charter board member qualifications.* Retrieved from http://newschoolsforneworleans.org/

New Schools for New Orleans [NSNO]. (2010b). *Our impact.* Retrieved from http://newschoolsforneworleans.org/

New Schools for New Orleans [NSNO]. (2012a). Charter school investments [Web page]. Retrieved from www.newschoolsforneworleans.org/charter-school-investments

New Schools for New Orleans. (2012b). National influence [Web page]. Retrieved from www.newschoolsforneworleans.org/national-influence

New Teacher Project [TNTP]. (2007, December 3). *The New Teacher Project wins Fast Company magazine and Monitor Group's social capitalist award*. Retrieved from www.tntp.org/newsandpress/120307_TNTP.html

New Teacher Project [TNTP]. (2010). *About us: Our business model*. Retrieved from www.tntp.org

Pocan, M. (2011, October). Inside the ALEC dating service: How corporations hook up with your state legislators. *The Progressive, 75*(10), 19–21.

Recovery School District [RSD]. (2007, June 13). *Two companies awarded the contract to develop master facility plan for Orleans Parish public schools* [Press release]. Baton Rouge: Author.

Recovery School District [RSD] and New Orleans Public Schools [NOPS]. (2008, August). *School facilities master plan for Orleans Parish*. New Orleans: Author.

Simon, S. (2012, August 16). Teach For America alumni at the head of the class. *Reuters*. Retrieved from www.reuters.com/assets/print?aid=USBRE87F05S20120816

Smith, N. (2012, January). The Louisiana Recovery School District: Lessons for the Buckeye State. Washington, DC: Thomas B. Fordham Institute. Retrieved from www.edexcellence.net/publications/the-louisiana-recovery-school-district.html.

Southern Poverty Law Center. (2010a). *P.B. et al. v. Pastorek*. [Complaint] Available at: http://cdna.splcenter.org/sites/default/files/downloads/case/pb_v_pastorek.pdf

Southern Poverty Law Center. (2010b). Special education in New Orleans public schools. Available at: www.splc.org/access-denied/special-education-in-new-orleans-public-schools

Southern Poverty Law Center. (2013, August 2). Memorandum of law in support of plaintiffs' renewed motion for class certification. Available at: http://bit.ly/19n3H6U

Thevenot, B. (2009, May 17). Local school principals' pay reaches new heights. *Times-Picayune*. Retrieved from www.nola.com

Underwood, J. and Mead, J. F. (2012). A smart ALEC threatens public education. *Phi Delta Kappan, 93*(6), 51–55.

United Teachers of New Orleans [UTNO]. (2010, March). *The New Orleans model: Shortchanging poor and minority students by over-relying on new teachers* [Report]. New Orleans, LA: Author.

United Teachers of New Orleans [UTNO], Louisiana Federation of Teachers [LFT], and American Federation of Teachers [AFT]. (2006, November). *"National model" or flawed approach? The post-Katrina New Orleans Public Schools*. New Orleans: Author.

United Teachers of New Orleans [UTNO], Louisiana Federation of Teachers [LFT], and American Federation of Teachers [AFT]. (2007, June). *No experience necessary: How the New Orleans school takeover experiment devalues experienced teachers*. New Orleans: Author.

Usdin, S. N. (2012). *Meet Sarah* [Orleans school board campaign material]. Available at: www.sarahusdin.com/meet-sarah

Vanacore, A. (2012a, October 26). New Orleans Mayor Mitch Landrieu endorses Usdin, Koppel and Marshall for school board. *Times-Picayune*. Available: www.nola.com

Vanacore, A. (2012b, October 9). Sarah Usdin draws $110,000 haul in Orleans Parish school board race. *Times-Picayune*. Available: www.nola.com

Wells-Barnett, I. B. (1900/2005). *Mob rule in New Orleans. With–Southern horrors: Lynch law in all its phases*. Cirencester, UK: Echo Library.

Whitman, D. (2008). *Sweating the small stuff: Inner-city schools and the new paternalism*. Washington, DC: Thomas B. Fordham Institute.

10

ENTERPRISE EDUCATION POLICY AND EMBEDDED LAYERS OF CORPORATE INFLUENCE

Patricia Burch and Jahni M. A. Smith

Introduction

It is 7:15 pm and a fifth-grade student, Lynette, sits in the middle of the living room with her father. They have just finished turning this room of their modest one-bedroom apartment into a learning center for a scheduled online mathematics lesson starting at 7:30 pm. The father, a Zapotec man from the southern state of Oaxaca, Mexico, has ensured that the internet connection is working properly, has set up a foldable table with enough scratch paper for his daughter to work with, and has opened the laptop (provided by a private vendor in order to complete the tutoring services) to the proper programs that the student will work on. This is their third session and both are eagerly waiting for the instructor to log on from his or her remote location and begin the hour-long session.

The session runs into technical difficulties from the instructor's end and begins at 7:40 pm. The instructor proceeds to assign the student 20 minutes of independent test-prep work. The program, however, runs into more technical difficulties and takes 7 minutes to load. The student answers multiple-choice questions that are unaligned to both her current schoolwork and grade level. Although her father's English proficiency is limited, he sits alongside her throughout the lesson and is showing some signs of unrest.

After the test-prep work, the one-to-one instruction begins. The instructor is either a voice or a presence acknowledged by instant messages displayed in the laptop. The instructor assigns Lynette a problem, but she mentions that she has already completed that specific problem. After three more attempts, the student begins to work on a word problem, which she answers in less than a minute. Her father helps. They both wait for the instructor to check the work and assign a new problem. The father is growing more concerned and visibly anxious. His daughter still has homework to finish. After 9 minutes, the instructor texts the student, "Good job man!" He doesn't realize that she is a girl and hasn't asked. For the remaining 20 minutes the student answers three questions. Most of the time is spent waiting. At 8:30 pm, the instructor signs off.

(Field notes, Supplemental Education Services Tutoring Session, May 23, 2012)[1]

This home digital instruction (engineered by a Silicon Valley start-up, the company providing tutoring to Lynette and over 7,000 low-income students in Los Angeles) is precisely the sort of item that policymakers and investors have identified as key to the future of public education. In the wake of No Child Left Behind (NCLB), policymakers increasingly have turned to digital education and other purchased private sector goods and services as a means to "fix schools." Digital education includes the use of technology in K-12 assessments and for the design and delivery of curriculum (such as e-textbooks), the use of new hardware and software (e.g., tablets and digital education games) to instruct in classrooms among other things. The transition to digital education is just the latest chapter in a decades-long trend to divest public education of its core management tasks and instead contract out with the private sector for these services, for a fee. The bill, as with other contracted-out education services and products, is paid for with government funds, in this instance funds that are meant for low-income students attending failing schools in the United States.

The processes through which government agencies, interest groups, and congressional staff collude in the creation of mutually beneficial policy has long concerned both political scientists and policy researchers within and outside of education. A core concept used in political science[2] for understanding the interaction of corporate and other special interests in national level policy processes is the "iron triangle." From the vantage point of the iron triangle, interest groups, congress, and bureaucratic agencies interpret and act on policies in ways that are mutually beneficial, and in their combined influence, create self-serving and seemingly impenetrable public policy. We use the concept of the iron triangle as a starting point for examining the channels and pathways through which state-corporate ties in K-12 education influence policy processes in the era of market-based education policy, or as we refer to it: enterprise education policy. Our aim is to help illuminate how these ties overlap at multiple points in the system, creating new commercial spaces within school settings and in other ways, and under certain conditions, working against the democratic purposes of education.

Framing Ideas

A core idea behind the iron triangle is that private and special interest groups have leverage over both elected officials and government staff because they represent powerful interest groups. In one corner of the triangle are government agencies that seek to do things that will bolster their own political power and so seek out alliances that will increase their clout. The second corner of the triangle is private or special interest groups. These powerful groups are eager allies already active in political affairs, which seek to influence legislation, for their own constituents through lobbying, voting and campaign contributions. In the third corner of the triangle is government staff; for example, staff within the Department of Education, which under the iron triangle principle, are also influenced by powerful interest groups.

Another dynamic that has long concerned policy researchers is the relationship between federal policy and local policy and action. Research on the impact of federal policy on local action concurs that policy is implemented and assumes significance as it works its way down the system from the Federal level to the local level (Berman and McLaughlin, 1976; Honig, 2006). In other work, Burch (2007, 2009) has argued that the implementation as a negotiation model of studying policy implementation has strengths. However, it has neglected an important layer or actor in these dynamics, mainly non-governmental agencies. Under this model, consistent with the iron triangle concept, private companies (both for-profit and not-for-profit) are directly involved in creating new markets for school improvement and, as we argue below, enacting policies in ways that support these markets. Rather than focus on either corporate–state ties, or implementation as negotiation dynamics, we link the two to better understand the influence of for-profits and not-for-profits on policies intended to benefit low income students.

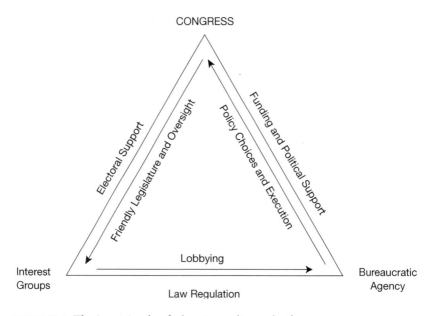

FIGURE 10.1 The iron triangle of education policy and reform

No Child Left Behind and Expanding Corporate Role in Public Instruction

Federal policy toward the contracting of local instructional services is changing along multiple dimensions. The Federal government has acted via spending conditions and new policies to influence what happens within classrooms and consolidate its own power in matters that founders of the education system in the United States typically have viewed as a state-level authority. With NCLB, Federal policy towards the contracting of local instructional services also now appears to more visibly and publically endorse the direct involvement of private companies in classroom practice and learning outcomes. In 2002, columnist Stephen Metcalf described No Child Left Behind as the "successful culmination of a decade of educational reform spearheaded by conservatives and business leaders." He captured a notable quote by then chairman of McGraw-Hill (formerly a major textbook publisher that now specializes in emerging digital technologies to guide assessment, teaching and learning), Harold McGraw, "It's a great day for education, because we now have substantial alignment among all the key constituents—the public, the education community, business and political leaders—that results matter."[3]

It was, as we know now and anticipated then, only the beginning of a broader trend within and outside of education. The larger context for the changes is a shifting center of gravity in public policy. Market principles of competition and consumerism have moved mainstream and become more accepted policy strategies for improving social outcomes. The idea is that public management and public policy should be modeled closely after marketplace principles. New public management theories, also called neoliberalism[4], envision a society in which third-party organizations (both for-profit and not-for-profit) play a much more central and government-endorsed role in designing, providing and evaluating government services (Guttman and Willner, 1976; Kettl, 2002; Salamon and Lund, 1989; Stoker, 1998). Governing agencies become nodes in a market-driven network of vendors. If public management is modeled more closely after market relationships, the story goes, then government will become more cost efficient and society will improve.

NCLB and Enterprise Education Policy[5]

The No Child Left Behind Act of 2001 (NCLB) is the decade's defining moment in education's gravity shift toward new public management or neoliberalism. George W. Bush knitted these ideas to political agendas for privatization of the Elementary and Secondary Education Act (ESEA) when he signed the No Child Left Behind Act into public law in 2002 "to close the achievement gap [in public education] with accountability, flexibility, and choice," (No Child Left Behind Act of 2001). In his advocacy for more corporate style management of ESEA,

President George W. Bush described NCLB's provisions as "based on the fundamental notion that an enterprise works best when responsibility is placed closest to the most important activity of the enterprise, when those responsible are given greatest latitude and support, and when those responsible are held accountable for producing results" (No Child Left Behind Act, 2001). The law offered school choice to those in persistently low-performing schools, and targeted federal funds on effective (evidence-based) practices for improving teacher and school quality. School districts and states were to be evaluated on the basis of standardized test scores and those that didn't pass based on state specified target goals were to close or be reconstituted.

NCLB created funding streams and mandates that had direct and immediate benefits for companies. Iron triangle dynamics can help explain these outcomes. Consider this example. From 2001–2007, 27 high-level U.S. Department of Education Officials resigned, all of whom were involved in integral ways in the design, administration, and oversight of NCLB. Sixteen of the 27 assumed positions at for-profit firms selling consultative or other services and products to schools linked to the mandates of NCLB. These private education firms gained the experience and knowledge of senior education officials with deep understanding of the law and its loopholes, and close political ties to both the U.S. Department of Education and to interest groups such as the Heritage Foundation with a pro-market agenda (see also Hogan, Sellar, and Lingard, Chapter 3, this volume). As employees of private non-governmental firms, the officials possessed the freedom to lobby for policy that would protect the financial interests of the firm.

To offer another concrete example, the provisions encapsulated by NCLB directly underpin initiatives propagated by President Bush's brother, Governor Jeb Bush in Florida, specifically the Florida Comprehensive Assessment Test (FCAT). More importantly, when considering the dynamics of the iron triangle with regard to NCLB, Governor Bush functions not only as an elected member of Congress, but also operates as a founding member for Foundation for Excellence in Education (ExcelinEd)—an interest group that lobbies for reform initiatives in education. Governor Bush's younger brother, Neil Bush, is also directly tied to the funding stream made available as he started a software company, Ignite! Learning, designed to provide testing solutions that are heavily mandated by NCLB.

NCLB continued to function as a governmental mandate until attempts to reauthorize in 2007 were unsuccessful due to congress. Consequently, when a deadline for reauthorization was set by President Obama in 2011, interest groups such as the Education Industry Association (EIA) mobilized. In an open letter to its constituents, the EIA cheered, "Education is rapidly becoming a $1 trillion industry, representing 10% of America's GNP and second in size only to the health care industry. Federal and State expenditures on education exceed 750 billion." And it wasn't just the EIA. According to a 2011 Open Secrets blog article by

Kathleen Ronayne, 153 organizations had lobbied on issues referencing NCLB by the opening quarter of Congress spending as much as $22.6 million.

The dynamics that produced NCLB's enterprise education legislation were further reflected and perpetuated in the design and implementation of the Supplemental Educational Services program. Supplemental educational services (SES) are part of the choice provisions of NCLB. Public schools that have not made adequate yearly progress in increasing student academic achievement for three years are required under NCLB to offer parents of children in low-income families the opportunity to receive extra academic assistance or to transfer to another public school. The guiding regulations of SES were specifically designed to minimize State influence and maximize free enterprise. Consistent with the design and intent of the law, the tutoring interventions were implemented at the local level and drew on the private sector to offer eligible students a range of choices for supplemental educational services (i.e., free tutoring outside of regular school hours). Although no new federal monies are allocated along with this mandate, the law lays out criteria and guidelines for state educational agencies (SEAs) and local educational agencies (LEAs) in choosing SES vendors and arranging for their services. It also obligates school districts to set aside 20 percent of their Title I funding for SES and to measure provider effectiveness in increasing student achievement. Reflecting theories of new public management, SES diverges sharply from original theories of change of ESEA in its emphasis on parent choice, regulations forbidding under certain conditions any public services (where districts don't make test score targets, they must contract with private vendors) and in all conditions government influence on the instructional content of tutoring services (districts and states by law can have no influence over vendors' chosen curriculum or price points). As discussed in the latter part of the paper, these provisions create commercial spaces inside of classroom settings, bootstrapping price caps by government agencies, and undercutting instructional time. While states typically establish specifications for provider applications and approval, the theory of action for SES tutoring situates the locus of decision-making largely at the parent and district levels, presupposing that they have sufficiently accurate and complete information on provider attributes and effectiveness to reap the benefits of choice, as well as adequate capacity or leverage for disciplining the market and rooting out ineffective vendors.

Executive Branch Acts to Enforce Enterprise Education

In the iron triangle of SES policy making, members of congress repay interest groups with legislation or rule making that will benefit them. As noted above, the original SES legislation included provisions that only allowed districts to be service vendors under certain conditions and disallowed districts with high numbers of students not making AYP. Districts such as Chicago with relatively successful after-school programs challenged the legislation in their requests for waivers.

The Department of Education ultimately allowed two school districts (Chicago Public Schools and Boston Public Schools) to provide after-school instruction within their district. Given that both districts had not met their test score benchmarks, Department of Education staff emphasized the waivers as an exception to the general rule—which was accompanied by the expectation of greater results. In the memorandum granting the waiver, Secretary of Education, Spellings, also specified penalties to be imposed on any states showing unwarranted resistance. Specifically, Spellings stated, "Given the technical assistance and support the Department has already provided to States and LEAs, and the poor and uneven quality of the implementation efforts we are seeing in LEAs around the country, we are prepared to take significant enforcement action." Here, Spellings operated under the assumption that the fidelity of implementation was a signal that States and LEAs were simply trying to undermine the initiative with lackluster effort. Spellings, in this statement, forcefully establishes an outcome-driven operation, perform or else. As the government proposed an outcome-driven ultimatum LEAs were forced to transition towards whatever solutions allowed them to report positive results under the program, solutions that could harm disadvantaged students.

Within the iron triangle of SES policy making, members of congress repaid interest groups with whom they were friendly with SES legislation that would allow companies to operate with minimal government regulation while making money from public funds. In the rule making following this legislation, public agencies were moved further from the center of public policy. School districts such as Chicago Public Schools, which had a long history of after-school programs, had to apply for waivers to simply sit alongside of companies as service vendors. Department of Education staff further reinforced the market-based paradigms of public policy by threatening to withhold funds from states such as California if they did not demonstrate full support (see Figure 10.2).

At the time of writing the future of SES is uncertain. Close to half of all states are being granted waivers to discontinue SES in exchange for other conditions (e.g., improved results, pro-choice policies) promoted by the Obama Administration. However, a future of expanded private engagement in public education seems to remain most certain. What was once a relatively hidden market is now, through legislations such as Race to the Top and other elements of the Obama Administration agenda, in full public view. Before NCLB, much of the policy talk was organized around the question of whether we ought to increase private engagement in the design and delivery of educational services. A decade later the conversation has shifted to how districts should coordinate and organize the engagement of private firms in the management and operation of public schools. While educational privatization has a long history in the United States, in the past decade much public and academic attention has focused on educational management organizations (EMOs). These firms typically assume full responsibility for all aspects of school operation including administration, teacher training, and

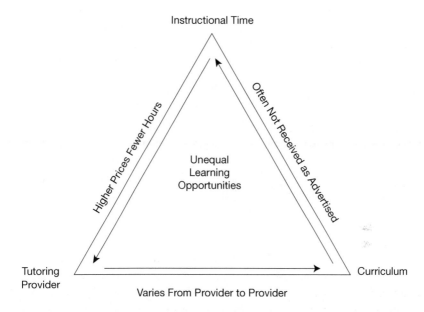

FIGURE 10.2 Enterprise education policy and education markets

non-instructional functions such as building maintenance, food service, or clerical support. However, with the passage of NCLB, the current chapter of NCLB is being written by firms of a different kind which have received less attention from the press, but cannot be ignored. These are specialty service vendors. Similar to other forms of district contracting, involving contract schools, districts in principle maintain control of funds by putting out bids, writing contracts, and overseeing payments to vendors.

Some firms specialize in a particular niche of specialty or wraparound services such as virtual schools (K12) and learning software (Blackboard). Increasingly, firms in the education marketplace are also operating across multiple segments of the market. Thus rather than primarily selling textbooks, a firm will also sell online curriculum as well as stand-alone assessment, management consulting, professional development and digital curriculum. Examples of firms already selling across different segments of the market include Pearson, which sells national and worldwide tests, curriculum software, and school management, and Educate, which sells after-school tutoring, teacher recruitment and test-related services for non-public schools.

Firms that once specialized in whole-school management are turning to less visible strategies where they contract with multiple districts for multiple specific functions in each. In some instances firms have given subsidiaries a variety of independent names. Consequently, the public or even school district personnel cannot easily see that a single for-profit firm is providing a large array of

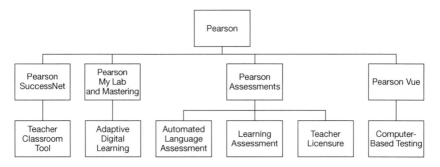

FIGURE 10.3 Pearson example of interlocking educational services

interlocking educational services to a district. Thus while a district may establish various contracts with seemingly different businesses and running for different terms, they could all be subsidiaries of a single company. Figure 10.3 demonstrates an example of this. Pearson has acquired several companies that have different products in the education marketplace. This diagram is a simplified version of the complicated business relationships that actually exist—there are instances where Pearson has stakes in a multimedia corporation, but no overt ownership, for example Nook Media. In these instances, it is plausible that a district may adopt several different products whose profits, and content control decisions, eventually flow back under the overall ownership of this one company. These products range from textbooks to teacher assessments, and just about every form of educational product in between.

These, in other words, inside the education market place, set local and regional dynamics that crisscross the public and private sector and parallel those at the national level. In the case of NCLB, companies responded to commercial opportunities by selling tutoring and other kinds of services and products to districts. They operated and continue to operate in ways that suggest little concern for corporate monopolies within particular jurisdictions and under-standably with little press to disclose what they were selling. Local education agencies responded to this commercial push by agreeing to purchase more services and products, and in doing so reinforced neoliberal ideas that education agencies should consume more and govern less.

Corporate-State Dynamics and Students' Opportunities to Learn

The dynamics of the triangle and its effects continue at the classroom level, exerting extraordinary influence on students' opportunities to learn. There has been much good work already done on classroom effects of particular segments of the K-12 industry. This includes studies of for-profit managers of charter schools, educational management organizations and test publishers (Gill et al., 2005; Heinrich and Nisar, 2013). However, in general, fewer studies have looked at how corporate–state dynamics originating at higher levels of government work their way into classroom settings. We try to take a more integrated approach here that knits corporate–state dynamics in policy processes with a focus on measured outcomes for low-income students' opportunities to learn. Drawing on our own and collaborators' work on a four-year study of the implementation and impact of supplemental educational services, we analyze patterns in how enterprise education policies and the corporate–state dynamics shape opportunities to learn at the classroom level.[6] The findings we report draw on a larger mixed-methods study of the implementation and impact of supplemental education services. The data included field work (observations, interviews, and focus groups) and analysis of administrative and student-level data in five urban school districts.

Charging High Prices

Alongside teachers, researchers tend to place intensity of instruction or hours of instruction as a central variable in opportunities to learn. Typically, the length of the class day, or hours of instruction that students receive over the course of a year is viewed as something that educational agencies, not outside vendors, can manipulate. However, our research on supplemental educational services shows that in the context of market-based education policy that limits district monitoring of product pricing, vendors can be primary influencers over how many hours of instruction students receive and what is in an instructional hour. When governments adopt policies that give education companies free reign in price setting, some companies leverage these opportunities for commercial gain in the absence of evidence that a higher price point translates to higher quality product or service. In the Chicago Public School District, where students routinely reached thresholds of 36 to 39 hours of tutoring (on average) and we consistently observed positive impacts of tutoring, provider hourly rates were the lowest on average (at $44 per hour). The number of hours students attended is directly influenced by the rate per hour charged by tutoring vendors and the dollars allocated per student by districts. For example, one district in our study allocated approximately $1,300 per student for tutoring; as over 70 percent of these students received tutoring from a provider charging $75 or more per hour, the maximum hours of tutoring a student could receive was about 18 hours over the school year.

In our study of classroom-level enactment of NCLB's tutoring program, we also observed differences between the advertised time of tutoring sessions and actual instructional time. Vendors are required to advertise the average length of their sessions, and districts are invoiced at an hourly rate based on the time spent in tutoring. In our sample, advertised sessions ranged from 60 to 240 minutes. Irrespective of the format, students tended to receive less instructional time than what was advertised by vendors, although the magnitude of these differences varied by format. Tutoring completed in the student's home most closely matched instructional time with advertised time (approximately three minutes difference on average). In school and community settings, average instructional time was often considerably less than average advertised time: approximately 19 minutes in the case of in-person, school-based tutoring and approximately 29 minutes in the case of in-person, community-based tutoring.

Hiring Decisions

Vendors operating in a context of market-based education policy also can exert influence via corporate policies regarding teacher hiring and selection process. This influence is amplified when, as in the case of SES, there are no standards for vendors to follow in hiring tutors or teachers, little calls for transparency in these processes, and no monitoring of how students are being assigned to teachers. In our study of SES, we found that when given the flexibility to hire their own tutors/teachers, vendors in our sample tended to hire certified teachers, teachers in training, and/or retired teachers. Certified teachers represented a clear majority of tutors. However, tutors certified as special educators were much rarer. In only 12 out of the 109 tutoring sessions that we observed were special educators present. In 89 sessions, instructors had a bachelor's degree or higher; only 8 tutors had less than a bachelor's degree. Considering that paraprofessional certification generally requires only two years of college-level courses, it is clear that the majority (82 percent) of observed SES instructors have higher qualifications than paraprofessionals. However, the 23 non-certified tutors with a bachelor's degree or higher may not have had any formal training in instruction for students with disabilities (SWD).

In other instances, preliminary findings suggest that companies made resource decisions that removed teachers entirely from the classroom or significantly limited students' interaction with them. This influence is particularly apparent in the growing market of digital instruction. The context of digital tutoring challenges traditional conceptions of a "tutor." Instead of falling into the models typical of in-person, non-digital tutoring contexts where the tutor is the primary guide or delivery system of the curriculum, our observations of tutoring sessions and interviews with provider staff indicate and illustrate a spectrum of enacted roles. Some digital tutoring platforms are structured where students have no interaction with a human during the tutoring session. Instead, students interact with instructional software, and may have the option of calling a helpline if they get stuck on a problem. Students also might interact with a provider staff member on occasions to upload progress reports or deal with technical needs (see below). In other instances, some tutoring platforms use personnel only for technical assistance, which could include a technical helpline or delivering/retrieving hardware from students' homes. In this instance, the role of the adult is a technician not a tutor.

We also observed sessions where students brought netbooks into a central location to have a provider personnel upload their progress in working through pre-loaded software. The role of a teacher in a digital setting is still developing, and as we have argued so far digital vendors are well poised to influence emerging ideas of what it means to be a teacher. In addition to the role of technician or no tutor, vendors may decide to hire personnel who are half tutors/half monitors. The tutor/monitor is beyond a technician, but not quite a full, interactive instructor. For example, tutor/monitors may respond to students if they need help on a specific question related to academic content, call families to discuss progress and encourage students, or answer questions via email. Finally, education companies might define a digital instructor as an instructor only if the tutor interacts with a student constantly throughout the session and the curriculum could not progress without the tutor, but in our research companies' investments in live, fully engaged instructors tended to be more the exception than the rule.

Deciding What to Teach

As noted above, the design of SES turns design and management of the enrichment curriculum over to the private vendors. For example, a district that has documented high failure rates in math for English Language Learners (ELL) cannot, by law, encourage or require specific vendors to make high-quality math enrichment available for these students. Vendors can select or teach the content that they want. The theory of action behind tutoring under NCLB is that variation between vendors creates a competitive marketplace from which parents can choose the most appropriate program for their students' needs. Variation within vendors confounds the assumption that the axis of parental choice lies on the provider level and also may complicate efforts to evaluate tutoring program effects at the provider level.

Vendors responded to flexibility around curriculum in expected ways. For example, sessions of very different instructional styles and quality were observed for one provider who offered services both in schools and homes. In one session at a school site, the tutor worked with three students together for one hour on a variety of math activities all focused on the same concepts around long division. This tutor was also the math specialist for the school and incorporated a number of activities and strategies from her day school resources to engage students in active learning. On the other hand, a tutor from the same provider worked with one student at home for two hours. She was not a certified teacher, although had coursework and experience in tutoring. She relied exclusively on the printed worksheets from the provider and jumped from concept to concept, even from math to reading, depending on the worksheet. The student was not actively engaged.

As this example illustrates, there was extreme variation in both instruction and in curriculum materials, as they come from a variety of formal (website or materials directly from provider administrators) and informal sources (tutors' own resources or students' work from day school). The in-use curriculum included formal materials supplemented by materials from the tutor, the latter being occasionally inconsistent with the formal curriculum. Due to regulations under NCLB, the *general content focus* of many digital vendors in the SES context is either language, arts or math. However, by law vendors are given considerable discretion in what they teach and how they enact the curriculum, contributing to considerable variation in terms of curricular format, curricular access, and curricular software. This can be interpreted to mean that equal opportunities to learn for students under SES are unevenly distributed and highly subject to vendors' own interpretations, their beliefs and/or commercial priorities.

As in the case of corporate decisions in the role of the teacher in an online setting, companies also exert influence on curriculum via choice of online software. In our study, curriculum ranged from highly structured and completely dependent upon software to "home grown" curriculum that is more fluid and dependent on the discretion of a live tutor. For example, one provider uses software that essentially is an online whiteboard through which the tutor and student interact by writing with the track pad/mouse, typing and speaking through headsets. The tutor can upload curriculum materials and prompts as needed. In terms of *source*, curriculum used by digital vendors comes from a variety of sources (purchased/leased from an outside source to curriculum developed in house and used only by tutors, and some combination of above). A number of vendors develop their own, proprietary curriculum used only by their tutors. We find that digital curriculum is often delivered outside of the traditional classroom and school context where teachers and principals can do a "walk through" to observe curriculum and instruction. For that and other reasons, it is much harder to "see" and analyze particular types of curriculum, and in particular, the enacted curriculum.

In addition, companies frame how students access the curriculum. In our study, one provider lent students used desktop computers; another provided a handheld device; two provided netbooks, and the remaining three vendors sent students laptop computers. Each of these vendors had either software pre-loaded onto the hardware or dedicated websites through which students would access the program. All but two of these vendors used internet-based programs.

In the outer rim of the iron triangle of NCLB and SES, corporate–state ties (interest group aligned with Department of Education rule making and Congressional action and inaction) produced and perpetuated enterprise education policy that had clear commercial benefits for private companies. By law public funds were set aside to pay private firms for teaching public school students. Corporate–state dynamics (and alignment of corporate–state interests) contributed to a changed public policy space. Companies were encouraged to withhold information from districts (such as how much business they were doing in the district) and expand their influence through interlocking contracts for testing, instruction, and curriculum. As described above, these dynamics also provided powerful frames for decision-making within classroom settings where public policy dollars are spent. Companies free to do so or emboldened at other levels charged prices that maximized companies' revenue while obstructing some students' ability to receive quality instruction. Companies prioritized spending in ways that reduces costs for the company, while denying or limiting essential teaching supports for students. For example, companies decided against hiring tutors trained to work with ELL and students with special needs. Some decided to use software where students get a computer rather than a live teacher.

We also find that while there are important exceptions to the rule, left to their own devices, some companies will adopt curriculum and hiring practices that replicate rather than address the opportunity gap that the original ESEA was in principle expected to address. In particular, the model of SES tutoring commonly observed took the form of traditional academic learning environments, with students being tutored in tested subjects—mathematics and reading—and typically instructed in a whole group format with more than one student and one focal activity. Students receiving tutoring who might learn best via project-based learning, arts integration, or links to community-based activities encountered few opportunities of this sort across the study districts. Further, curriculum and instruction were rarely tailored to the unique needs of students with disabilities or English Language Learners. In focus groups, parents of students with special instructional needs, such as students with disabilities, felt the information about tutor qualifications and vendors' ability to make appropriate instructional adaptations was mixed and at times misleading.

In summary, our research on SES provides further confirmation that absent regulations and monitoring, companies in the education space can easily prioritize commercial imperatives as opposed to emphasizing acting on equity imperatives to close the opportunity gap between low-income and middle- and higher-income students. By charging high hourly rates, hiring teachers without skills or training to work with ELL or SWD, delivering curriculum via online platforms that minimize student interaction with live teachers, companies can and are using their expanded authority and revenue in ways that reinforce, rather than counter, existing educational inequities.

Figure 10.2 shows how macro and micro levels of corporate influence combine to work against high-quality learning opportunities for students in the case of the Supplemental Educational Services Initiative. Specifically, in Figure 10.2 we see how limited regulation created the space for variability across corporate levels of influence including in advertised hours of tutoring versus actual hours, planned curriculum versus enacted curriculum, the role of the teacher, student access to curriculum, and cost. This variation in implementation is well noted in policy research literature on State policy processes, the implementation as negotiation model identified at the beginning of the chapter. However, the role of corporate actors (supported by corporate–state ties) in contributing to uneven implementation and unequal learning opportunities, has received much less attention. Left unchecked, these dynamics can work against the democratic purposes of education, in particular equal access to challenging instruction that helps students develop as learners and individuals. In the case of NCLB, policies originally designed to level the playing field are reauthorized and rewritten in ways that heighten educational disparities while benefitting commercial interests. Policies designated in principle name to expand parents' "rights" to information provide a cover for companies engaging in false marketing, where actual instructional time does not equal advertised time. Allowed to cut costs that protect their own bottom line, companies make decisions that further discriminate against historically and culturally disadvantaged students such as English Language Learners and Students with Disabilities via hiring policies that give them unequal access to qualified live tutors and curriculum.[7]

Pushing Back

Currently, the relationship between state level policy and companies, as depicted (see Figure 10.2), is facilitated by legislation (and a broader environment) that creates an environment that allows these relationships, and their effects, to persist. However, the harmful effects of corporate influence on instruction, bolstered by enterprise education policy, are not inevitable. Pushing back against the current structure requires political and institutional work at multiple levels, classroom, community, district and state, and at different pressure points—within policy, outside of policy, or some combination thereof. This is already happening and with good results. In the community in which Lynnette and her father live, the father–daughter pair that was shortchanged by the online tutoring provider, pushing back involved organizing to inform other parents about companies' false claims and advertising. At the city level, districts such as the Chicago Public School district, have instituted policies aimed at compelling vendors to deliver more hours of tutoring via guidelines for using district space and the district provider's own rate setting (which has driven down market rates charged by other tutors). Following waiver approvals in Wisconsin and Minnesota, Milwaukee Public Schools and Minneapolis Public Schools now require tutoring vendors to comply with maximum hourly rates and other requirements that will ensure students are offered a minimum of 40 hours of tutoring. Milwaukee has also taken actions to reduce provider direct costs of delivering tutoring (e.g., eliminating facility rental fees), and Minneapolis is establishing performance-based contracts with bonuses. At higher levels of policy making, some states have begun active debates requiring greater transparency on the part of all vendors doing business with schools, instituting standards of practice that go beyond basic compliance that both vendors and district staff agree to before signing a contract. For example, in February 2014, the Tennessee Department of Education held meetings to begin to consider pilot projects requiring that districts and vendors jointly commit to rigorous evaluations of contracted products and their benefits for students.

Vendors of educational services and products can contribute to policy talk and action. Not-for-profit organizations, which can be expected to operate under a different set of incentives than for-profit companies, can lead this work. For example, in Wisconsin, a not-for-profit provider of digital curriculum is working with districts to revise eligibility criteria for its online courses, with the deliberate intent of making them more accessible to low-income students.

Inside the big iron triangle, we have argued, are deeply disturbing state-corporate ties that can serve to "lock in" the privileging of commercial interests as part of "public" policy. The embedded layers of corporate policy influence are complex and connected to large political and institutional forces. However, there can be, and is, effective pushback so that commercial interests don't trump students' interests. As researchers, reformers, and social activists continue to challenge the relationship between the larger political structures and local instantiations a heightened awareness is created for accountability and overall system change. These collective efforts can work to reshape an educational policy landscape that once felt impenetrable.

Notes

1   The proceeding vignette also appears in Burch, P., and A. G. Good. *Equal scrutiny: privatization and accountability in digital education.* Cambridge, Mass.: Harvard Education Press, 2014.
2   "A Glossary of Political Economy Terms." Iron triangles: www.auburn.edu/~johnspm/gloss/iron_triangles (accessed June 2, 2014).
3   Metcalf, S. "Reading Between the Lines." Reading Between the Lines. www.thenation.com/print/article/reading-between-lines (accessed June 2, 2014).
4   Our characterization of NPM as synonymous with neoliberalism is supported by public policy analysis and use of the framework to trace of economic principles in the public sector.
5   Aspects of this discussion also appear in Burch, P. *Hidden markets: the new education privatization.* New York, NY: Routledge, 2009.
6   This analysis, research and methods are from the following: Good, A. B., Burch, P., Stewart, M. S., Acosta, R., Heinrich, C., Robertson-Kraft, C., Duckworth, A., Cherng, H.-Y., Turney, K., and Kao, G. (2014) Instruction Matters: Lessons from a mixed-method evaluation of out-of-school time tutoring under No Child Left Behind. *Teachers College Record, 116*(3).; Heinrich, C. J., Burch, P., Good, A., Acosta, R., Cheng, H., Dillender, M., Kirshbaum, C., Nisar, H., and Stewart, M. (2014). Improving the Implementation and Effectiveness of Out-of_School_Time Tutoring. *Journal of Policy Analysis and Management, 33*(2): 471–494.
7   This analysis draws directly on Supplemental Educational Services: Integrated Qualitative and Quantitative Study of Implementation and Impact funded IES Education Policy, Finance and Systems Research Program. Fuller description of research and methods appear in Burch, P., and Good, A. G. (2014). *Equal scrutiny: privatization and accountability in digital education.* Cambridge, MA: Harvard Education Press; Good, A. B., Burch, P., Stewart, M. S., Acosta, R., Heinrich, C., Robertson-Kraft, C., Duckworth, A., Cherng, H.-Y., Turney, K., and Kao, G. (2014) Instruction Matters: Lessons from a mixed-method evaluation of out-of-school time tutoring under No Child Left Behind. *Teachers College Record, 116*(3).; Heinrich, C. J., Burch, P., Good, A., Acosta, R., Cheng, H., Dillender, M., Kirshbaum, C., Nisar, H., and Stewart, M.

(2014). Improving the Implementation and Effectiveness of Out-of-School-Time Tutoring. *Journal of Policy Analysis and Management, 33*(2), 471–494.

References

Berman, P., and McLaughlin, M. W. (1976, March). Implementation of educational innovation. *The Educational Forum*, 40(3), 345–370.

Burch, P. (2007). Supplemental education services under NCLB: Emerging evidence and policy issues. Retrieved August 15, 2007 from http://epsl.asu.edu/epru/documents/EPSL-0705-232-EPRU.pdf

Burch, P. (2009). *Hidden markets: The new education privatization*. New York: Routledge.

Gill, B., Hamilton, L. S., Lockwood, J. R., Marsh, J. A., and Zimmer, R. (2005). *Inspiration, perspiration, and time: Operations and achievement in Edison Schools*. Santa Monica, PA: Rand Corporation.

Guttman, D., and Willner, B. (1976). *The Shadow Government: The government's multi-billion-dollar giveaway of its decision-making powers to private management consultants, "experts," and think tanks*. New York, NY: Pantheon Books.

Heinrich, C. J., and Nisar, H. (2013). The efficacy of private sector providers in improving public educational outcomes. *American Educational Research Journal*, doi:10.3102/00028 31213486334.

Honig, M. (2006). *New directions in education policy implementation: Confronting complexity*. Albany: State University of New York Press.

Kettl, D. F. (2002). *The transformation of governance: Public administration for twenty-first century America*. Baltimore, MD: John Hopkins University Press.

Metcalf, S. (2002). Reading between the lines. *The Nation, 274*(3), 18–21. Retrieved June 2, 2014 from www.thenation.com/print/article/reading-between-lines

No Child Left Behind Act of 2001, Pub. L. 107–110, 115 Stat. 1425

Ronayne, K. (2011, July 20). *Lobbyists push congress, administration on No Child Left Behind*. Retrieved June 2, 2014 from www.opensecrets.org/news/2011/07/no-child-left-behind-lobbyists.

Salamon, L. M., and Lund, M. S. (Eds.). (1989). *Beyond privatization: The tools of government action*. Washington, DC: The Urban Insitute.

Stoker, G. (1998). Governance as theory: five propositions. *International Social Science Journal, 50*(155), 17–28.

INDEX

abuse 183–184

accountability 9–10, 52–54, 69, 114–117, 158–159, 203

ACER *see* Australian Council for Educational Research

ACT Inc. *see* American College Test Inc.

actors 12, 72, 74–78; boundary spanners 43–51; China 92–94, 97–100; SIMCE 109–114, 117–121

affiliation networks 12, 14; correspondence analysis 14, 134, 139–140 *see also* network

American College Test (ACT) Inc. 95–96, 98, 101

Appadurai, A. 45

Apple, M.W. 3

Asking More 57–61

Aspen Institute 78, 175

Australian Council for Educational Research (ACER) 120–122

Aylwan, M. 119

Ball, S.J. 2, 54, 61, 70, 89–90, 97–98

Banfield, E. 167–168

Barber, M. 43–51, 54–55, 60–61

Barkan, J. 157

Beck, U. 40

Bevir, M. 24

Bezos Foundation 155

Bill & Melinda Gates Foundation 1, 9–10, 80, 152–155, 171

Bingler, S. 177–178

Bishop, M. 54

Blanco, K. 170

BNOB *see* Bring New Orleans Back Commission

Bosworth, D. 10, 159

boundary spanners 43–51

Bourdieu, P. 45–48, 129, 143

Brandt, D. 156–157

Bring New Orleans Back Commission (BNOB) 170–171

Broad, E. 152

Broad foundation 80, 152, 171

Brown, J. 129

Bunyad 35

Burch, P. 192

bureaucracy 67 *see also* iron triangle

Bush, G.W. 166, 169, 193–194

business *see* corporate education

Candler, M. 176

capital 44–51, 61–62, 129–130, 172–173

capitalism 3–5, 67–68 *see also* corporate education; neoliberalism

Catholic Church 121

Cavett-Goodwin, D. 39

Center on Reinventing Public Education
  (CRPE) 149, 152, 154–156
CFCRS *see* Chinese-Foreign Cooperation
  in Running Schools
Charles, R. 167
charter management organizations
  (CMOs) 71–74, 78–82, 174–175, 178,
  181–183
charter schools 1, 6, 66–69, 72–80;
  effectiveness 159–160; New Orleans
  80–82, 169–173, 175–184; WA State
  147–153, 157–160 *see also* Ren2010
Cheung, P. 110
Chicago 126–128, 143–144; economists
  109; Ren2010 discourse 130–131,
  139–142; schools 135–139; social space
  128–129, 132–134
Chile 2, 105–109, 121–122 *see also*
  SIMCE
China 86–89, 91–98, 100–101; global
  education markets 88–89, 100–101
Chinese-Foreign Cooperation in Running
  Schools (CFCRS) 87–89, 93–94, 100
choice 67–69, 195, 201
civil rights 180–181, 183
class 2, 7, 88–89, 108, 167–168, 172–173
CMOs *see* charter management
  organizations
coding 132–133
commodification 107–108, 128 *see also*
  corporate education; neoliberalism
community 36–37, 67 *see also* Chicago;
  New Orleans
competition 107–108
Connell, R. 107
conversations 130–131, 141–142
corporate education 7–10, 67–69, 127;
  China 96–101; NCLB 193–197;
  networks 43–45, 49, 51–62; New
  Orleans 80–82; responsibility 53–54,
  62; sponsorship 78–80, 156–159; state
  dynamics 198–205 *see also*
  philanthropy; Ren2010; SIMCE
correspondence analysis 14, 134, 139–140
corruption 159, 181–182
Cowen Institute 171–172, 177
Cowen, S. 171
Cox, C. 118, 122

critical cartography 15, 90, 132, 144
critical research 11, 69–70
CRPE *see* Center on Reinventing Public
  Education
cultural politics 167–169, 183
curriculum 92, 96, 101, 108, 201–204

data 71–72, 91, 150
decentralization 86
Delpit, L. 148
democracy 121, 156–159
density 13
development 33–34, 86
digital education 191, 200–202 *see also*
  mEducation
disabled students 180–181, 203–204
discourse 129–131, 139–142
dispossession 170, 179–184
diversification 86
donations 150–152
Duncan, A. 131

economic development *see* development
economists 109
Ecuador 111
Ed-Tech 25–26, 28–30
education *see* corporate education;
  mEducation
educational management organizations
  (EMOs) 196–197
Education For All 33–34
Education Innovation Summit 29
Education Reform Now! 151–155
Education Week 25, 27–28
efficacy 51–61
Efficacy Framework 46, 51–54; *Asking More*
  57–61; *Incomplete Guide* 54–57
Elementary and Secondary Education Act
  (ESEA) 193–195
elites 3–4, 117–121, 127, 147–149,
  157–160; I-1240 150–6
Elliot, A. 62
EMOs *see* educational management
  organizations
enterprise *see* corporate education;
  neoliberalism; Teach For America
ESEA *see* Elementary and Secondary
  Education Act

ethnography 14–15, 24, 43–44, 90–91
evaluation *see* SIMCE; tests
events 12
Eyzaguirre, B. 119–120

Fabricant, M. 3, 5–7
Faust, K. 11
federal policy 192–195
Feinberg, M. 171
field 129–130
Fine, M. 3, 5–7
Finn, C. 131
Fordham Institute 130–131
formality 130
Forster, M. 120
free market *see* markets; neoliberalism
Friedman, M. 2
Froemel, J.E. 119
funding 178–179 *see also* philanthropy

GAC *see* Global Assessment Certificate
gangsta culture 167–169
García-Huidobro, J.E. 119
Gates, B. 9–10
Gates, B. jnr. 150–152, 159
Gates Foundation 1, 9–10, 80, 152–155, 171
GATS *see* General Agreement on Trade in Services
Gee, J. 130
General Agreement on Trade in Services (GATS) 88–89
gentrification 137–139, 142
Geographical Information Sciences 15
Global Assessment Certificate (GAC) 87, 92, 94–96, 98–101
Global Literacy Professional Development Network 36–37
globalization 88–89, 100–101, 106–107
governance 4–5, 8–12, 23–25, 70, 169–173; iron triangle 191–192, 194–196, 202, 205 *see also* network governance; policy
graphs 70–72
Green, M. 54
Grek, S. 62
Groupe Speciale Mobile Association (GSMA) 30–35

GSMA *see* Groupe Speciale Mobile Association
GSV Advisers 26–30

habitus 129–130
Haddad, W. 111
Harden, K. 181–182
Harvey, D. 3–5
Henderson, K. 66
Heritage Foundation 169
Hill, P. 149
Himmel, E. 109, 113, 118
hiring 200–201
Holsinger, D. 111
Holzer, B. 53
Howard, P.N. 14
Huggins, R. 48
Husain, S. 110

I-1240 148–150, 156–160; campaign network 153–156; funding 150–153
IAP program *see* International Access Project
The Incomplete Guide 54–56
individualism *see* choice; markets; neoliberalism
inequality 2–4, 69, 88–89, 108, 203
Inkpen, A. 48
International Access Project (IAP) 87–88, 91–98, 100–101
international curriculum 89, 92
international high schools *see* International Access Project
International Society for Technology in Education (ISTE) 25–26, 28
Inzunza, J. 113
iron triangle 191–192, 194–196, 202, 205
Isaacson, W. 175
ISTE *see* International Society for Technology in Education

Jacobs, L. 177–178
Jindal, B. 177
Junemann, C. 54, 90

Karier, C.J. 158
KIPP *see* Knowledge is Power Program
Kissinger, H. 2

Klaf, S. 140–141
Klein, J. 66
knowledge 36, 39, 87
Knowledge is Power Program (KIPP) 81,
    168, 171
Kopp, W. 65–66, 171

Landrieu, M. 176–177
Latin America *see* Chile; SIMCE
leadership 74
learning *see* teaching
legislation 115 *see also* policy
Leonardo, Z. 168–169
Lingard, B. 61
linguistic markets 130–131, 141–143
Lipman, P. 3–5, 8–9
local policy 192, 196
low-income students 69

McCann, E. 24–25, 29
McGraw, H. 193
McKinsey & Company 30–31, 44
management *see* governance;
    neoliberalism; policy
Manzi, J. 119
mapping 15, 90, 132–136, 144
Mapping Corporate Education Reform 16–18
Marginson, S. 107
markets 2–6, 88–89, 130–131; China
    88–89; Ed-Tech 25, 28–29; philosophy
    66–67, 169, 171, 193 *see also*
    neoliberalism
Marx, K. 19
Matte, P. 120
Mead, M. 26–27
measurement *see* SIMCE; tests
media 127–128, 130–132, 136–142
mEducation 23–24, 30–35, 38–40, 191,
    200–202; Alliance 35–38
meetings 62
Mekes, L. 122
Metcalf, S. 193
methodologies 10–15, 44–45, 70–71
    see also critical cartography; social
    network analysis
Mexico 4
Microsoft 150–151
Mobile Network Operators 31–32

mobile networks *see* mEducation
Mobilink 35
mobilities 45–48
Monroe, K.R. 23
Mos Def 165–166
multivariate techniques 13–14

narratives 23, 26–30; media 127–128,
    130–132, 136–142
NCLB *see* No Child Left Behind
neoliberalism 2–10, 18–19, 67–68, 193;
    Chicago 128, 133, 142–144; Chile
    106–109, 121–122; China 86–90,
    94–101; networks 44, 51–52, 61 *see also*
    markets; Ren2010; SIMCE
network 66, 70, 82; analysis 12–15;
    campaign 153–159; capital 44–51,
    61–62; efficacy 51–61; ethnography
    14–15, 24, 43–44, 90–91 *see also*
    social network analysis
network governance 8–12, 43–44,
    106–109; China 89–90, 98;
    consequences 179–184; mEducation
    23–25, 34–35, 39–40; New Orleans
    173–179
New Curriculum Reform 86–87, 92
New Orleans 80–82, 165–166;
    dispossession 179–184; network
    governance 173–179; racial politics
    167–169; state aggression 169–173
newspapers 127–128, 132, 136–142
No Child Left Behind (NCLB) 193–197,
    199, 201–202, 204
no excuses model 74
nodes 12–13
Nokia 33–34, 36–37
NOLA 81, 168, 171, 173
NSNO 172–182

Olivia, W. 120
Olmedo, A. 54
Orange 38
Orange Jones, K. 177
organization ties 72–83, 151–152 *see also*
    actors; network governance

Partnership for learning 149
paternalism 168

Patterson, M. 23
Pearson 36–37, 43–51, 61–62, 197–198;
   efficacy documents 51–61
philanthropy 54, 68, 78–81, 149,
   152–153, 157–159
Pinochet, A. 2
policy 101, 110–111, 121; convergence
   89; iron triangle 191–192, 194–196,
   202, 205; mEducation 34, 38–40;
   network analysis 11–12, 44–45, 61–62,
   156–159; New Orleans 173–179; TFA
   66, 69–74, 78–83 see also neoliberalism;
   network governance
Pontific Catholic University of Santiago
   see PUC
poverty see class; inequality
power 90–91, 97, 158–160; iron triangle
   191–192, 194–196, 202, 205
prices 199–200
privatization 5, 67–69, 80–82; Chile
   114–120; China 90, 97–101; NCLB
   191–193, 195–197, 202–203
public-private partnerships 98–101, 114,
   116–118
PUC 109, 111–113, 115, 118–119
Putnam, R.D. 48

race 67, 69, 159–160; Chicago 129, 134,
   137, 142; New Orleans 167–170,
   172–173, 180, 183
Ravitch, D. 51, 158–159
Recovery School District see RSD
reform see corporate education;
   neoliberalism
relations 11–12
Ren2010 126–128; discourse 130–131,
   139–142; schools 135–139; social space
   128–129, 132–134
resistance 204–205
Return on Education 29–30
Rhee, M. 78
Rhodes, R.A.W. 24, 70, 89–90
Rizvi, S. 53
Ronayne, K. 194–195
RSD 166, 170, 173, 179–180

Samsung 35
Scardino, M. 44

Scherping, G. 120
Schiefelbein, E. 111
Schnur, J. 66
school choice see charter schools;
   Ren2010
School Quality Measurement see SIMCE
schools 133–139
Scott, J.T. 158
Scuzzarello, S. 27
segregation 159, 168, 181
Sellar, S. 59
SES see Supplemental Educational Services
SIMCE 107–114, 121–122; adjustments
   114–116; private-public 116–121
Sistema de Medición de la Calidad de la
   Educación see SIMCE
SNA see social network analysis
social capital 44–51, 61–62, 129–130,
   172–173
social network analysis (SNA) 1, 10–15,
   70–71, 90–91 see also network
social space 128–129
sociology 40
Somers, M. 26
Somerset, A. 112
space 15, 90, 128–129, 132–137,
   139–144, 180
sponsorship see philanthropy
state 4–10, 18–19, 128, 198–205; Chile
   106–109, 116, 121; New Orleans
   169–173
Stewart, M. 131
stories see narratives
students 69, 198–202
Supplemental Educational Services (SES)
   195–196, 200–203

Teach For America (TFA) 65–74, 78,
   80–83, 171, 175–177; affiliations
   75–77, 79; New Orleans 80–82
teaching 6, 198–204; termination 171,
   173, 179–180
technology 151, 191, 200–202 see also
   mEducation
Telefonica 31
termination 171, 173, 179–180
tests 69, 106–109, 137, 194 see also
   SIMCE

TFA *see* Teach For America
themes 132–134, 137–140
ties 72–83, 151–152
transnational advocacy networks 36, 39
Tsang, E. 48
Tulane University 171–172

UNESCO 33–35, 110–112
Urry, J. 45–48, 62
Usdin, S. 81–82, 171, 175–178

Varas, H. 120
vendors *see* corporate education
venture philanthropy *see* philanthropy

WA State 1, 148–149 *see also* I-1240
Wacquant, L.J.D. 46–48
Walton, A. 152
Walton Foundation 152–153, 155
Ward, K. 24–25
Washington Post 165–166
Wasserman, S. 11
wealth *see* elites; inequality
White, J. 176–177
Whitman, D. 168
Williams, P. 89–90
working groups 36–37
World Bank 110–112, 117

Made in the USA
Columbia, SC
30 August 2019